D0891995

DATE DUE

WITHDRAWN

THE TEMPTATIONS OF TYRANNY
IN CENTRAL ASIA

DAVID LEWIS

The Temptations of Tyranny in Central Asia

Columbia University Press
New York

Columbia University Press
Publishers Since 1893
New York

Library of Congress Cataloging-in-Publication Data

Lewis, David.
  The temptations of tyranny in Central Asia / David Lewis.
    p. cm.
  Includes index.
  ISBN 978-0-231-70025-2 (cloth : alk. paper)
  1. Asia, Central—Politics and government—1991- 2. Asia,
Central—Foreign relations—1991- I. Title.
  DK859.56.L49 2007
  958'.043—dc22

                          2007044200

⊚

Columbia University Press books are printed on permanent and durable acid-free paper.
This book is printed on paper with recycled content.
Printed in India

c 10 9 8 7 6 5 4 3 2 1

References to Internet Web sites (URLs) were accurate at the time of writing.
Neither the author nor Columbia University Press is responsible for URLs
that may have expired or changed since the manuscript was prepared.

CONTENTS

PREFACE

This book is designed to give an overview of the complexities of Central Asia, while addressing some of the problems and challenges posed by Western policies after 2001. It is not a purely academic study, but where possible I have sourced controversial points to easily accessible literature. However, much of the source material for this book came from thousands of interviews and conversations while I was living in Central Asia between October 2001 and May 2005, when I was working for the International Crisis Group, based initially in Osh, and later in Bishkek.

Not surprisingly, many of those interviewed while I worked in Central Asia preferred to remain anonymous. Many of those whom I talked to extensively in Uzbekistan in 2002-5 are now in prison, or have been forced to flee the country. I would like to thank all those who contributed to this volume, through their candid conversations, frequent hospitality and open discussions.

Particular thanks are due to all my former colleagues at the International Crisis Group, notably Robert Templer, Azizulla Gaziev, Saniya Sagnaeva, Kathleen Samuel and Michael Hall, Volodya Kultugin and Aibek Sultanov. Their invaluable work can be found at www.crisisgroup.org. I would also like to thank those who read the manuscript and contributed their comments.

Transliteration of names has been based on common sense rather than strict criteria. In most cases, relatively well-known geographical names are used in their Russified forms, which are still in use in most atlases. Names have tried to follow the person's own most frequent usage.

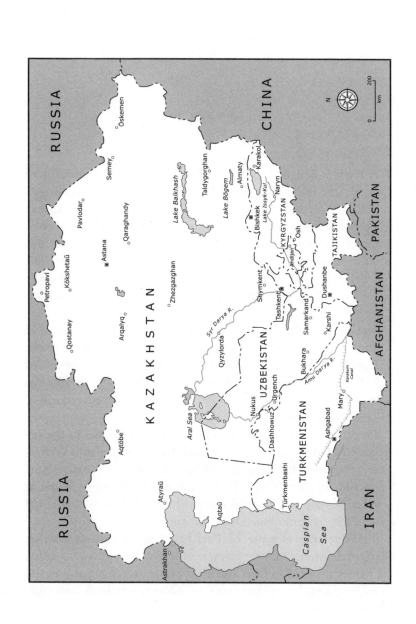

INTRODUCTION:
CENTRAL ASIA REDISCOVERED

At the end of August 2001, as the summer's unbearable heat finally began to fade, Uzbekistan celebrated a decade of independence from the USSR. The celebrations mixed Soviet-style parades and firework salutes with long speeches on the achievements of independence by the president, Islam Karimov. Around the same time, the other Central Asian states also celebrated their first 10 years of independence. The same fireworks, the same parades, the same speeches, the same litany of unqualified success.

But behind the façade of official statistics, problems were rife. When the USSR collapsed in 1991, the Central Asian states had independence thrust upon them almost overnight. As other Soviet republics declared their independence from Moscow, they had little choice but to follow suit. Since then their economies had collapsed, bloody conflicts had flared up, and any initial idealism that independence had brought had largely faded. At the beginning of the 21st century most of Central Asia was ruled by a collection of brutal feudal leaders, while much of the population remained in extreme poverty.

These five states—Kazakhstan, Kyrgyzstan, Uzbekistan, Tajikistan and Turkmenistan—were usually lumped together as an unwieldy entity called "Central Asia", stretching north of the Amu-Darya river (marking the northern border of Afghanistan) up to the southern borders of Russia. The muddy, silted waters of the Amu-Darya and its more northerly counterpart, the Syr-Darya, meander sluggishly across the region, their waters, and the occasional ancient oasis, providing the only areas of fertile land for habitation. Downstream, in

1

the west, much of the land is arid and inhospitable, fatally damaged by the environmental disaster of the disappearing Aral Sea. Upstream, in the east, the headlands of these great rivers are the glaciers and forbidding mountain ranges of the Tien-Shan, on China's most westerly frontier.

Modern Central Asia is an artificial colonial construct. Culturally and geographically, the boundaries of a broader region of Inner Asia spread much further. To the east there are historical links with Mongolia and the Turkic peoples of southern Siberia, as well as the Muslim Uighurs of western China. To the south, political history divided the Tajiks of Tajikistan and the Uzbeks of Uzbekistan from their compatriots in Afghanistan. In medieval times this had been a unified region of trade and culture, which romantic 19th century historians had dubbed the "Silk Road", named after the silks and other luxury goods that travelled on camel trains from China through Central Asia to the markets of Europe.

The region's remoteness had always conjured up wild legends and fables in Western literature. But writers such as James Elroy Flecker, who dreamed of the "Golden Road to Samarkand",[1] never visited the region. The few Western explorers who did penetrate its fabled cities and despotic khanates often wished they had stayed at home. The tale of the British officers Col. Charles Stoddart and Capt. Arthur Conolly, who were executed in 1842 in Bukhara, apparently because their presents to the Emir were not lavish enough, became a staple of imperial literature for Victorian children in England. Generations of Western readers had sat through Christopher Marlowe's *Tamburlaine*, the definitive exploration of medieval despotism. Subsequent travellers to Uzbekistan were surprised to see him feted as a national hero.

If Central Asia was a prime subject for Western orientalism, it was also defined geographically and politically by European imperialism. By 1878 most of the ancient khanates of Central Asia—Bukhara, Samarkand, Khiva and Kokand—were effectively under Russian rule.

---

1   "...We travel not for trafficking alone/By hotter winds our fiery hearts are fanned:/For lust of knowing what should not be known/We take the Golden Road to Samarkand", James Elroy Flecker, *Hassan, The Story of Hassan of Baghdad and how he came to make the Golden Journey to Samarkand* (1922).

The Russian imperial conquest was brutal, and it began to transform the lives of the Central Asians, with more settlement of nomads and a huge expansion of cotton cultivation, but it treated religion and culture with a relatively light touch. The Russian expansion reached the Amu-Darya, before negotiations with the British, in what came to be known as the "Great Game", established Afghanistan as a buffer state between the two great empires.[2]

Although China's western frontier remained disputed until after the Second World War, the main contours of Russian-dominated Central Asia were decided by the Tsarist regime. The revolution of 1917 brought only a short interlude of chaos before the Soviets reasserted control and instituted a repressive regime that began to root out what the Communists called "vestiges of the feudal past": the veiling of women, the patriarchal leaders, the mosques and the religious Sharia courts. This caused outrage in these conservative societies, but periodic revolts were put down swiftly by the Red Army. It was under the Soviets that the modern borders of these states were first drawn on maps, when they were carved out into Soviet Socialist Republics (SSR), which served as the basis for today's independent states.

The Soviets built schools, railways, roads and hospitals, and developed an infrastructure and level of education that still distinguish Central Asia from other countries of similar levels of economic development. But much of the Soviet legacy was calamitous: collectivisation bred mass famine, particularly among the nomadic Kazakhs; thousands of Central Asians were incarcerated or killed in Stalin's purges; Soviet industrial agriculture, particularly cotton cultivation, brought environmental disaster; and for seven decades the region was almost completely cut off from foreign influences. Its rediscovery of the world was always going to be a traumatic and dangerous process.

---

2   On British-Russian rivalry in the region in the 19th century, see Karl E. Meyer and Shareen Blair Brysac, *Tournament of Shadows: The Great Game and the Race for Empire in Central Asia* (Washington, DC: Counterpoint, 1999).

The five new states that emerged in 1991 from the wreckage of the USSR faced huge challenges. None had a tradition of statehood in the modern sense: political formations in the past had either been the khanates—small feudal statelets, in which the *khan* was the unchallenged ruler, and outsiders were seldom welcome—or loose nomadic formations that had a greater tradition of freedom, but little sense of permanency. New leaders of these states had to begin everything from scratch: borders, passports, national flags, a diplomatic service, foreign relations, national armies, and much else. Above all, they had to retain stability in states that suffered from considerable social and ethnic fractures underneath the Soviet façade of unity and homogeneity.

Perhaps those least prepared for independence were a number of former nomadic tribes, the Turkmens, who gave their name to the USSR's most remote and undeveloped republic, the Turkmen SSR. The Turkmens had once been praised by Marco Polo for their carpets and their fabled horses, but latterly had been more feared for their rapacious attacks on traders' caravans. They had been quelled by brutal Russian conquest and Soviet repression. After independence, the one-time head of the local Communist Party, Saparmurat Niyazov, declared himself *Turkmenbashi* (Father of all the Turkmen), and retained all the most disastrous features of Soviet rule, only lightly covered in a veneer of Turkmen national culture. Instead of reading Lenin, schoolchildren learned their president's writings off by heart. Instead of statues of Marx and Lenin, they worshipped at the shrines and portraits of Turkmenbashi. The old KGB was renamed, and the Communist Party became the Democratic Party, but their activities were unchanged. By 2001 Turkmenistan was one of the world's most repressive states.

Living on Turkmenistan's huge eastern plains were many ethnic Uzbeks, another Turkic people. There were other Uzbek minorities in all the region's states, but most lived in their eponymous republic, Uzbekistan. Uzbekistan was the pivot of the whole region. Its 25 million people made up nearly half of the Central Asian population. It bordered all the other Central Asian states, and acted as the main conduit for transport and trade among them and with the outside world. It was in Uzbekistan that travellers could find the ancient cities of Samarkand, the capital of Timur's great medieval empire,[3] and Bukhara, a world centre of Islamic learning in medieval times that had long fallen into a dark age of isolation and repression. The Uzbek capital Tashkent, in the centre of the country, was rebuilt in Soviet style after a massive earthquake in 1961. Many of the Russians and Ukrainians who came from all over the Soviet Union in the 1960s to build its towering apartment blocks and grandiose architecture stayed to live, turning it into a Russified city, with little hint of its more exotic Eastern past.

The rest of the country was less cosmopolitan. Every morning, on the eastern fringes of Tashkent, headscarved women and skull-capped men wait patiently at the side of the road for crowded cars to take them over the mountain pass to the Fergana Valley, Uzbekistan's most fertile and densely populated region. It is a six-hour journey from Tashkent, punctuated by numerous road-blocks and police checks, for Fergana is Uzbekistan's most volatile and politically restive region. It was in the Fergana valley that Islamist unrest first broke out in the early 1990s, only to be brutally suppressed by the Uzbek president Islam Karimov, and it was in Andijan, the valley's main town, that an uprising in 2005 was crushed by Uzbek troops, with hundreds of unarmed civilians killed.

Soviet planners had divided the Fergana valley between three different republics. The bulk of its territory was held by Uzbekistan, including the towns of Andijan, Kokand and Fergana. Just a few miles from Andijan was the town of Osh, where almost half the inhabitants were also Uzbeks. But since 1991 Osh had been part of a new state, the Kyrgyz Republic. In the Soviet period these borders were meaningless, and people crossed back and forth without even noticing. After independence all the paraphernalia of state sovereignty—passports, visas and customs—came to divide the two cities. As relations worsened, barbed wire and land-mines also appeared along the frontier.

---

3   Timur is generally known in the West as Tamerlane or Tamburlaine, a nickname referring to his lameness (Timur(-i) Leng).

The new international borders in the southern portion of the Fergana valley were a cartographer's nightmare. Soviet governments had designed a series of exclaves in Kyrgyz territory that made travel through the region hugely difficult. From Rishtan in Uzbekistan a ten-mile ride to the Uzbek exclave of Sokh in 2002 involved nine border crossings, as the road tracked in and out of Kyrgyz territory. Just to confuse things further, the Uzbek citizens of Sokh were mostly ethnic Tajiks.

The Tajiks are an Iranian people, speaking a dialect of Farsi, and they frequently set themselves apart from the Turkic peoples of the rest of Central Asia. Their ancient centres of learning and civilisation, however, were Samarkand and Bukhara, whose mainly Tajik inhabitants sometimes chafed at their inclusion in the Uzbek state. Tajik nationalists occasionally dreamed of a greater Tajikistan, passing round fanciful maps showing a Tajik state with Samarkand as the capital. In reality, Tajiks were left with a collection of remote territories that were not even connected to each other by road for most of the year. The charming capital, Dushanbe, was growing rapidly, but it was still essentially a one-street town. Much of their territory was uninhabitable, dominated by the massive plateau of the Pamir mountains, and descending to the most formidable part of the Afghan border, across which heroin, guns and Islamist militants flowed with worrying freedom.

No former Soviet republic had been as traumatised by independence as Tajikistan. By 1992 it had descended into a bloody civil war, which pitched region against region, and half-hearted Islamists against one-time Communists. More than 50,000 people died in the fighting, until a hard-won peace was crafted in the late 1990s. But in 2001 clashes with rebel groups were still common, and foreigners in Dushanbe still observed a night-time curfew for fear of kidnapping. Drug barons and Islamists mixed uneasily in the corridors of power, where a compromise government was dominated by its colourful leader, President Imomali Rahmonov.

With neighbours like these, Kyrgyzstan perhaps deserved its epithet as "the island of democracy" in Central Asia. Its leader, Askar Akaev, was a highly educated physicist, who could not have been more different from the thuggish leaders of the southern Central Asian states. After 17 years living in what passed for the *beau monde* of Soviet culture in Leningrad, he returned to Kyrgyzstan, and emerged in 1991 as a compromise leader who suited other rival factions. His aspirations for a more politically open regime, and his support for engagement with the outside world, gained him many Western supporters. During his first decade in power, his early enthusiasms waned and his grip on power got tighter. With little industry and few resources, 60 per cent of the population lived below an already minimal poverty line.

In the Soviet period, the vast state of Kazakhstan was not considered part of Central Asia proper, and today it still stands apart, closer perhaps to Russia than to the southern arc of Central Asian republics. Kazakhstan's development is considered only in passing in this book, since its history and contemporary trajectory in many ways place it apart from the rest of Central Asia.[4] However, its economic development has had a major impact on the rest of the region. Its biggest city, Almaty, offers a growing culture shock to visitors from the rest of Central Asia. Its property prices are soaring, and its luxury shops mock poorer visitors. While the other Central Asian states try to cope with mass poverty, by 2005 Kazakhs were among the richest citizens of the major post-Soviet states. Kazakhstan's new-found wealth was mainly due to major reserves of oil, which were starting to come on stream in greater volumes by 2001.

Western companies were the first investors in Kazakh oil, and there were widespread allegations that they paid millions of dollars in bribes to the country's leadership in exchange for lucrative contracts. But in Kazakhstan there was at least the beginnings of a trickle-down effect, and ordinary people were seeing some of the financial benefits of economic reforms and foreign investment. But economic growth was not converted into democratic development. Instead, President Nazarbaev did everything to block the emergence

---

4   Martha Brill Olcott, *Kazakhstan: Unfulfilled Promise* (Carnegie Endowment, 2002) provides a comprehensive analysis of the first decade of Kazakhstan's independence.

of any serious political opposition. His family controlled the media, political parties and a good deal of the business world. Challengers to his lucrative position were dealt with in unceremonious fashion. At first, few outsiders ventured into this complex region. In the 1990s it was largely ignored; only Germany, Russia and the US had embassies in all five states. Aid agencies developed some small development programmes, and the major international financial institutions handed over money to local governments, often with little regard to how it was spent. A few brave multinationals invested, primarily the oil majors in Kazakhstan. Further south, few succeeded.

All this changed in September 2001, when it became clear that Afghanistan was to be a prime target of military action following the terrorist attacks in the US. While the US began searching in the region for logistical bases for its troops, journalists from all over the world gathered in Tashkent and Dushanbe, ready to cross the border to join US forces and the Northern Alliance in their push against Taliban forces inside the country.

Central Asian leaders were quick to respond to the new geopolitics. They had long sought ways to increase their international respectability and improve their security, and they wanted alternatives to their heavy dependence on Russia. In 2001, much to the irritation of Moscow, they offered basing facilities to the US-led coalition. The US Central Command toured the region's Soviet-era airstrips, many of which had been developed to support the Soviet invasion of Afghanistan more than 20 years previously. The US settled on Manas, the main civilian airport for Bishkek, and Khanabad, a largely disused military airport in southern Uzbekistan, to host US and coalition forces in support of the Afghanistan operation.

Alongside the military came diplomats, officials, aid agencies, and non-governmental organisations. In the US, in particular, military engagement was viewed by some officials as more than just a purely temporary logistical exercise: it was a fundamental strategic shift that would promote democracy and Western values in the region, and enhance permanently the US position, not just in relation to Afghanistan, but towards Russia, Iran and China. The first delegations that travelled through to Tashkent and Bishkek were optimistic and idealistic, convinced that local leaders would make the most of this unexpected "window of opportunity". Many Central Asians, desperate for meaningful reform of their repressive states and sclerotic economies, were equally convinced that this new relationship would be a breakthrough, a decisive move away from Soviet isolation and totalitarianism towards the global economy and open societies. On both sides, expectations were high. Perhaps predictably, it did not take long for disappointment to set in.

1
THE ROAD TO ANDIJAN

Either Karimov is a reformer, or this country is going to hell in a handcart.
US diplomat, Tashkent, 2003.

On 5 October 2001 the US Defense Secretary, Donald Rumsfeld, and President Islam Karimov of Uzbekistan gave a press conference in Tashkent. All the journalists present already knew what the two politicians had agreed: US forces would begin using the Khanabad airbase, near Karshi, in southern Uzbekistan. Karimov insisted that this was only for the delivery of humanitarian aid to Afghanistan. He denied categorically that there were any secret deals with the Americans to allow combat troops to operate from the base.[1] Few of the reporters believed him. The two men had secretly agreed that Khanabad would be the main forward base for US special operations to operate in northern Afghanistan. A new US air base, later dubbed Camp Stronghold Freedom, was born. Symptomatically, its very inception was introduced with a lie.

To the first arrivals at Khanabad, it seemed the edge of the world. "A dust bowl with nothing, in the middle of nowhere" was how one engineer described it.[2] There was concern about disease; the stench

---

1   US Department of Defense, News Transcript, "Secretary Rumsfeld Press Conference with President of Uzbekistan", accessed at www.defenselink.mil/transcripts/2001/t10082001_t1005uz.html .

2   Cited in Dr Forrest L. Marion, "Building USAF 'Expeditionary Bases' for Operation Enduring Freedom-Afghanistan 2001-2002", *Air & Space Power Chronicles*, 18 November 2005.

11

from a stinking ditch hung over the camp for weeks; there were rumours that the camp still contained the remains of old Soviet chemical weapons; the first contingent of 600 soldiers shared a single toilet. But within 100 days American engineers had set up a working base. Over 1,000 soldiers were soon stationed there. The US military, for the first time since 1918, was operating on the territory of the former Russian empire.

For President Karimov, the US intervention was a godsend. Just months earlier, concerned about the approach of the Taliban towards his southern border, Karimov had secretly begun negotiations with their leadership over possible diplomatic recognition.[3] One group allied to the Taliban, the Islamic Movement of Uzbekistan (IMU), was formed of old enemies of Karimov, such as the Islamic radical Juma Namangani, who had humiliated Karimov at a public rally in 1992 and subsequently led an Islamist rebellion from across the border in Tajikistan. Since 1999 these rebels had been based in Afghanistan, forming an important part of al-Qaeda 055 international brigade, but still attempting to stir up rebellion in Uzbekistan itself. Karimov's security fears were compounded by economic woes: foreign investment and international assistance had dried up and the IMF had just closed its Tashkent office in protest at the government's failure to carry out any economic reforms.

With one US air base, Karimov seemed to be free. In early US bombing in Afghanistan, camps belonging to the al-Qaeda 055 international brigade, including the IMU, were among the first targets. Many IMU fighters, including Namangani himself, died during the battle for Kunduz in November 2001. The remainder fled to remote areas of Afghanistan, such as Badakhshan, or to the southern Afghan-Pakistan border. The threat of the IMU to Uzbekistan seemed to be significantly reduced, if not eliminated.

The new security relationship with the US also gave Uzbekistan the international recognition and economic help that Karimov had

---

3   See William D. Shingleton and John McConnell, "From Tamerlane to Terrorism: The Shifting Basis of Uzbek Foreign Policy", *Harvard Asia Quarterly*, Volume V, No. 1, Winter 2001.

long sought: successive delegations of US officials and congressmen arrived in the capital, profuse in their thanks to the Uzbek leader for his support. The US offered hundreds of millions of dollars in aid, and promised to encourage the IMF and other multilateral lenders to back the government with new soft loans.

For strategists in Washington who could think beyond the immediate conflict in Afghanistan, the relationship offered much more than just a temporary base. Even before 9/11 the Pentagon had been seeking forward-basing facilities in Central Asia for use in future conflicts: General Tommy Franks, head of US Central Command, was reported to have discussed possible use of the base with Karimov back in September 2000.[4] The Afghan conflict provided the perfect opportunity for an expansion of US military reach into the region.[5]

Much of US policy towards Central Asia in the 1990s, suffused with Cold War thinking, was focused on keeping Russia out of its former colonies. The Russians were not consulted on the US air base in Uzbekistan, and the new US presence was seen as an affront in Moscow, even if President Putin expressed a grudging acceptance of the US *fait accompli*. The base would allow the US to gain a new ally in Central Asia, and ease Uzbekistan out of the Russian sphere of influence permanently. The problem, hardly acknowledged by the delegations of US officials who swept through Tashkent in late 2001, was that Karimov's regime was a brutal dictatorship that sat oddly with the values that the US was ostensibly fighting for in "Operation Enduring Freedom".

Dealing with the West: the discourse of stability

Karimov had run the old Communist Party in Uzbekistan, and his rule after independence differed little from the old days. He was elected president in December 1991 in a rigged vote: his opponent

---

4   Marion, "Building USAF 'Expeditionary Bases' for Operation Enduring Freedom-Afghanistan 2001-2002", *Air & Space Power Chronicles*, 18 November 2005.

5   For some citations of such views, see Vernon Loeb, "Footprints In Steppes Of Central Asia", *Washington Post*, 9 February 2002, p. 1.

in the poll, Mohammed Solih, fled the country, as did many other opposition figures. Karimov had won the latest presidential election in 2000 with 91 per cent of the vote. The election turned even more farcical when his sole opponent, a political ally who had been drafted in to give the appearance of some democracy, even admitted on television that he too had voted for Karimov.

The government blamed this lack of political progress on the security situation, and indeed they did face a serious security threat from the IMU, which was blamed for a series of bomb attacks in Tashkent in 1999. The terrorist attacks merely provoked greater repression, not just against Islamic activists, but against any secular opposition as well. The government clamped down hard on any sign of an independent press, and had as many as 7,000 political and religious activists locked up in Uzbekistan's expanding network of prison camps. Many of those in prison were arrested on charges of belonging to Islamist groups: a large proportion were convicted on the flimsiest of evidence, and only a tiny minority had been involved in groups committed to violence or terrorism. They were subject to appalling conditions, particularly in the Jaslyk prison, located in the inhospitable desert of Karakalpakistan, where Human Rights Watch concluded that "dozens of inmates reportedly died from mistreatment and disease [and] there were several shocking reports of torture causing the death of detainees and prisoners."[6]

Karimov was a small man, with a rather pudgy face and restless, bead-like eyes. But he had a certain charisma, and was adept at playing to the prejudices and simplistic notions of foreigners. He brushed aside allegations of human rights abuses, by asserting that prisoners were "terrorists", and simply denied that maltreatment was taking place. He always asserted that it was too early for democracy to be launched, while he was surrounded by powerful enemies: the Taliban and Islamist militants on the one hand, and the former colonial power, Russia, on the other. These arguments were often accepted blindly by foreign delegations, and were also useful domes-

---

6   Human Rights Watch, "World Report 2001 – Uzbekistan", accessed at www.hrw.org/wr2k1/europe/uzbekistan.html.

tically. In 2001 there was still a broad swathe of the population who believed that Karimov was the lesser of two evils: the twin spectres of Islamic fundamentalism and civil war were used repeatedly by the government to frighten the population into support for the government. But much of this scare-mongering was based on myth. Many Uzbeks were relatively secular, following 70 years of Soviet anti-Islamic campaigns and widespread non-religious education, and there was little support—outside pockets of the Fergana valley—for any form of Islamic state.

Even in 2001 there were signs that the new relationship with the US would not be easy. The US could not persuade the Uzbek government to open its border with Afghanistan to allow humanitarian aid to be transported to Afghans in the northern provinces, who were facing a bleak winter. The border had only one crossing; its name, the Friendship Bridge, was belied by the curls of rusting barbed wire that decorated the entrance, and by the heavily-armed special forces that blocked access to the frontier. Only after the US Secretary of State, Colin Powell, had travelled halfway around the world to plead with Karimov in person did the first transports begin to roll across the bridge. The difficulties posed by this minor issue were a warning that dealing with the Uzbeks was not going to be easy.

Although the regime was highly repressive, there were small pockets of independent thinking. Groups of human rights activists and a few local journalists struggled to gather information on the government's widespread abuses. Human rights groups operated in a legal grey zone: to operate legally they had to register formally with the Ministry of Justice, but they had always been refused permission to register, and so were always at risk of arrest, harassment or worse. Many of them were brave and principled, but not surprisingly, in this repressive environment, such movements also attracted some strange characters. Some were consumed by paranoia, sure that rival groups were working with the government. Others were scarcely credible. One, an ageing vegetarian with the white hair of a would-be prophet, dispatched increasingly bizarre emails, accusing his rivals of everything from prostitution to corruption.

By comparison, Western delegates found that officials at the Uzbek Ministry of Foreign Affairs were sophisticated and well-educated. In most cases they knew more about the West than any visitor knew about Uzbekistan, and they used their knowledge to their advantage. Many were convinced that US rhetoric about human rights and political reform was just that: rhetoric. They were used to dealing with the annual human rights report from the US State Department, which routinely detailed the abuses of the government. They were used to the occasional diplomatic démarche about the arrest of another human rights activist. Now Uzbek officials openly talked about a new relationship, in which their country would be "something like Israel": security and aid would flow, and political problems would be raised only as a formality.[7]

A first test of the new relationship came in a referendum in January 2002. Voters were corralled into polling booths to support a proposal to extend Karimov's term in office by an extra two years, until 2007, avoiding the need for an election in 2005. This move was unconstitutional, but there was no discussion of such legal niceties in the tightly controlled media. The referendum was reminiscent of old Soviet patterns of voting: the heads of local communities (*mahallas*) were responsible for making sure that people turned up to vote and voted the right way. Any minor lapse in the result could anyway be corrected during the counting. As with previous votes, an unlikely 93 per cent of the population supported this undemocratic measure.

This seemed to be a direct snub to the new relationship with the US, which was already being couched in the rhetoric of human rights and democracy. However, the calculations of Uzbekistan's leaders that the US would overlook abuses in exchange for military cooperation proved to be correct. Beth Jones, the Assistant Secretary of State for Eurasian Affairs, turned up in Tashkent two days after the referendum to announce an extra $160 million in US aid to the Uzbek government. A delegation led by US Senator Joe Lieberman admitted that it had not raised the issue with any officials ahead of

---

7   Personal communications, Tashkent, March 2002.

the vote. Thus was set in pattern a game of rhetoric and reality that continued for the next four years.

In March 2002 Karimov received his ultimate accolade: a long-sought visit to Washington. His visit to the White House to meet President Bush was hardly noticed in Washington DC—Karimov was just another far-away leader driving down Pennsylvania Avenue—but in Tashkent it produced wall-to-wall coverage. Less well advertised—the text was not made public by either side for several months—was a rather strange document, the "Declaration on the Strategic Partnership and Cooperation Framework Between the United States of America and the Republic of Uzbekistan", signed during the Washington visit.[8]

This agreement included far-reaching promises from both sides. The US offered a security relationship and economic assistance, and Tashkent made promises to "...further intensify the democratic transformation of society", develop a multiparty democracy and expand the role of independent media. US officials were strangely optimistic about this document, even claiming that the Uzbek side had insisted on the inclusion of a section on democratisation. But US officials still had a lot to learn about negotiating with the Uzbek government, which routinely ignored a whole raft of international conventions that it had signed. The Uzbek government would sign almost anything, if it felt signing was advantageous, but seldom had any intention of implementing it. An important point was that none of the proposals in the document had any timing attached, and there was no mechanism for monitoring Uzbekistan's commitments.

Karimov was brilliant at using the rhetoric of political and economic reform when necessary. Many Western diplomats, particularly at the US embassy, thought that he was an embattled reformer, surrounded by powerful clan leaders who restricted his natural preference for modernisation. He was advertised as a south-east Asian style authoritarian moderniser, who would delay democracy for the

---

8   For reasons that were never clear, the Declaration was only made public in July 2002. Available at: http://www.fas.org/terrorism/at/docs/2002/US-UzbekPartnership.htm

sake of political stability and rapid economic growth, but would push through modernising reforms that would take the country forward. In truth, while the bureaucrats and mafia figures around him certainly did have power and influence, Karimov was far from being the puppet ruler of other forces. Karimov himself had no commitment to political or economic reforms, and even his semblance of a national vision had largely faded by 2001, when his sole remaining ambition seemed to be to cling onto power.

Western officials were easily duped by Karimov's charismatic style and by the slick presentations of his more cosmopolitan aides. Among them was Sadyk Safaev, the urbane Ambassador in Washington, and later foreign minister, who was a favourite among US diplomats: fluent in English and willing to discuss problems that no other Uzbek government official cared to address, he had a reputation as a reformer in the Western categorisation of government officials. Akmal Saidov headed something called the National Centre for Human Rights, which spent most of its budget—much of it coming from international organisations—on glossy brochures about the Uzbek legal system, but did nothing to prevent widespread human rights abuses. The National Ombudsman, a tough woman called Sayyora Rashidova, the daughter of Uzbekistan's former Communist Party leader Sharif Rashidov, fulfilled a similar role. A few academics from government think tanks were also used to spread the message: that the government was committed to reform, but needed time, as well as political and economic support from the West.

These officials were sometimes very persuasive. They openly admitted to failings by the government, but suggested that these were exaggerated and that there were no easy solutions. They pointed out that much of the repression was aimed at Islamist extremists; this fell on fertile ground with many visiting delegations. The government's commitment to secularism, its good relationship with Israel and its suspicion of the UN, did much to persuade visiting Republicans that this was an ally they could do business with.

The illusion of progress

While delegations of Westerners skipped between Tashkent's only five-star hotel and the foreign ministry, ordinary people got on with their lives. There was little change on the ground as a result of Karimov's shift in foreign policy priorities towards the West. Taxi drivers complained about the constant road closures to accommodate visiting motorcades, but they were used to that anyway: whenever Karimov left his residence, half the city came to a halt. The more optimistic Uzbeks believed that that the US base would be followed by major investment in the economy, and that US pressure would gradually produce a more open political environment.

At first the optimists seemed to be right. In March 2002 one local human rights group was legally registered. The small community of human rights activists enjoyed slightly more freedom than in the past, and there were fewer arrests of political and religious opponents of the regime than in previous years. This was presented as significant progress by the government and by the US embassy, although the latter admitted that there were still as many as 600 arrests of opponents of the regime during 2002,[9] most of them being sentenced on the flimsiest of evidence and usually convicted on the basis of a confession, frequently produced by using torture. The one human rights group that had been registered subsequently became more pro-government in its views, and other groups were denied registration later in the year. In a strange twisting of reality, the US State Department blamed the groups themselves, rather than the government, for this failure to legalise their activity.[10]

What seemed to be another breakthrough came in May 2002, when the official body that censored all newspapers was abolished, to much applause from Western diplomats. In reality, censorship now became the responsibility of newspaper editors and owners, and by extension every individual journalist: any deviation from the of-

9 US State Department, "Country Reports on Human Rights Practice – Uzbekistan, 2002", 31 March 2003.

10 US Department of State, "US Engagement in Central Asia: Successes", 27 November 2002.

ficial line would still produce a heavy-handed response. As a result, there was no significant change in the official press, although a few more adventurous articles on social problems briefly appeared in Russian-language papers in Tashkent, before they too were gradually expunged. As before, the security services blocked any critical internet sites, and television and radio outlets were almost exclusively dominated by government propaganda.

During 2002, there was no evidence of any deep commitment to serious change on the part of the government. Instead, a slightly cynical diplomatic game seemed to be developing: US officials would "urge" reforms in polite meetings with the government, and government officials would promise unspecified changes at an unspecified future date. These proposed reforms were of a largely symbolic, legalistic nature. No US diplomat ever proposed that perhaps the regime might begin moving towards some kind of democratic elections; what the US needed was enough symbolic change to assure Congress and human rights groups that slow but steady progress was occurring. The last thing anybody wanted was a change in regime.

These tiny, cosmetic steps were relentlessly advertised by US officials. The ending of formal censorship and the registration of a human rights group were repeatedly used as evidence of progress by a series of congressional and government envoys, who passed through Tashkent during the year. Few offered any critique of the Uzbek government; some were downright obsequious in their comments. The US Administration's senior economics official, Treasury Secretary Paul O'Neill, used a visit in June 2002 to praise Karimov's disastrous economic policies and attack journalists who suggested that reality was a little more depressing than he had imagined. After batting away yet another critical question, he dismissed the reporters in his own unique way:

I would suggest one thing to you, for those of you who transmit these questions and events and are interested in the development of social policy in countries around the world. It would be well for you to go and make inquiries of people across the region who have realized the difference from living in a welfare state or one that's controlled by totalitarianism to the freedom that they feel when they have their own land, and they own their own land and they have the ability to create a good life for themselves and their families. Maybe I haven't been looking in the right places, but I haven't found anyone who has had the opportunity to become a land-owner instead of a slave to a government who prefers to be a slave to a government.[11]

This was typical of some Western rhetoric towards Central Asian states, which equated independence from Russia with "freedom", without acknowledging that post-Soviet reality, whatever a country's foreign policy orientation, could retain many of the most objectionable elements of Soviet politics, and even add some new repression. Clearly nobody had briefed O'Neill at the US embassy that most people in rural areas lived on state-run cotton plantations, which differed only in nomenclature from the Soviet experience of working on collective farms. Even the small number of semi-private farmers had to fulfil government orders for cotton cultivation, for which they seldom received payment.

Despite the lack of progress, the US continued to promote its positive view of Uzbekistan, which concentrated on progress in human rights and the country's role in the "war on terror". On 8 September 2002 Secretary of State Powell reported to Congress on the situation in Uzbekistan, as he was required to do under the appropriate legislation, and asserted that there had been substantial improvement on human rights. He pointed to fewer arrests of religious and political activists in 2002 and to an amnesty conducted in December 2002, in which several hundred prisoners were released. But all these measures were essentially symbolic, trying to burnish the image of the regime, without affecting the system itself. In any case, the number of arrests seemed to grow again in the last few months of 2002, and again in 2003. The positive assessment of the situation from Powell allowed US aid to continue flowing, with $219m allocated in 2002, followed by $86.1m in 2003, a big increase from the $55m that Uzbekistan had received in 2001, although still far less than the Uzbek government was seeking.[12]

---

11 "Joint Press Conference With President Islam Karimov of Uzbekistan: Paul H. O'Neill, Secretary of the Treasury", Tashkent, 17 July 2002. Accessed at http://www.state.gov/e/eeb/rls/rm/2002/11945.htm.

12 US State Department, Bureau of European and Eurasian Affairs, Fact

The minor signs of progress in early 2002 hid a grim reality. Political prisoners were still regularly being tortured and abused. According to Mamadali Makhmudov, a writer who had been imprisoned in 1999 for 14 years because of his friendship with opposition leader Muhammed Salikh, abuses of political prisoners imprisoned under article 159 (Infringement of the Constitutional Order of Uzbekistan) actually intensified in 2002: "The oppression increased when [Karimov] returned from America. Although Chirchik [prison camp] is relatively better, an order came from on high to torture the 159-ers. Each day ten people are taken away. I was on yesterday's list. Olim Nurov, Olim Khasanov, Muktor, Ikrom, Ladgar also...."[13]

Uzbekistan's repression went beyond ordinary brutality, and was often marked by a peculiar sadism. Muzafar Avazov and Husnidin Alimov, who were both imprisoned under Article 159, died in August 2002 in Jaslyk prison. According to prison officials, the seventy per cent burns on their bodies were the result of an accident with some hot tea. After British Ambassador Craig Murray started investigating the case, it emerged that Avazov and Alimov had actually died after being immersed in boiling water. Avazov's mother was later sentenced to six years in prison, apparently for trying to seek justice for her son.[14]

In a concession to outside pressure, the UN Special Rapporteur on Torture, Theo van Boven, was allowed to visit Uzbekistan in November-December 2002. Despite not being able to visit the notorious National Security Service (NSS—the former KGB) cells in Tashkent, van Boven produced a damning report that concluded that torture was "systematic" within the law enforcement system, and called for radical changes, including a public acknowledgement by the Uzbek leadership that torture was a serious problem and that measures would be taken to tackle it. The government effectively re-

---

Sheet, 17 February 2004; Fact Sheet, 9 December 2002, "US Assistance to Uzbekistan—Fiscal Year 2002". Figures for total aid allocation are complicated by multiple agency expenditure.

13 Letter from Mamadali Mukhmudov, written from Chirchik prison.

14 Jim Lobe, "Conviction of 62-year-old mother focuses attention on Uzbekistan's human rights record", *Eurasianet*, 17 February 2004.

jected the report, but admitted there was a problem in isolated cases with the use of torture. The authorities began a fairly meaningless consultation programme on an "action plan" against torture, which engaged the international community in a further spate of seminars, conferences, and offers of training and assistance for the police.

The conclusions of van Boven's report were supported by countless reports by former prisoners. One prisoner, the journalist Ruslan Sharipov, described what happened during his time in police detention:

One detainee was severely beaten in front of me and then—in handcuffs and leg-irons—hung out of a third-floor window, head down, and told he was about to be dropped, at which point he lost consciousness. After he came round, he was tortured further with the gas-mask suffocation method and by having his feet placed in an iron bucket in which a fire had been started. He fainted again, and at this point he was taken away. Two days after I arrived, a detainee from my cell, Shahruh, was taken up to the second floor for one of the regular interrogation sessions. When he came back—carried into the cell by a couple of policemen and dumped on one of the bunks—he was in a terrible state, covered in blood and with all his clothes torn. All his toenails had been ripped out. He was unable to stand, and said he thought his legs were broken from a beating with a metal hammer. Shahruh explained that interrogators were trying to get him to confess that he murdered an 18-year-old-girl, but he had held out, insisting his innocence. He screamed all night but was given no medical attention. In the morning, he was taken away on a stretcher and never returned to the cell.[15]

This behaviour was simply routine in most prisons, particularly in the early stages of detention when the police were trying to get the accused to sign a confession. Other reports suggested that rape of both men and women was common; human rights groups reported that threats to kill or rape children and wives of prisoners were frequently used. Sometimes criminals were hired to deal with recalcitrant prisoners. Sharipov talked to one such "agent":

He told me that such agents will carry out any orders, and that he himself had killed many detainees and made it look like suicide. In fact, he had killed a man just the previous week, he said. The man was a devout Muslim, and refused to confess to any crime. [The agent] received orders to get

---

15 Ruslan Sharipov, "Uzbek prisons – a survivors guide", IWPR, 10 December 2004, at www.iwpr.net.

a confession at any cost. He raped the man, and then threw him from an upper bunk, head first into the toilet. The fall killed the man immediately. [The agent] smiled as he recounted the incident, and was visibly proud of what he had done.[16]

The evidence of abuses was reported regularly by human rights groups, but their accounts represented only a small proportion of the real horrors of Uzbek repression. Only the bravest or most desperate families informed human rights groups of their situation. Prisoners were regularly told that things would only get worse if they complained to international organisations of their position, and most tried to avoid provoking any reprisals. Only the grossest abuses tended to receive any real publicity, and the everyday abuses suffered by many ordinary people were routinely ignored. Well known journalists or activists in Tashkent at least had a chance of international action on their behalf, but lowly farmers in the provinces or ordinary people picked up for criminal offences had almost nobody to speak on their behalf.

Some of the torture and brutality in prisons had no rationale at all. It was simply the result of a deliberate government policy of brutalisation and impunity. But initial police torture was often the result of the system. The police tortured people because they had little motivation to try and establish guilt or innocence. Instead, they were forced to meet quotas for arrests and convictions for each quarter. To meet the quota they were encouraged to get a confession from the accused; courts almost never rejected these confessions as evidence, and conviction rates were close to 100 per cent. Not meeting the quotas would entail serious reprisals from the Interior Ministry leadership; using torture to force confessions out of prisoners was unlikely to lead to any repercussions at all. Occasionally, a few unlucky officers were singled out for exemplary punishment for torture: usually they had somehow fallen out of favour with their superiors for other reasons, and this was an easy way to get rid of them.

Not all the police were happy with the corrupt, ineffective and brutal system of which they were a part. Older, more professional

---

16 Ibid.

officers were often deeply disillusioned with the roles they were required to play. Many looked back on the Soviet period as a "golden age" of more honest policing, an indictment indeed of contemporary Uzbek reality. The Soviet system had developed a brand of professionally trained policemen, even if they operated in a system where justice was decided by the one-party state. In the Uzbek system, many appointments were filled by the politically well connected, who used the position for its many perks, but had no professional training or interest in the job itself. The Interior Ministry thus became a hugely corrupt bureaucracy, which depended heavily on continued high levels of repression for its existence and funding, much of it gained from illegal sources. The system was totally brutal and totally corrupt. Brutality began at the top, and reached down to the lowliest village policeman. Money was collected at the bottom, and cascaded up to the top, to the enormous enrichment of senior officers.

The US, the UN and other international agencies offered a variety of proposals to tackle torture in prisons and places of detention, but they ignored the systemic reality that ensured that torture would always be present in the law enforcement agencies, until there were wholesale reforms of the system. While Western engagement concentrated on providing human rights training for officers, or improving forensic facilities to allow other evidence to be collected, almost nobody pointed out that under such an authoritarian regime there would be little change unless the media could freely report on police abuses, and there was a real parliament or other political institutions with the power and willingness to hold the security forces accountable. Instead, the approach to both police and military reform was largely technical, with no real sense of the broader political environment in which they operated.

This whole system was rotten, but nobody in the diplomatic community in Tashkent was keen to point it out. Few were prepared to challenge the actual structure of governance that gave rise to all the problems of human rights abuses and lack of political openness. Instead, small victories were sought at the margins—a conference on religion here, a meeting of human rights activists there—but none of this challenged the monopolistic power of the government to abuse its population on an everyday basis.

The US government was not alone in its acceptance of the status quo. With a few exceptions, most European embassies were happy to go along with this tacit recognition that "nothing could be done". In private, European diplomats were cynical about the regime, but many believed that any alternative could only be worse.

This rather cosy consensus was shattered in mid-2002, when a new British Ambassador, Craig Murray, arrived in Tashkent, and began to take a more critical line. In October, in a speech at the opening of a US non-governmental organisation (NGO), Freedom House, Murray gave a speech that criticised the egregious human rights abuses in the country, and called for real change, including:

...releases of political prisoners; registration of political opposition parties and human rights groups; the opportunity for people to express their opinions in free elections and through a free media and the right to free assembly; and to practice their religious beliefs without fear of persecution.[17]

None of this was very controversial in the abstract. And he was not stepping out on his own: the speech had been cleared with the Foreign Office in London, albeit after something of a fight. But it immediately made Murray something of a hero among human rights activists in the audience. However, another attendee, listening with a stony face, was the US Ambassador John Herbst, whose own speech on the same occasion had again underlined the "progress" that Uzbekistan was making. Their differing views of policy towards Uzbekistan, and indeed on global politics in its entirety, were accentuated by their contrasting diplomatic styles.

Herbst was a sincere and cautious diplomat, who firmly believed in the the danger faced by the Uzbek government from Islamist activism. He claimed that he had good access to the regime, through his weekly meetings with the foreign minister, but he never seemed to have the kind of instinctive understanding of the political system that would

---

17 Speech by Ambassador Craig Murray, Freedom House, 17 October 2002, available at http://archive.muslimuzbekistan.com/eng/ennews/2003/10/ennews18102003_2.html

have given US policy a much needed dose of scepticism. Murray was a different figure altogether, a *bon viveur* who became a familiar sight in the city's nightclubs. But he also spent a good deal of time trying to understand what was going on in Uzbekistan. He developed a wide range of informal contacts, and travelled outside the capital, something only a few diplomats ever did extensively. But Murray was an isolated voice in the diplomatic community in Tashkent, and some other embassies did their best to undermine his credibility.

"The Year of Economics"

The US embassy, privately fearing that there would be no rapid movement on human rights issues, began to say that 2002 would be "the year of economics" in Uzbekistan. This approach was based on a false premise, that somehow economic reform was much more feasible than progress on political change or human rights. In reality, the regime was even more fearful of economic reform than of improving the human rights situation. Serious changes in economic policy would substantially undermine the dominance of the economy by the small elite close to Karimov, and start the emergence of a new, independent business class that could potentially challenge their political dominance.

New US aid programmes funded foreign advisers and consultants in everything from statistics to banking reform. Most of them had little idea of the political context in which they were working, and found it almost impossible to understand what was going on in the real Uzbek economy. Although reports, PowerPoint presentations, and pie charts were produced in some abundance, there was little impact on the real decision-makers, and even less on the average Uzbek, who still eked out an existence on an average salary of less than a dollar a day.

Long-suffering officials at the Finance ministry used to complain that the country's main problem was that their president thought he was an economist. Karimov's many years in *Gosplan*, the Soviet state planning ministry, had convinced him that he understood better than anybody the intricacies of economic policy. He had developed

27

his own "Uzbek model" of economic development, which was largely a warmed-up version of Soviet economics: everything still revolved around the state, with just a veneer of private enterprise. By 2001 these policies, although superficially attractive because of their apparent concern for social stability and welfare, had simply avoided difficult choices, and instead delivered the economy into the hands of a corrupt and kleptocratic elite. Economic growth was down, foreign investment was minimal, and the IMF had left the country, its advice on economic reform having been consistently ignored. It seemed that things could not get much worse, but the next four years would see a further attack on ordinary Uzbeks' already miserable living standards.

Unlike Russia, Ukraine or Kazakhstan, Uzbekistan had opposed any idea of "shock therapy" and mass privatisation. Although homes and small-scale enterprises had been passed to private hands, a large part of major industry remained under state control. The state also retained huge powers to intervene in business, and the average entrepreneur spent much of his or her time dealing with the rapacious officials in this overweening bureaucracy. Nevertheless, avoiding the accelerated privatisations undertaken by Russia and other former Soviet states seemed initially to have preserved a certain level of stability in the economy. By 1999, according to official figures, Uzbekistan had recovered to 95 per cent of its 1991 level of GDP, while the average in the former Soviet Union (without the Baltic states) was just 65 per cent. The so-called Uzbek economic model even garnered a small Western fan-club, led by Chicago economist Martin Spechler, who praised the idea of gradual economic reform with no serious impact on social stability.[18]

---

18 The "Uzbek paradox ... is this: although Uzbekistan has been very reluctant and slow to adopt the neo-liberal economic reforms recommended by the 'Washington consensus' in general and by the IMF in particular, its measured economic growth has been surprisingly rapid and robust. By contrast, Kazakhstan and Kyrgyzstan have not achieved the economic rebound predicted by IMF models and advice". All this was news to the thousands of Uzbeks who travelled to Kazakhstan in search of work in its booming economy, or even to Kyrgyzstan, widely seen, outside Uzbekistan, as an economic failure. Martin Spechler *et al.* 'The Uzbek Paradox', p. 1, at http://www.gdnet.org/pdf/draft_country_studies/Uzbekistan_final.pdf.

In reality, the Uzbek economic model was a disaster, and the statistics were largely mythical. You only had to ask an ordinary farmer to find out the grim reality. A majority of Uzbeks worked in agriculture, and most of those were caught up in a system of cotton plantations that differed little from the old Soviet agricultural system of collective farms. Effectively "farmers" worked for almost nothing on these vast state-owned farms, often receiving cotton oil or other side products in lieu of wages. They survived only by retaining small private plots of land, on which they grew vegetables and kept a couple of cows. A small number had family farms on land, which they leased from the government, but even they were forced to grow what the government ordered, inevitably cotton, from which they received almost no profit at all. The cotton sector earned Uzbekistan up to $1,000 million a year in hard currency earnings, but most of the profit went to a few powerful individuals close to the government and the security forces. Western cotton buyers, such as Switzerland's Reinhart, also did well out of this exploitative system, but seemed impervious to the reports of abuses in the cotton fields: child labour was regularly used, and workers were subject to physical abuse and shocking conditions.

The countryside had a high birth rate, and there was a frightening growth in rural unemployment among young men. It was these youngsters who made up the bulk of increasingly high migration, both inside Uzbekistan to the cities, but also further afield, to Russia, Kazakhstan and Kyrgyzstan, and on to Turkey and Europe, when possible, and to South Korea and other Asian states. You could see them on the edge of any town, these so-called *mardikorlar* (casual workers), usually standing by a roundabout or crossroads. Cars would pull up, the crowd of workers would surge forward, and a lucky two or three would be picked to work for the day, earning up to two dollars each for a long day at a construction site. Other times the police would pull up and workers would scatter: those who were caught would be thrown out of the city, where they had no legal right to reside, and probably have to pay the police not to spend time in prison.

Slightly luckier than those caught in the rural plantation system were those who worked at state-owned factories, although they sel-

29

dom received anything like a living wage. Most received less than $20 per month, and some went for months without getting their salaries. Almost all these factories—which made everything from aircraft to bad, Soviet-style shoes—were loss-making, especially against competition from Chinese producers. But the government feared even greater social discontent if they were closed.

Like any decent Soviet-era economist, Karimov believed that an economy really meant factories, the bigger the better. There was a huge amount of pride in a new Daewoo factory in Andijan, which produced small cars and minibuses, but the only way it could stay in operation was by putting extremely high tariffs on any car imports. Thus a small Daewoo car cost about $10,000, while in neighbouring Kyrgyzstan better-quality foreign cars could be had for much less. But once Daewoo had begun its production, it was impossible to allow it to fail. Protectionism was bound to follow, but Uzbekistan's geographical position made it highly dependent on trade for any real economic growth. The contradictions in this economic policy were obvious to most ordinary Uzbeks, but not, it seemed, to their rulers.

While some Western economists found this economic model strangely alluring, any Tashkent taxi driver could point out the flaws inherent in the policy. Many drivers were highly qualified: engineers and specialists who had left their poorly paid jobs at state enterprises. They could propound at length on the advantages of a convertible currency (Uzbekistan's som was not convertible, and a thriving black market operated), the need for trade liberalisation measures, and ways to attract foreign investment. And they all seemed to have intimate knowledge of the machinations of Uzbekistan's economic elite.

Karimov's economic policies may have offered little for ordinary people, but they were extremely lucrative for the small ruling elite, which was able to manipulate the state to its own advantage. In 2002 the whole economic apparatus was managed by a small number of powerful political figures, who controlled key income-producing parts of the economy. Deputy Prime Minister Mirabror Usmanov was a typical example. He had worked his way up through the Soviet trade sector, and after independence presided over an empire of import-export operations and retail outlets in Tashkent. Other major players included Gafur Rakhimov, the head of the Uzbek Olympic Committee, who was once denied a visa to the Sydney Olympic Games because of his alleged links to organised crime (which he strongly denied). His ally, Salim Abduvaliev, had also built up a wide range of legal business interests, and expanded into sport. He was often linked to the mini-jet-set that circled around the presidential daughters, Gulnora and Lola Karimova. Gulnora, in particular, began to develop her own business interests when she returned from the US in 2001, after a messy divorce.[19]

This small elite lived in luxury mansions in Tashkent, and often owned property abroad. In contrast to neighbouring Kazakhstan, however, too ostentatious displays of wealth were frowned on. When one British cotton trader arranged a deal to buy cotton with one of the mafia leaders who controlled such arrangements, he was met by a couple of slightly down-at-heel young men—both multimillion-aires—driving an old Lada car. But businesspeople of this kind were vastly rich—one owned an island in the Indian Ocean, others had major investments in property in Dubai.[20]

This general tendency not to display ostentious wealth within the country may have informed the view—popular in the US embassy at the time—that the leadership in Uzbekistan was not corrupt in the same way as in say, Kazakhstan. This convenient myth was finally undermined when details emerged of the financial affairs of the president's daughter, Gulnora, after her financial adviser defected to the US in 2003. Even her 10-year-old son had $1 million in the bank, and she had been involved in a host of machinations that had netted her tens of millions of dollars in profits.[21] This was not much compared with

---

19 The divorce from Mansur Maqsudi also caused problems for Coca-Cola's investment in Uzbekistan. Maqsudi was forced out of the joint-venture after the divorce. Karimova's refusal to agree access to the couple's children led to the issue of an arrest warrant by a US court. See Edward Alden, Andrew Ward, "Bottled up: why Coke stands accused of being too cosy with the Karimovs", *Financial Times*, 16 June 2006.

20 Personal communication, cotton trader, Tashkent, October 2002.

21 David Stern, "Rich pickings for Uzbek leader's daughter", *Financial Times*, 18 August 2003.

the Nazarbaevs in Kazakhstan perhaps, but Gulnora had started late in business, and was catching up with her rivals quickly.

Economic reform, in theory, would mean everybody getting a piece of a larger pie, but in reality it would ensure that the exclusive access to wealth that the presidential family and other leading political players enjoyed would no longer be guaranteed. There was no rational reason for any of these figures to change a system that suited them very well. Reform was only necessary for national development and for the broader population, but very few people in the elite had any real vision for the future of Uzbekistan. Most were narrow-minded, greedy and rapacious.

There were some genuine reformers in the elite, but they seldom held serious decision-making positions. Those who remained in the system were inevitably corrupted by it. Those who supported more principled positions were gradually weaned away from power, and most ended up in meaningless academic institutes, with little influence on real policy-making. Those labelled as "reformers" in the government in 2002-3 had little real interest in reform at all, although many diplomats liked to view the government as involved in a struggle between "reformers" and "conservatives". This formula, much loved by Western commentators on Russia, was deeply misleading when transferred to the Uzbek context. Those favoured by the US, as "reformers", were hardly more reformist than those labelled as conservatives. They were simply better at concealing their general antipathy to any change in the economic structure that would damage their own personal positions.

With little understanding of the dynamics at work, the US embassy began to press for economic change. It encouraged the IMF to resume contacts with the government: negotiations in early 2002 resulted in a "staff monitored programme", an agreement by the government to follow a reform programme, but with no financial assistance attached. The government was not happy with this arrangement: it wanted the money up front, with reforms perhaps to follow later. However, the IMF programme promised that if the government completed some basic reforms, such as currency convertibility, it would be eligible for significant assistance. The World Bank and the Asian Development Bank also offered substantial assistance if reforms were initiated.

There was plenty of positive rhetoric from the government, and some minor improvements—the complex exchange rate mechanism was at least simplified—but overall the rhetoric outstripped reality. Life was still tough for the private sector, with little access to hard currency, massive bureaucracy and corruption, and semi-criminal protection rackets operating in many sectors. Despite the lack of significant progress, in the late summer of 2002 the US pressured the IMF and other multilateral lenders to provide significant financial support to the government, but the sceptical head of the World Bank office, David Pearce, and the British Ambassador, Craig Murray, argued that it would be foolish to commit funds without any evidence of serious commitment to reform.

Throughout 2002 the IMF continued to work with the government on its reform programme, but despite US pressure for a charitable view of Uzbekistan's largely illusory economic reforms, the IMF was not sufficiently impressed to offer any financial assistance.

The IMF had concentrated on persuading the government to make the Uzbek som convertible, which would in theory have allowed improved trade and encouraged foreign investment. However, the powerful mafia groups that controlled much of the economy were highly reliant on the multiple-exchange regime for their flow of illicit income. In a normal import-export regime their businesses would probably not survive; at the very least they would be far less lucrative. The government pushed ahead with a limited devaluation of the som, as a prelude to restricted convertibility, but officials feared that too great a devaluation could bankrupt the dysfunctional banking system, which had for years been giving out hard currency loans to privileged businessmen whose businesses were only viable under artificial exchange rates. More important, they were concerned that under a more liberal exchange regime the consumer goods sector would be dominated by informal traders at the bazaars, and existing government-linked business empires would not be able to compete.

Although the government liked to showcase its failing industry, such as the Daewoo car plant, the real centre of the economy remained the bazaar, as it had done for centuries. Hundreds of thousands of people scraped a living through casual import-export trade, selling cheap Chinese and Turkish goods at huge open-air markets. The biggest market, a sprawling mass of stalls and traders at the Hippodrome outside Tashkent, offered almost anything you could imagine, at prices that even Tashkent's impoverished middle classes could afford.

In May 2002 the government introduced a raft of new tariffs on imports of consumer goods, reaching as much as 90 per cent, although the highest rate was later dropped to a still prohibitive 70 per cent. The new laws also forced traders to procure a raft of new documentation to regulate their trading, which in reality simply meant paying much higher bribes to state organs. The tax police swooped on bazaars across the country and seized any goods that did not have the right documents. The authorities closed down the Hippodrome bazaar, making thousands of traders unemployed.

Anti-government protests were almost unprecedented in Uzbekistan, but in July 2002 bazaar traders in the capital went on strike and held protests, and there were reports of scuffles with the police. Some ringleaders were reportedly arrested; others were persuaded to go back to work. The new rules had left some traders effectively bankrupt: they often bought goods on credit, but now that these had been seized by the police, they would be unable to repay their loans. Many were absolutely desperate. One man in Khorezm reportedly set fire to himself in front of the tax office, after tax police had seized his goods three times, leaving him completely destitute.

It was not just the traders who suffered; consumers were now faced with much higher prices. Prices for basic goods rose by two or three times, and canny shoppers began to cross the border to shop at cheaper markets in neighbouring countries. Tashkent housewives travelled in packed minibuses a couple of hours north to Shymkent in Kazakhstan, where prices were now much lower and the choice of goods much greater than back home. From the Fergana valley, shoppers in search of bargains travelled to the huge market at Kara-Suu in Kyrgyzstan, where Chinese goods from Urumchi and Kashgar were on sale at extremely cheap prices. The border crossings became crowded with shoppers every weekend, and one diplomat calculated that at least $100 million flowed out of the country to Kara-Suu and Shymkent in October 2002.[22]

Such disastrous economic consequences would have made any other government think again about its policies. Not in Uzbekistan, however. In December 2002 the government went further, effectively outlawing any small company from being involved in cross-border wholesale trade, leaving only three or four companies legally running import operations, all of them linked to leading members of the government or their relatives.

In a final blow against the traders, the government simply closed the borders with Kazakhstan and Kyrgyzstan, ending the weekend shopping trips and impoverishing the large part of the population that depended on trading to make ends meet. Uzbek troops destroyed the bridge across the Shakhrikhansay river, which divided Kyrgyz Kara-Suu from Uzbek territory. Traders now had to travel 20 miles to the nearest crossing, or try and get across the river illegally: many did so, and there were reports of dozens of elderly women, laden with goods, drowning when they fell from makeshift wire bridges. The destroyed bridge at Kara-Suu was symbolic of Uzbekistan's self-imposed isolation. Government propaganda made much of the ancient Silk Route from China across Central Asia to Europe: in one stroke, the government had ended any chance to resuscitate a once great trading route.

Throughout this period, international criticism of the government's economic policy was muted, although polite diplomatic noises were made when the borders were finally closed in December. But it was clear that the "Year of Economics" had failed miserably: the US policy of positive engagement was not producing any results. In many ways, indeed, the situation seemed to be getting worse. The European Bank for Reconstruction and Development (EBRD) was particularly worried, since it was planning to hold its Annual Meeting in Tashkent for the first time, in May 2003. It was feared that the Annual Meeting might be a major embarrassment for the EBRD,

---

22 Personal communication, Tashkent, November 2002.

given Uzbekistan's movement away from economic reform and its terrible human rights record.

The EBRD was a good example of why it was difficult for international organisations to start pushing for economic reforms in 2002. The Bank—which was set up to assist post-Soviet economies in their transition to market economies—had for years uncritically given money (over 500m euros by 2003) to the Uzbek government and to Uzbek companies linked to the regime, without demanding much in return. Uniquely among international financial institutions, the EBRD had a specific commitment in its charter, under Article 1, to invest money only in countries with a commitment to democracy and market economics. The Uzbek government had demonstrated no commitment to either tenet, but prior to 2003 the Bank had made little effort to promote a reform agenda. By the time the Bank began setting out conditions for lending, in 2003, it was far too late to have any real influence.

The May 2003 EBRD meeting itself was a slightly surreal affair. The government conducted its usual showcase politics, investing millions in new hotels that would subsequently be half-empty, and issuing Soviet-style speeches on the country's vibrant investment climate. But the government was on the receiving end of bitter criticism from human rights activists, who were allowed to speak in several of the forums. Western officials, including Clare Short, the British International Development Secretary, were publicly critical of Uzbek government policy. But the government was not listening: Karimov demonstratively removed his headphones during their speeches. In a concession to the EBRD, these speeches had been broadcast live on television, shocking many viewers, used more to the usual pro-government propaganda. "I thought all these foreigners always supported Karimov," one young man told me afterwards. "It turns out they don't believe him either."[23]

The international criticisms went down badly with government officials. At a reception afterwards, government ministers sat in the Japanese garden bemoaning the foreigners' lack of understanding of Uzbek

---

23 Personal communication, Tashkent, May 2003.

political culture. This line was common among Uzbek government supporters, claiming that Westerners could never fathom the mythical "Uzbek mentality". They had a few supporters, especially among the Americans, who had been conspicuously quiet throughout the meeting, and had not overtly backed the stronger European line.

The EBRD meeting was the high point of international engagement with Uzbekistan after 2001. With hundreds of delegates, businesspeople and bankers, the government had a chance to make a breakthrough in its economic policies, and attract much needed foreign investment. With that moment lost, Uzbekistan now began to blunder badly, caught in the contradictions of its own policy. The economy probably shrank in 2003: the IMF suggested it had grown by 0.3 per cent,[24] but anecdotal evidence suggested that overall economic activity had collapsed. Official figures, as usual, suggested surging growth, but only the most gullible of observers believed these statistics. The reason for the collapse in activity was the all-out attack on cross-border trade, and the virtual closure of borders to private traders with Kazakhstan and Kyrgyzstan. The result was to push much of the bazaar trade into the illegal sector, with massive bribery the only way to ensure that goods still reached markets.

About 20 miles from the ancient city of Bukhara, the town of Gulistan was home to one such market. Buyers came from miles around to browse among its enormous varieties of clothes and cheap consumer goods, mostly from China. One man, Rustam, who was selling an array of colourful Chinese rucksacks, grinned and admitted: "I'm a contrabandist", using the Uzbek government's label for these illegal private traders. "Everybody here is illegal really", he laughed, waving a hand around the stalls around him. There were plenty of police around, but they seemed much more intent on getting their cut than on implementing unpopular legislation. But profits were down. Rustam still made a useful $300 a month, but he had to pay far more bribes than before and support a big extended family with

---

24 It later revised this figure to 1.1 per cent.

the money. It was not just the bribes, he explained: "People have less money in their pockets. The economy is terrible".[25]

The decline in the informal trade economy had only a limited impact on government revenue: most income still came from the export of cotton and gold, and this revenue was more dependent on world prices than anything else. But trade restrictions hit the population hard, including the middle classes, many of whom were also involved in trading activities. Uzbekistan needed an economically prosperous small and medium business class to build a more stable economic and political future. But the government was concerned that such a socio-economic development would undermine its own control over the economy, and also lead to potentially troublesome pressure for political change.

The economic situation was particularly bad in border areas such as the Fergana valley. Towns such as Andijan, which had once been among the most prosperous in Uzbekistan, suffered disproportionately. Now Uzbeks from Fergana villages were more than happy to cross the border and work on Kyrgyz farms for a dollar a day. Some 80 per cent of prostitutes working in Osh's lively red light district were from Uzbekistan, according to local NGOs. They also made up the bulk of the passengers on Osh's only international flight, a weekly charter to Dubai that was presumed to be a one-way ticket for sex trafficking.[26]

Some people were still making money in the Fergana region, but most of it was illegal. Unsanctioned cotton exports across the border to Kyrgyzstan were extremely lucrative. Some of this risky cross-border trade was carried out by local farmers, but most of it was in the hands of a powerful mafia that held official posts in Andijan. Border guards and police were all involved in the trade, but much of the money came back into Kyrgyzstan. Osh's casinos did a roaring trade for visiting Uzbeks, laundering their money through the roulette wheel.

---

25 Personal communication, Gulistan, June 2003.

26 When police finally stopped this regular flight, in 2006, almost all the girls on board were citizens of Uzbekistan, many of them under age.

This hugely unequal economy—divided between a small, enriched, corrupt elite and a mass of increasingly impoverished ordinary citizens—was hardly a recipe for stability. And everybody knew that things were getting worse. But the US was still putting a brave face on the unfolding disaster. As one of its more cynical diplomats put it to me in late 2003: "If you want good news, come to the US embassy". By the end of that year, it was in short supply elsewhere.

Democrats and diplomats

Western embassies often intervened on behalf of arrested activists or journalists, bringing up their cases with officials, or sometimes helping them leave the country. Individual officers at the US embassy were particularly helpful in several cases, where Uzbeks faced arrest over their political activities. Gradually, these critical voices were leaving Tashkent, as governmental pressure increased. Foreign journalists were finding it harder to get visas. NGOs came under increased pressure.

The range of alternative voices in the city was narrowing quickly. In August 2003 the British Ambassador Craig Murray, one of the most outspoken critics of the government, was asked to resign by the Foreign Office. Murray had become increasingly critical since his first speech in October 2002; he regularly castigated the government, and was influential in pushing a more critical line at the EBRD meeting in May 2003. The Uzbeks had long tried to gather discrediting information on Murray, with little success.

A whispering campaign against Murray was kept alive by the Uzbeks, supported by some diplomats from other embassies, who told me that he "did not understand the situation", "was an alcoholic" or "had lost all influence with the government". True, relations between government officials and the UK were frosty, but Murray understood the dynamics of the situation much better than many other diplomats.

Murray refused to resign, claiming that a list of allegations against him, including a claim that he gave out British visas to Uzbek girls in exchange for sex, were untrue. An investigation disproved all the allegations, but his increasingly open opposition to the use by Western security services of information obtained by Uzbek security services under torture left him in a constant battle with London. In October 2004 Murray was sacked, after a secret memo outlining his opposition to obtaining intelligence from the Uzbek security service was published in British newspapers.[27]

By 2004 even the most optimistic US diplomat was becoming disillusioned: it was clear to most that the Uzbek government was extremely resistant to any change that might pose a political threat to its monopoly of power. There seemed no sign of a let-up during the year, with the government concerned about stability ahead of parliamentary elections due in December 2004. In July 2004 Secretary of State Colin Powell admitted to Congress that he could no longer certify that Uzbekistan was achieving "substantial and continuing progress" on human rights, as congressional legislation demanded; as a result, all US assistance to the central government would be cut. This amounted only to about $18 million, but the cut was a serious setback for the relationship, and came as a shock to many Uzbek officials, who considered that their support for the US in the "war on terror" and on the diplomatic front should ensure that the aid kept flowing. Many officials had not taken the US stance on human rights too seriously, presuming that it was simply a formality that had to be endured. One foreign ministry official told me: "We voted for every single US proposal in the UN: no other Muslim country had done that. And this is how we are rewarded."[28]

All was not lost, however. Just one week later, the Department of Defense (DoD) announced that it would provide $25 million to the Uzbek government, under legislation that was not subject to the human rights proviso. The DoD had campaigned strongly against any cut in aid, and now signalled openly that it did not agree with the State Department decision. The DoD aid decision effectively undercut the State Department, leaving the US government looking divid-

---

27 Craig Murray has written an engaging autobiographical account of his time in Tashkent. See *Murder in Samarkand* (Mainstream Publishing, 2006).

28 Personal communication, Uzbek official, Almaty, Kazakhstan, 2004.

ed and incompetent. These divisions between different departments made it extremely difficult to develop a consistent line towards the Government of Uzbekistan. Uzbek officials, understandably, tended to believe that the Pentagon would inevitably sway the administration, and tended to underestimate the power of Congress and the State Department, not to mention that of civil society activists and non-governmental organisations.

The DoD's overriding priority was the retention of the base at Karshi, and it had little direct interest in the human rights situation or commitments to reform. By mid-2003 negotiations on the base had begun to get difficult, with Karimov seeking financial compensation (rumoured to be extremely high) for use of the base. The DoD was resisting these demands.[29] Karimov had expected considerable economic benefits from the US relationship. The increase in US aid in 2002-3 was not really significant for the Uzbek leadership, particularly as a large proportion went on technical assistance or even democracy programmes. In terms of personal enrichment for leading members of the regime, the funds were negligible.

On the other hand, the German government, which had taken over an air base in Termez in support of German troops stationed in Afghanistan, was investing money in the base, amounting to at least 10 million euros by mid-2006, a portion of which was allegedly going to various government ministers.[30] The US-led coalition base in Bishkek, capital of Kyrgyzstan, was earning considerable sums for that state, with much of the money allegedly going to the country's most influential individuals. Karimov's deal with the US over Karshi was looking like a poor bargain.

According to one US military official, Karimov wrote to President Bush with a plea for funding in the spring of 2003, but was apparently rebuffed because of the lack of movement on human rights.[31]

---

29 Kurt Meppen provides a good analysis of the base negotiations in "Anatomy of a Crisis, US-Uzbekistan Relations 2001-2005", at http://www.silkroadstudies.org/new/inside/publications/0602Uzbek.pdf

30 Christian Neef, "Germany's Favourite Despot", *Der Spiegel*, 2 August 2006, at http://www.spiegel.de/international/spiegel/0,1518,429712,00.html

31 Meppen, op. cit., p. 31, ft. 33.

The US seemed not to understand that Karimov was primarily interested in the financial side of the relationship, assuming that the politico-military aspects of the relationship were too important for Karimov to oppose the US: "US negotiators were mystified by Uzbekistan's repeated attempts to extract financial concessions, particularly after explaining...that in other theaters, sovereign nations paid into the US Treasury for American troops to stay on their soil as a security guarantee and not vice-versa."[32] But the US had always overestimated Karimov's commitment to issues of global concern, and misunderstood his much more serious attachment to the well-being of the Karimov family.

Party politics

In 2003-4 the US embassy had been almost begging the government to make some symbolic concession on human rights to allow US aid to continue, but by 2004 the government was in no mood to make concessions. It may have been misled by DoD officials into thinking that these human rights concerns were merely rhetorical. Either way, the government was more concerned about upcoming parliamentary elections, and ensuring that the opposition remained under strict control, than it was about foreign policy issues.

The government's repression had decimated opposition movements over the previous decade. The original independent parties that had emerged in the late 1980s had focused on cultural and linguistic politics; they gradually evolved into two proto-parties, Birlik (Unity) and Erk (Liberty), but by 1993 both groups had been forced out of political life, and they continued to operate only sporadically and in practice illegally. Of the two, the government put more pressure on Erk, largely because its leader Mohammed Solih was still feared as a potential opponent of Karimov—he had stood in the 1991 presidential elections, the last poll that was semi-contested, before fleeing into exile in Western Europe. Subsequently the government accused him of masterminding the 1999 bombing in Tashkent, in league with the IMU. The evidence for his involvement was non-existent;

---

32 Ibid., p. 32.

although he had developed some contacts with Islamist opposition groups, he was committed to secular politics.

Birlik did not have a well known leader inside the country either, and had dwindled to just a few supporters, most of them human rights activists in the Fergana valley region. Often these opposition activists were involved in convoluted intrigues against each other, and few could be considered real politicians-in-waiting. Their frequent feuds often exasperated the international community that provided them with some limited political support, but it was not surprising that the opposition would find it difficult to develop an open and cooperative movement in the atmosphere of repression that they had to face. They had no legal way of raising money, no opportunity to appear in any media, no chance to publish a newspaper, and were not allowed to hold demonstrations. They also faced the possibility of arrest and imprisonment, usually by being labelled as Islamic extremists, or by having drugs planted on them.

In theory, the March 2002 US-Uzbek declaration promised the development of multi-party democratic elections. In practice, very little emphasis was placed on political pluralism in talks between US diplomats and the government. Indeed, a senior US diplomat in 2004 suggested that the US should stop dealing with independent political parties, since they had limited popular support.[33] All this missed the point, which was that these limited opposition movements, for all their drawbacks, provided the last flickering flame of secular opposition politics in an otherwise sterile environment of repression. Of course, it was likely that if change were to come, it would emerge primarily from within the regime, but nevertheless, the existence of some independent forces on the outside ensured that pressure for change continued to be articulated inside the country.

Parliamentary elections were due in December 2004, and during the year there were rumours that Birlik would be registered as a political party, and thus be able to compete in the elections. The government claimed that the new parliament was a major step forward from the old Oliy Majlis, which had met only a couple of times

---

33 Personal communication, senior US diplomat, Tashkent, October 2004.

a year to rubber-stamp laws. The new legislature was to be bicameral, with one chamber working full-time as a professional legislature. In theory, this was a positive change, but in reality there was little hope that it would actually promote greater debate or allow independent voices to be heard in the legal political arena.

Two US-financed NGOs, the International Republican Institute (IRI) and the National Democratic Institute (NDI), began programmes to help Birlik and other parties get through the registration process. When this failed, opposition parties sought ways to put up independent candidates. All these efforts led nowhere, as the government blocked the registration of Birlik, claiming that many of the signatories on their registration documents were forged. In reality, the NSS had visited many of those who had signed in support of the party, and forced them to renege on their support. Any hope that independent candidates might have been permitted to contest the elections had always been unfounded. Instead, the government created a new party to give some semblance of multiparty elections.

There had been four "official" parties in the old parliament, created and controlled by the presidential administration. They had no differences in policy, all slavishly supporting Karimov. In 2004 a new party emerged, the Liberal Democratic Party, which at first showed some signs of independence, having emerged from among some younger business people. It was quickly co-opted by the government, and soon became the dominant party in the election campaign. Although it claimed to represent the business class, it had no criticism to make of the overtly anti-business agenda of the government. The government promoted the new party as a step towards multiparty democracy, but it merely represented another development in the government's increasingly shaky façade of managed pluralism.

There were always some Western observers willing to take all this at face value. The EU provided 1.5 million euros to the new parliament. Most of the money seemed to disappear on state-of-the-art translation equipment for the conference chamber. Some US observers, such as Frederick Starr at Johns Hopkins University, provided propaganda coups for the government, as when he claimed that the Liberal Democratic Party somehow represented a real political force for change,[34] but locals were not so easily fooled.

The Uzbek elections were overshadowed by events in Ukraine, where a flawed second-round ballot in late November 2004 had sparked off a massive demonstration in support of opposition candidate Viktor Yushchenko. The widespread reports of support by US-funded NGOs for the opposition, although misrepresenting the role of the US in such events, further deepened suspicion of US intentions in Uzbekistan itself. There had always been pressure on international NGOs working in Uzbekistan; now things got much worse.

Given the overwhelming power of the state in most areas of life, non-governmental organisations played an important role in providing space for citizens to discuss issues of concern, and also plugged huge gaps in welfare and education programmes. There was almost no local financing for such organisations, and in most cases they depended on international organisations to provide grants for their activities. Many of the NGOs had already faced considerable pressure from local authorities and government officials unhappy with some of their activities; more traditional officials often looked suspiciously at work with young people and with women.

In May 2004 the Open Society Institute (OSI), a programme that promoted a wide range of educational and other initiatives funded by the billionaire George Soros, had been closed down by the government, despite considerable international support. This move seemed to be partly a response to reports claiming that Soros had supported the opposition in Georgia in the overthrow of President Shevardnadze in 2003, but it also satisfied long-standing opposition among some government officials to the kind of work that the OSI was engaged in.[35] After the Ukraine events, pressure mounted on other NGOs also.

---

34 See discussion at American Enterprise Institute, 28 July 2005, on events in Andijan at www.aei.org.

35 None of the Soros Foundation programmes were really controversial and

Some NGOs were trying to remain operational by cooperating as closely as possible with the government. In the internet room in Freedom House's office in Tashkent, there were notices banning visitors from visiting opposition websites. The office's director Mjusa Sever began organising seminars with the law enforcement agencies; human rights activists who were involved found themselves sitting opposite their potential torturers. Her continual cooperation with the government even led to an audience with President Karimov in March 2005. In a low point for US engagement policy, human rights activists picketed Freedom House, claiming that its director was "an accomplice of Islam Karimov's dictatorial regime who discredits the whole human rights movement".[36]

With increased pressure on NGOs and on opposition parties, there was no possibility of any upsets at the parliamentary elections in December 2004. The candidate list was prearranged, and no independent candidates were registered. The elections passed off without any significant sign of a democratic process: as usual, people were told who to vote for and more or less forced to go to the polls by local *mahalla* committees. Nevertheless, the government's claim of a high turnout was questioned by many local residents, who claimed that the poll had been marked by widespread apathy.

For the first time, there was a limited OSCE mission of observers at the elections, who gave a critical view of the process. There were no other independent observers, although there was the usual motley collection of foreigners, who were flown in by the government to provide some façade of democracy. The presence of such people was believed by the government to provide their polls with some credibility. In reality, it usually undermined the credibility of the observers

---

usually they steered well clear of overt political activity, concentrating on educational, youth and health initiatives. However, even these programmes were unpopular with some officials. Others were upset by some publications, notably a *Dictionary of Ethnic Minorities in Uzbekistan* that challenged official claims about this sensitive topic. Personal communication, Uzbek official, Tashkent, May 2004.

36 Andrei Kudryashov, "Uzbek human rights activists organized a picket in front of the Freedom House mission in Tashkent", *Ferghana.ru*, 29 March 2005, at: http://enews.ferghana.ru/article.php?id=887

themselves, who were widely mocked by local political activists for their attempts to put a positive gloss on the electoral farce.[37] But while the US and other Western states had expressed outrage over the Ukrainian elections, there was no international protest over the Uzbekistan poll. There was no statement from the US State Department, in marked contrast to its overt interventions in Ukraine.

Popular protests

Most Uzbeks had no interest in events like the elections. They either dismissed them as a joke, or went along with the process without giving it much thought. Many lived in an essentially private world, revolving around family, friends and work, with as little engagement as possible with the repressive state. No sensible person was likely to mount a protest against rigged elections. It was only when the government again clamped down on the livelihoods of bazaar traders in late 2004 that ordinary people took to the streets.

By mid-2004 many people were increasingly squeezed, by increased pressure from the government on traders and business, on the one hand, and increased payments for utilities, delays in salary payments, and lower welfare benefits on the other. There were also increasingly frequent power cuts and shortages of gas and other crucial utilities. Small protests broke out around the country during late 2004 and early 2005. Most of these were fuelled by basic socio-economic problems, while others were linked to perceived injustices meted out by local authorities, particularly towards farmers and traders.

The primary reason for initial protests was the continuing clampdown on private traders. In August 2004 the government announced a new decree, the innocuous-sounding Decree No. 387, to be introduced on 1 November. Tax inspectorates were ordered to enforce more rigid control of all traders: new rules meant that the sale of imported goods would only be allowed to individuals who went through an expensive bureaucratic process to get an import-export

---

37 See, for example, Aftab Kazi, "Uzbekistan's parliamentary elections: glass half-full or half-empty?", *Central Asia-Caucasus Analyst*, 9 February 2005.

license, and could produce documents showing that all their goods had passed customs inspection.

Under the new rules, all proceeds from the sales of imported goods had to be deposited in bank accounts. If given the choice, no Uzbek would ever put their money in the bank, since it was never easy to predict whether the bank would be able or willing to repay the money. On the other hand, banks were forced to give customers' money to the tax authorities, without even informing their clients. Hence traders preferred to stick to the cash economy—or, even better, inflation-proof gold jewellery—wherever possible.

Kokand is an ancient city in the Fergana valley that had once been the centre of the Kokand khanate, and later the centre of a major revolt against the Russians in 1920; only the ruins of the Khan's palace remain to indicate the town's former status. There is little opportunity for its young men to find work, but it remains a traditional trading town, where the bazaar remains the main source of employment.

On 1 November tax officials arrived at the bazaar to demand the new customs documents from traders. Those who did not have them had their goods confiscated. A large crowd soon surrounded the warehouse where the confiscated goods were being stored and tried to break down the doors. When police tried to intervene, they were pelted with stones by the angry crowd. Thousands of people marched down the main street, setting fire to two police cars, and stoning any policeman who approached. Eventually, the crowd were calmed by the local mayor, Maruf Usmonov, who promised that enforcement of the controversial decree would be temporarily suspended.

Similar standoffs with officials and police were seen in the Guravval bazaar, in nearby Marghilon, where officials also promised a delay in implementing the decree to calm angry crowds. In the town of Fergana more than 1,000 people were reported as protesting against the new decree, with some women threatening self-immolation; again the crowd only dispersed after the Fergana mayor promised that implementation of the decree would be delayed.[38] There were

---

38 See International Crisis Group, "The Andijan Uprising", *Asia Briefing* No. 38, 25 May 2005.

reports of unrest at other bazaars across the country, including Bukhara, Jizzakh, Karshi and Khorazm. Protests of this sort were rare in independent Uzbekistan, and the local authorities' reluctance to implement those new central decrees showed their concern that popular discontent was growing to dangerous levels.

In many cases local officials were in an unenviable position. They understood the rising level of tension much better than government ministers in Tashkent, but they had little chance to express their anxieties. Caught between a counter-productive government policy and an angry population, they had nowhere to turn.

There were further protests throughout the winter, mostly over gas and electricity shortages. Uzbekistan's Soviet-era energy system was gradually collapsing—it was subsidised by the government budget, but was hugely expensive to run. Attempts to increase tariffs met fierce opposition, and most people were simply unable to pay the bills out of their miserly salaries. The winter of 2004-5 stretched the system almost to breaking point, a situation compounded by an export deal for gas signed with Russia, which left Uzbekistan without enough for domestic consumption.

On 1 December 2004 villagers blocked the main road between Osh and Fergana, protesting at the lack of electricity, and stoned any cars that tried to pass their roadblock. Their electric power was eventually restored after the authorities relented. Similar scenes occurred the next day on the Samarkand-Tashkent road, when residents of the village of Bakht blocked the main highway with burning vehicles. There were further protests in Andijan province, and elsewhere, over utilities and energy, but for the most part they were easily contained by the authorities.

From a distance this kind of protest seemed not terribly significant. The protests were relatively small, and in any other country would not have signified any impending upheaval. Western diplomats in Tashkent certainly did not think they would lead to anything, claiming that they would die down once winter was over.[39]

---

39 Personal communication by email, Western diplomat based in Tashkent, December 2004.

It was easy to dismiss such minor incidents from the relative comfort of Tashkent. In the Fergana valley there was a sense that the situation could not last much longer—the consistent attacks by the government on traders and ordinary people over the past three years had pushed many people to the edge of their legendary patience. Everybody was frustrated, but there were no political groups to channel their distress. Even local officials were concerned that violence could break out; they understood that the situation could quickly slip out of control. One human rights activist in Fergana told me: "There will be no democratic revolution here: people will rampage down the street, burn down the police station and hang the *hokim* [governor] from the highest lamppost."[40]

---

40 Personal communication, May 2004.

2
THE END OF THE AFFAIR:
ANDIJAN AND ITS AFTERMATH

I watched TV and I wondered, "Why are they lying? Why aren't they telling the truth? Why aren't they telling the truth about the people who opened fire on children, the ones who fired at the people?"

Mahbuba Zokirova, court witness, October 2005.

At one time Andijan was a prosperous city. In the 15th century, the founder of the Mughal empire, Zahiruddin Muhammad Babur (1483-1530), wrote warmly of the town's sybaritic charms, recalling its famous melons and grapes. The pheasants, he claimed, were so fat that four people could not eat one between them.[1] Much of the ancient town was destroyed in an earthquake early in the 20th century, but even under Soviet rule, although it lost much of its charm, it was an important industrial centre for the region.

However, as Soviet-era factories closed or cut production, many of its specialist workers, particularly Russian-speakers, left the city. Gradually, as life got more difficult, many former factory workers turned to trade to make ends meet. Given Andijan's position—right on the border with Kyrgyzstan—much of its population relied on

---

1   See Babur's remarkable memoirs, Zahiruddin Muhammad Babur [Wheeler M. Thackston, trans.], *The Baburnama: Memoirs of Babur, Prince and Emperor* (Washington, DC, The Smithsonian Institution and Oxford University Press, 1996).

buying goods in the markets of Osh, Jalalabad and Kara-suu, just over the border in Kyrgyzstan, and reselling them in Uzbekistan. The new restrictions on trade introduced in 2002-4 hit the town hard.

In the narrow alleyways of its old town, in the *mahalla*s, life was slow, and the people were generally conservative and often religious. In the 1990s there was a resurgence of conservative Islam, and the first appearance of more radical Salafi groups. The government had clamped down hard on these alleged Wahhabis in the aftermath of bomb attacks in Tashkent in 1999. Several well-known mosques in the old town remained closed, much to the chagrin of locals. There were still some active Hizb ut-Tahrir members in the town, and there was a well developed network of women—mostly relatives of prisoners—who occasionally mounted small protests against their continuing detention. But politically, in 2004, the city had been quiet for years; the long-term *hokim* Kobiljon Obidov was unpopular, but he was also experienced at getting government funding to his city and ensuring political stability.

Most regional *hokim*s were only in their posts for a couple of years, before being moved on. Karimov rotated governors to avoid them building up a strong regional powerbase. In Uzbekistan's political culture, local patronage networks were extremely powerful and a long-term governor could stymie the central government if he gained a sufficient network of power. Obidov was an exception to the other governors: he had been in power for more than eight years and ruled Andijan largely as his own personal fiefdom.

On 25 May 2004 there were an unusual number of police on duty in Andijan. Roads in and out of the town were blocked by police checkpoints. President Karimov was visiting the city for an extraordinary session of the local parliament, at which he intended to dismiss Obidov, and he was taking no chances: Obidov had plenty of supporters among the mafia clans that controlled the region's economy. The charges against Obidov were numerous, claiming that he was corrupt and had repeatedly prevented any prosecution of his son, who was allegedly involved in contraband and racketeering. All of this was common knowledge, and Obidov was probably not much worse than any other regional governor. But he had clearly upset somebody in the presidential administration or the ruling elite, and a more malleable figure, Saydullo Begaliev, was to be installed. Obidov was placed under house arrest.

Once in power, Begaliev began to move against businesses that had been loyal to Obidov, becoming more closely involved with them. In one such instance, police arrested 23 local businesspeople in Andijan, and accused them of membership in what police termed an Islamic extremist group, Akromiya. At first the case gained little attention: accusing businessmen of membership in an Islamist group was a very common way for the police to extort bribes; usually the money would be paid and the case hushed up. This time, however, the case gradually gained publicity, perhaps because the businessmen refused to pay, or because Begaliev wanted to win plaudits in Tashkent for "uncovering" an Islamic cell.

Whether they really formed a coherent network called Akromiya remains unclear. Some of them certainly knew Akrom Yuldashev, whose name gave rise to the label Akromiya, and had read his work, which combined Islamic teaching with social activism. Yuldashev had been in prison for years on charges of Islamic extremism. He was a former member of the radical Islamist group Hizb ut-Tahrir (HT), but had left the group, disagreeing with some of its more grandiose schemes, and instead advocated a kind of community-based Islamism, in which mutual self-help and business would lead to a more Islamic society. He had never been involved in any violence or terrorism.[2] His ideas seem to have had some resonance among people in the Fergana region, because they effectively mirrored most people's social reality, but there is still little evidence that Yuldashev had succeeded in establishing a really coherent network of followers, with serious political goals. Instead they seem to have established a kind of business cooperative movement, based on Islamic values.

---

2   According to Bakhtiyor Babadjanov, a scholar who works for the Uzbek government, one of Yuldashev's writings calls for the overthrow of the government and the launch of jihad. This seems to be based on a rather deterministic reading. See Martha Brill Olcott, "The Andijan Uprising, Akramiya and Akram Yuldash", accessed at http://www.carnegieendowment. org/publications/index.cfm?fa=view&id=18453&prog=zru

To understand groups such as Akromiya, it is important to understand how society works in the fairly conservative Fergana valley. One of the basic operating units of society—apart from the family—is groups of men who have common interests and are often united by kinship ties. They meet regularly to eat plov, the national dish of rice and meat, and discuss issues of common concern. These meetings, called *gap* in Uzbek, are important arenas for building up mutual trust and establishing business deals. This type of organisation is also at the heart of some religious groups, who gather in houses to discuss Islamic ideas: mostly these are harmless lessons in traditional Islam, but occasionally they stray into more controversial political issues or unorthodox ideas. The *gap* is also seen in the organisation of some opposition groups, whose traditional meeting place is also around the table for plov. Again, it is usually a men-only affair.

Small, closed groups of men, united by business links and mutual trust, often resemble mafia groups in their structures. And certainly, in some Fergana towns what were essentially mafia groups had long had considerable influence. The small town of Marghilon had a reputation in the Soviet Union for some of the most formidable mafia bosses in the country. Much of their power had been broken by the Uzbek state—or, more accurately, by more powerful mafias from elsewhere in the country—but at a local level influential "informal authorities" continued to hold sway, both over business and over some aspects of social life. When a disco opened in Kokand, a group of thugs forced the owner to close it, claiming it led young people astray.[3] But nevertheless, life remained pretty secular on the outside, and Islamic thinking was largely confined to everyday issues, particularly the conduct of women, the attachment to the family and other cultural issues.

Some of the businessmen accused of being members of Akromiya were linked in an informal group, where ideas such as those of Yuldashev's may have been discussed. One of the 23 businessmen arrested commented:

---

3   Personal communication, local activist, Kokand, May 2003.

The Uzbek authorities put the label 'Akromiya' on us. We did not think that we belonged to such an organization. It was rather a club of friends with similar views made up of wealthy and pious businessmen. Our main idea was that all Muslims must help each other. There must not be poor people among the righteous! We constantly transferred money to orphanages, boarding houses... The minimum salary in Uzbekistan is $8 per month—you cannot even buy bread for that much money.[4]

Yuldashev's ideas reflected many common norms among conservative Uzbek men: there was little space in these ideals for Western values, including democracy, but they put great store by justice and fairness and support for one another in a local community. Many of the businesses seem to have been generous in their social activity, but this kind of social activism outside the state was viewed with considerable suspicion by the Uzbek authorities. They were well aware of the support that Middle Eastern groups such as Hamas and Hizbullah had gained from their social activity and viewed any charity work with a religious bent as dangerous. The authorities preferred businessmen to be highly dependent on the state, and preferably corrupt. This made them vulnerable to the authorities, and ensured that they had little popular support. However, as the Uzbek state's ability to meet its own limited social contract diminished, the role of local activists and businessmen in providing employment and some rough and ready welfare became increasingly important for their supporters.

Occasionally small protests of a few dozen people, mostly by wives of members of Hizb ut-Tahrir, had been staged in towns like Andijan. Usually they were quickly dispersed by the police. With the 23 Andijan businessmen things were different. These business leaders employed huge numbers of people, who were all threatened with unemployment if their employers were convicted. The general economic situation in Andijan, the restrictions on traders and the bazaar, and the high level of unemployment simply amplified the possible consequences of the businessmen's arrests. In February 2005 the 23 were finally put on trial after months in prison on remand. As

---

4   Cited in Igor Rotar, 'Yuldashev testimony played at trial', *Eurasia Daily Monitor*, 27 October 2005, at www.jamestown.org/edm/article.php?article_id=2370397.

the trial neared its close, employees and relatives of the accused began a mass vigil in the streets leading to the court. Journalists reported as many as 4,000 people protesting, in a remarkably civil manner, lining the streets leading up to the courtroom. Old men with wispy white beards stood with their middle-aged sons and young grandchildren. Women stood separately, some with babies. Nobody was shouting, there were no political demands, there was just silent disapproval of the injustice being done in the courtroom.

These trials were always unfair, and nobody expected anything different from the Andijan trial. Defendants were expected to plead guilty to save time, and the rest of the trial looked just like Stalinist show trials of the 1930s. Defence lawyers had almost no chance of putting together any legal defence, and most prisoners were tortured to make sure they confessed and gave the "correct" testimony in court. Once a trial came to court almost 100 per cent of those charged were found guilty. Sentences were stringent, even for minor crimes. For membership in an alleged Islamic extremist group, the businessmen could expect 15-20 years in the appalling conditions of an Uzbek jail, effectively a life sentence.

Massacre on Bobur square

On 12 May the court was due to pronounce its sentences on the men, but it announced that it was postponing the decision, apparently concerned that the sentence might provoke unrest. The situation was tense. According to some reports, on the night of 12 May the NSS began arresting some of the protestors. Rumours of the arrests spread quickly, and a crowd of demonstrators moved towards the prison where the businesspeople were being held.

It remains unclear whether this was a spontaneous movement or a planned attack. The official version claims that a trained group of armed men attacked the prison; other reports claim the prison break was more spontaneous. Certainly a large group of men entered the prison, apparently encountering little resistance, although some reports suggested prison guards were shot. They released prisoners, seized guns from the guards, and moved on to attack an army garrison, where they apparently seized more arms from the military. There were some indecisive armed clashes early in the morning around the main headquarters of the NSS in central Andijan, but the insurgents failed to take the building. Instead, they seized the local administrative centre and a local theatre, which they set on fire.

Who were these armed men? None of the subsequent investigations provided any conclusive evidence. The official version claimed that they were a trained group of Islamist militants, who had undergone training in Kyrgyzstan, at a disused rifle range near Osh and at Osh football stadium. This news was treated with some contempt by the Kyrgyz, who found the notion preposterous. Certainly Osh stadium, an open football pitch in the middle of the city, was hardly the place for clandestine terrorist training. And the militants on the streets of Andijan hardly seemed to be an elite terrorist force. Some had guns, mostly easily-available Kalashnikovs, but there was little evidence of any other explosives: mostly they were armed with home-made Molotov cocktails.

The most likely version remained that this was an ad hoc grouping of friends and partners of the arrested 23, including some who might have been influenced by, or read some of the works of, Akrom Yuldashev, plus some local thugs perhaps from among the Uzbek community in Osh, who may have also had some links to groups of the Akromiya type. Another version suggested that followers of Bayaman Erkinbaev, a Kyrgyz mafia boss, who was reputedly close to Obidov's grouping, had sent some armed men. A more conspiratorial version suggested that some armed men had staged a "provocation", as locals liked to put it—an attack staged with the connivance of the NSS to discredit the protestors, but there was of course no evidence for this. There were certainly outstanding questions, however: given the build-up to the unrest over several days, it is hard to imagine the NSS not having a good idea, through its ubiquitous informants, of the demonstrators' plans, if indeed the plot was really planned in advance. And if, as the government alleged, infiltrators from Kyrgyzstan were involved in the unrest, NSS networks in Osh and Jalalabad, which were reported to be extensive, should have been able to interdict any action.

Whatever the reality of what happened during the night, the next morning a crowd of supporters and onlookers gathered on Andijan's central square, named after Babur, Andijan's most famous resident. Most of the protestors were unarmed, with only a few militants with guns mixing with them at the edges of the crowd. Other armed men were inside the administration building situated on the edge of the square. They had taken some policemen and officials hostage, and were holding them inside the building. Some of the demonstrators were those who had been protesting for many days prior to the armed attack on the prison. Others joined them simply out of curiosity. Demonstrators started making speeches about their difficult economic situation. Mostly they talked about unemployment and injustice. There was little talk of religious ideas, although a later video appeared to show occasional refrains of *Allahu akbar* (God is great). For the most part, pent-up thoughts from years of repression poured out as men and women launched into speeches against the government.[5]

Meanwhile, government troops were beginning to group in roads around the square. At around 8.00 am the first interior Ministry troops arrived, and apparently fired into some of the crowd, killing or wounding some people. The first journalists arrived in town about 10.00, to find the demonstration in full flow, and heard confused accounts of fighting between the two sides. During the day there were reports of telephone negotiations, with Interior Minister Zohirjon Almatov apparently offering the leaders of the uprising safe passage to Kyrgyzstan, but they reportedly demanded that Akrom Yuldashev should be brought to Andijan to give evidence at the trial.

---

5 Some film footage of the protests has been released by the Uzbek government. It has been extensively edited, but gives some idea of the nature of the protest: Marina Barnett, Martha Brill Olcott, "The Andijan Uprising, Akramiya and Akram Yuldashev". Available online at www.carnegieendowment.org. On the Andijan events, see OSCE/ODIHR Report on "Preliminary Findings on the events in Andijan, Uzbekistan, 13 May 2005," Warsaw, 20 June 2005, at http://www1.osce.org/documents/odihr/2005/06/15233_en.pdf; Human Rights Watch, ""Bullets Were Falling Like Rain", The Andijan Massacre, May 13, 2005," June 2005, Vol. 17, No. 5(D), at http://hrw.org/reports/2005/uzbekistan0605.

"The authorities said he was the leader," one report quoted a participant as saying, "so we demanded that he come and tell the truth about the situation and say whether or not these men really were his people".[6] In truth, the rebels seemed to be confused about what to do next: there was no sign of a bigger plan to seize power or to link with supporters in other cities.

There were rumours that President Karimov was coming to Andijan, and many of the people who were in the square later claimed that they were waiting for the president to come, presumably naively expecting that he would intervene and solve their problems. This belief that Karimov was somehow not to blame for the misery of their everyday existence, and that if only he knew about their problems they might be solved, remained in existence—an echo of many authoritarian systems, where the myth of the good Khan or the good Tsar, surrounded by mendacious advisers, was an important source of legitimacy for failing regimes.

The speeches on the square continued for most of the day. At about 5.00 pm local time I was on the phone to a journalist in the square. "Something is happening, I have to go," she said. And the phone went dead. Only later did I discover that she was fleeing for her life as armoured personnel carriers entered the square and began shooting indiscriminately at the protestors. Another journalist, Galima Bukharbaeva, dived into a ditch to avoid the shooting. Later she discovered a bullet embedded in her rucksack. There was no warning given, despite later government claims to the contrary. And there was little response to the attack by the militants: several dozen men in total seem to have got hold of some kind of arms, but they were no match for the massed ranks of the Uzbek troops in their tanks and APCs.

The result was a bloodbath. Initially the shooting targeted the crowds on Bobur square. Many of them then fled down the one street that was still not blocked by troops—Cholpon street. The demonstrators moved down the road, with militants in front of

---

6   Cited in International Crisis Group, "Uzbekistan: The Andijan Uprising", 25 May 2005.

them, holding many of the hostages as human shields, assuming that the troops ahead of them would not fire on the policemen and other officials who had been taken hostage. But troops who had taken up position blocking the route suddenly began firing at the advancing demonstrators, killing many of the hostages as well as their captors. Unarmed civilians in the crowds, including women and children, were also killed. Refugees claimed that the shooting continued for another hour and a half. One survivor claimed the dead were lying in front of him piled three bodies high. Another who found his way out via a side street, told a journalist: "I had to climb over the bodies. There were dead women and children; I saw one woman lying dead with a small baby in her arms."[7]

Another survivor recalled his experience:

I crawled behind a tree and stood, looking at what I saw. Dead people everywhere, and some alive, just moving. I felt sick, because of all the things splattered on my clothes. I went into the college and saw the APCs moving over the bodies. They wanted to kill anyone who was wounded. Soldiers walked down the sidewalk, firing single shots at anyone moving. It was a scene from hell, but I saw it...[8]

Hundreds fled the city, trying to break through to the Kyrgyz border, and cross to the relative safety of Kyrgyzstan. Many were reportedly killed as they walked through the night, including a group of defenceless women, who were shot at by Uzbek troops.[9] Several hundred did get through to the border and managed to escape to the comparative safety of Kyrgyz territory.

The government claimed that 187 people had died in the carnage, blaming most of the deaths on "militants". Locals put the figure much higher, with human rights activists claiming 750 or more might have died. Bodies were allegedly cleared quickly from the streets, and some reports suggest they were taken out of the city to an unknown desti-

---

7   Ed Vulliamy, "Death in Bobur Square", *Guardian* (London), G2 section, pp. 10-15, 13 September 2005.
8   Ibid.
9   Ibid.

nation. Others were reportedly piled up in their hundreds in a local school, the mortuary being full. Nobody knows the true death toll.

The unrest threatened to spread to neighbouring towns. In the Uzbek village of Qorasuv—just across the border from the Kyrgyz market town of Kara-Suu—demonstrators stormed the town hall, and took the mayor hostage. The local police station and the tax office—the most hated symbols of state power—were set on fire. The first move of the demonstrators—indicating the real concerns of most protestors—was to rebuild the destroyed bridge across the Shakhrikhansay River, thus opening up trade again with the Kyrgyz on the other side. The leader of the Qorasuv uprising was a local maverick, Bakhtiyor Rahimov, who excited journalists with his proclamations about establishing an Islamic state. On 19 May 2005 Uzbek special forces entered Qorasuv, arresting Rahimov and other protestors. By the next day the situation on the border seemed to be back under the control of Uzbek government forces.

International response

As the bodies were being cleared from the streets of Andijan, the US White House spokesman Richard Boucher announced that the US was worried about the possibility that terrorists might have escaped from the prison in Andijan, and called on "both sides" to exercise restraint. His statement summed up everything that was wrong about US policy-making: a lack of independent information; an embassy staff that was out of touch with reality on the ground; and a security-led relationship that saw most events through the prism of the "war on terror". Only as Western media started picking up the story, and asking awkward questions, did the US start responding with some concern for the victims of the crackdown.

The EU was also slow to react. The UK's Foreign Secretary Jack Straw was the first to issue anything like the kind of condemnation the events required, but others were slow to follow. A few days after the massacre, the Uzbek authorities, who had rejected requests by the International Committee of the Red Cross and other international organisations to visit Andijan, escorted a group of ambassadors to the city to show them that the situation was under control. They were not allowed to talk to anyone and were lectured by Interior Minister Almatov on the government's firm handling of terrorists.

Finally, in mid-June, as pressure mounted for a more robust response, the EU issued a statement calling for an independent inquiry. Both the OSCE and the UN Commission on Human Rights began investigations, but neither was permitted to visit Andijan and they had to base their reports on interviews with refugees in Kyrgyzstan. Nevertheless, enough information had emerged to make even the most fervent Karimov supporter doubt the government version of events. Eyewitness reports from journalists and interviews with survivors gave credible evidence that there had been a massacre of hundreds of unarmed civilians in Andijan.

Nevertheless, despite all evidence to the contrary, some Western observers chose not to question the official line. The British academic and Central Asia specialist Shirin Akiner outlined her own assessment of what happened in Andijan in a research-based report.[10] Her version was based on a day's visit to Andijan some time after the event and included the following comment: 'the United States and Europe have systematically discredited the Uzbek government's version of what happened and relied instead on the testimony of human rights activists and partisan journalists, many of them with long histories of opposition to the government of Uzbekistan.'

Nevertheless, after the first uncertain response, the US began to make a more public stand. President George Bush's calls for dictators to be challenged and for the US to lead a "war on tyranny", and Condoleezza Rice's assertion that dictatorship was intimately linked to terrorism, made it increasingly difficult for the US to be so supportive of the regime. Neoconservative foreign policy writers, such as William Kristol at the *Weekly Standard* and even Ariel Cohen at the Heritage Foundation, came out with critical stances towards Karimov.

---

10 Shirin Akiner, "Violence in Andijan, 13 May: An Independent Assessment".
    Available at www.silkroadstudies.org/new/inside/publications/0507Akiner.
    pdf.

Over 400 people who had fled the massacre to Kyrgyzstan, were refusing to return home, fearing that they would be arrested if they did. The UN set up camps for the refugees, but Uzbekistan was putting enormous pressure on Kyrgyzstan to return them, claiming that they were criminals and terrorists. However, the US embassy in Bishkek and other international organisations were trying hard to convince the Kyrgyz authorities to give them refugee status. The Kyrgyz authorities were unsure how to respond. However, they finally agreed to allow most of the refugees to be transported to safety in Romania, from where they would be distributed to final destinations in several states. Meanwhile, hundreds more refugees remained in the Uzbek communities of southern Kyrgyzstan; others had fled farther afield in Kazakhstan or Russia.

The US support for the refugees upset the Uzbek government. From then on the US-Uzbek relationship, already in trouble, went downhill fast. Relations had not been helped by an ill-fated trip to Uzbekistan by three influential US Senators, John McCain, Lindsey O. Graham and John E. Sununu, in late May. At first the government tried to refuse them visas; after much pressure they were allowed to visit the country, but no government official was willing to meet them. They responded with a combative press conference in Tashkent, calling on the government to allow an independent international investigation into the Andijan massacre.

The government responded with claims that the US had somehow been involved in planning the Andijan uprising, as part of an attempt to mount a Ukraine-style revolution against the government. This unlikely claim was at first obliquely suggested by government spokesmen, which blamed "destructive external forces" for provoking the violence. Who these forces were was not spelled out, but innuendo suggested a long-held conspiracy theory—popular in some circles in Russia—linking US intelligence agencies with Islamist extremists. Western human rights organisations were also implicated in the events, with government officials claiming that they were waiting on the Kyrgyz side of the border for something to happen. Western media outlets were also accused of knowing ahead of time that something was about to happen, with the BBC in particular accused of stirring up dissent and perhaps instigating the uprising. Although it was clearly fanciful, foreign visitors to Karimov later in 2005 reported that he really did seem to believe this unlikely version of events.[11]

While Congressmen and the State Department were becoming increasingly critical of the Andijan events, and of the regime in general, the US Department of Defense seemed to remain oblivious to reality. Even in June 2005 a spokesman, Bryan Whitman, commented: "When you look at the totality of what Uzbekistan has been doing, they've been a very valuable partner and ally in the global war on terror…Clearly, our continued engagement we feel is pretty important."[12] Indeed, in June 2005 US military officials were still trying to negotiate a long-term deal for the K-2 air base with the Uzbek government, after months of wrangling over payments. In a final low point, at a NATO meeting in mid-June, US military representatives blocked a move by the rest of NATO to issue a condemnation of the Andijan massacre.[13]

Meanwhile, other powers in the region, keen to see the US retreat from its military engagement in the region, took full advantage of events. Both Russia and China issued supporting statements after the massacre, claiming that the government had acted correctly in suppressing an Islamist uprising. A week after the events in Andijan, Karimov visited Beijing in a move designed to demonstrate Chinese support for his position. A trip to Moscow followed soon afterwards. The two powers made their position clear: in return for political and economic support, the Uzbeks would have to get rid of the US military. In late July the Uzbek leadership announced that it was giving the US six months to leave the base. America's romance with the Silk Road seemed to be over. In November, a month ahead of schedule, the last US aircraft left the base.

---

11 Personal communication, Western diplomat, December 2005.

12 Cited in Editorial, "Decision on Uzbekistan", 8 June 2005, *The Washington Post*, p. A20

13 R. Jeffrey Smith and Glenn Kessler, "US opposed calls at NATO for Probe of Uzbek Killings", *The Washington Post*, 14 June 2005, p. A15.

Sanctions and repression: Andijan's aftermath

The US had lost its military base, but Washington did not respond to the Andijan debacle with any talk of sanctions or limitations on other areas of engagement. The Uzbek government did little to help keep the relationship alive, however. It expelled Peace Corps volunteers, and began closing some of the last remaining US NGOs active in Uzbekistan. In September 2005 IREX, an education and exchange programme sponsored by the State Department, was suspended, after it refused to provide the government with lists of people who had attended its seminars and participated in educational programmes. Freedom House and other NGOs soon followed. The US embassy was effectively isolated, finding it almost impossible to get meetings with government officials.

The EU, which had initially seemed so hesitant, took more concrete action. Its statement in mid-June 2005 threatened unspecified actions unless the Uzbek government permitted an international inquiry by the end of the month. The end of the month passed, and nothing emerged from the EU. In September reports circulated that any action in the EU had been blocked by Germany, which still maintained its military base in Termez, servicing its troops in northern Afghanistan. Eventually, in early October, the EU adopted a series of sanctions against the government, blocking sales of arms or military-related equipment to the country (this had only limited impact on the military, which continued to rely heavily on Russia for its equipment needs). Other sanctions included a suspension of the EU Partnership and Cooperation Agreement with Uzbekistan, and the imposition of visa restrictions on 12 officials who were deemed responsible for the killings in Andijan. This last provision was somewhat undermined by the revelation that Zohir Almatov, the Interior minister, who headed the sanctions list, was already in Germany undergoing medical treatment. The EU also did not include Karimov in the list, apparently to "keep the door open" to further dialogue. Despite the loopholes, the sanctions were a major break with previous EU policy, and the move was a shock for Uzbek officials, who had been used to a more compliant policy from Brussels.

The Andijan events were followed by a new round of repression against journalists, human rights activists, and political opponents of the regime. Many journalists and activists fled the country. Those who stayed faced arrest and worse. The Andijan-based human rights activist Saidjahon Zaynabitdinov, who had briefed foreign media about the killings, was arrested in May, and reportedly sentenced to seven years in prison in a secret trial in January 2006. In Tashkent the human rights activist Elena Urlaeva was arrested and locked in a mental hospital for drawing a cartoon lampooning government officials; Radio Free Europe's correspondent in Namangan, Nosir Zokirov, was arrested and sentenced to six months in prison for "insulting a security official". Sanjar Umarov, leader of a newly formed opposition coalition, Sunshine Uzbekistan, was also arrested in October 2005, and subsequently sentenced to 14 years in prison on trumped-up tax evasion charges. Mukhtabar Tojibaeva, a feisty human rights activist from the organisation "Flaming Hearts", was also arrested in October, and sentenced to eight years in prison. There were many other detentions and prosecutions.

Foreign journalists and researchers also faced severe problems getting visas or maintaining their credentials. Local staff faced much more serious threats. The pressure on the BBC was so strong that in October 2005 it finally closed its office in Tashkent, and many of its journalists were forced to leave the country. The reporting of Radio Free Europe was also suspended, and the country lapsed into a new era of isolation.

Any last vestiges of doubt about the Andijan incidents were largely undermined by the show trial of the first defendants in a packed courtroom in Tashkent. The 15 defendants all duly confessed their guilt to charges of membership in an extremist Islamic group, terrorism and murder. Carefully rehearsed testimony from witnesses backed up the government version of events, in which the defendants were no longer simply businesspeople but were allies of Taliban-linked Islamic extremist groups, who had undergone training in special terror training camps in Kyrgyzstan and elsewhere. There were allegations that the confessions were extracted under torture; there was no other way to force them to confess to these charges. Usually a combination of torture and threats to persecute family members still at liberty had the required affect on almost any prisoner. The careful preparation of the security services ensured that the theatre of the court remained undisturbed by any vestige of the truth.

Until 14 October, that is, when Mahbuba Zokirova, a mother-of-two in her early 30s, was called to testify. Her testimony suddenly blew a hole in the whole prosecution case, as she recalled what had really happened on the square on 13 May:

Words can't describe it. It wasn't like that even during the war. It was horrible, bloody. When we were lying down, blood was flowing on the ground where we were lying. I was so scared that I didn't know what was going on. We said, "They [the troops] shot their own guys [the hostages—DL]. What's going to happen to us now?" Everyone ran in all directions to save their lives. There were about 10,000 people there and they went running away. Most of the people there fled. They got killed. In that situation, the crowd turned, wondering where to run and how to save themselves. They turned down this one street to get away from the shooting. My kid was in the crowd in the middle of the shooting. A guy who picked him up was shot. My 3-year-old and my 7- or 8-month-old were with me. But the guy who picked up my other kid was either shot or fell down on the ground. My kid stayed there. I took my kid and went ahead. "Oh, my child!" I said. People were dying. Shots were ringing out. A child went running and took my kid. My kids were crying. They were all terrified. When I remember it now, I'm scared. (Lowers her voice.) I'm not afraid of you. When I remember those events, I get scared.[14]

This sudden rush of truth in the court was a shock. She understood that she was now in some danger. She concluded:

The thing is that I'm afraid to live here because now I've said things no one has talked about. I watched TV and I wondered, "Why are they lying? Why aren't they telling the truth? Why aren't they telling the truth about the people who opened fire on children, the ones who fired at the people?[15]

The rest of the trial passed off in expected fashion, although the prosecution did not demand the death penalty as was normal in cases of alleged terrorism, instead seeking sentences of 15-20 years for each

---

14 Daniel Kimmage, "Uzbekistan, One Witness's Testimony Forces Courtroom Collision", RFE/RL, 23 October 2005.

15 Ibid.

defendant. This was only the first of several trials. At least 100 people had been detained in connection with the Andijan events; dozens more had been arrested in the subsequent clampdown on journalists and political activists. Most subsequent trials seem to have taken place in secret, the authorities perhaps being concerned that more glimmers of the truth might emerge if the public were allowed to attend.

In 2006-7 the repression continued, with human rights activists, journalists and NGO workers under extreme pressure. Some had fled the country after the Andijan events; others quietly left during 2006. But those who had remained or returned were at serious risk of arrest. In December 2006 Umida Niyazova, a human rights activist, who had worked for a number of international NGOs in Tashkent and was well known in the international community, was arrested at Tashkent airport. She had left the country after an initial detention, but had been persuaded to return, apparently reassured that there would be no charges against her. But she was arrested, found guilty at a farcical trial, and sentenced to seven years in prison.

While the situation worsened, and the arrests continued, some EU member-states nevertheless tried to push for sanctions to be relaxed. Germany retained its military base in Termez, and this military relationship seemed to be of much greater importance than the human rights situation in Uzbekistan. The Germans claimed that a "human rights dialogue" with Uzbekistan was producing some results. At an EU meeting in early May 2007 Germany led efforts to relax the restrictions, despite the lack of movement from the Uzbek government. One European Commission official, Rolf Timans, reportedly said in relation to Niyazova's imprisonment, "One should not expect that the Uzbek authorities will release such prisoners overnight."[16] In fact, given Niyazova's innocence of any crime, that is exactly what the EU should have expected. In a typically cynical move the Uzbek authorities released Niyazova just before the EU was to review its sanctions regime against Uzbekistan later in May. She was forced

---

16 Andrew Retman, "Germany keen to relax Uzbek sanctions despite crackdown", *EU Observer*, 3 May 2007, accessed at http://euobserver. com/9/23989.

to make a confession and to criticise her erstwhile employers, Human Rights Watch. But there was no leniency for another activists sentenced at about the same time: Gulbahor Turaeva, a doctor and human rights activist, was imprisoned for six years.

On the eve of the second anniversary of the Andijan killings, the EU relaxed sanctions slightly, lifting the travel bans on three of the 12 officials on the original travel sanctions lists. The EU's retention of the arms embargo and the other travel bans prompted a strenuous protest by Uzbekistan, but human rights groups were concerned by this limited shift by the EU. Uzbekistan had not responded to any of the EU's concerns over Andijan, nor had it improved its overall human rights record. In fact, if anything, there had been a serious deterioration since 2005.

The US meanwhile had not followed the EU lead, and had imposed no sanctions. Senator John McCain introduced a bill in the US Senate proposing targeted sanctions, but it got nowhere. The US maintained its demands for an independent inquiry into the Andijan events, however, and relations remained difficult.

The struggle for power

The government made various spurious attempts to make its cover-up of the Andijan events more credible. A video was released purporting to prove that the uprising was an attempt by Islamists to seize power. Some pro-Karimov Westerners tried to make some mileage out of this, but in reality the footage did not differ from eyewitness accounts of the event. More interesting were a series of dismissals and promotions that indicated the link between Andijan and the power struggle around Karimov.

There had always been rivalry between the key security structures in Uzbekistan, but before Andijan there seems to have been an increase in tension between the two forces.[17] The Minister of the Interior, Zokir Almatov, and the Chairman of the NSS, Rustam Inoyatov, seemed to be jockeying for power. The internet was full of what the

---

17 "A power struggle brews in Uzbekistan," *Eurasia Insight*, Eurasianet.org, 1 May 2005.

Russians call *kompromat* (compromising materials) apparently put out by agents of both sides against each other. Rivalry between the two was linked to control over resources and business as well as positioning for influence ahead of a possible post-Karimov succession. Inoyatov had seemed to be winning the battle for influence, gaining control over border forces in 2004 for example. But it was Andijan that really cemented NSS influence, and finally ended Almatov's career once and for all.

Although Karimov had reportedly been on the ground in Andijan during the May 2005 events, the subsequent blame for what happened fell directly on Almatov. It was already clear that he was destined to be the scapegoat when he was forced to show Western ambassadors around the town in the aftermath of the massacre. Almost immediately, interior ministry troops were transferred to NSS control. Almatov then apparently fell ill, and by December 2005 he had been "retired", on the grounds of ill-health. He was reported to have been replaced by Anvar Salikhbaev, a former deputy head of the NSS. With that, it seemed, Inoyatov's victory was complete.

But things were never that clear-cut in the murky corridors of Uzbek politics. A few days later it was announced that Bakhodir Matlyubov, head of the customs agency, had actually taken over the ministry. Matlyubov was from the interior ministry establishment, having served there earlier as deputy minister. The customs agency was also traditionally an Interior ministry fiefdom. Inoyatov's complete control over the security structures had clearly been blocked at the last minute, probably because Karimov feared having such a powerful figure in his entourage: traditionally he preferred to balance powerful interests against each other.

All this backroom politics suggested that the Andijan events had been cleverly used by Inoyatov to get rid of his chief political rival, and cement the power of the NSS at the centre of Uzbek politics and business. In a further surprising move, in October 2006, Karimov dismissed Saidullo Begaliev as governor of Andijan, and implied that mistakes by the local administration had partially provoked the

Andijan unrest. Meanwhile, reports claimed that former governor Obidov was transferred from house arrest to a Tashkent prison. [18] This entire sordid power struggle among the elite was about power and resources, and who would control them after Karimov left office. His term as president expired in January 2007, but nobody seemed to notice. Officials suggested that elections would be held in December 2007, when, according to the constitution, Karimov would have to step down. With no obvious successor in place, except for his aspirant daughter, it seemed only ill-health might end his disastrous rule.

The failure of engagement

The US military and strategic partnership with Uzbekistan had lasted almost exactly four years, from October 2001 until the Andijan trials and the withdrawal of US troops in late 2005. It had started with great optimism, with the signing of a grandiose statement of mutual intent, and a naive belief that Karimov and his cohorts were ready for serious political change. Instead of inducing political and economic reforms, the relationship turned into a grotesque irony, with a US air base called Camp Stronghold Freedom operating in one of the world's worst dictatorships, and ended in desperation when Uzbek troops, some of them trained by the US in counter-terrorism, massacred hundreds of civilians in Andijan.

There had been no progress on any of the ambitious aims of the US-Uzbek agreement. By 2005 Uzbekistan was more repressive, with more political prisoners in its colony of camps; it had less interaction with the outside world; the economy was in much worse shape, with vastly increased levels of discontent. This was true even before the Andijan killings; afterwards Uzbekistan was in a downward spiral of self-isolation and political repression, from which it seemed almost impossible to recover.

None of this was directly the fault of the US: it was the failure of the Uzbek government to respond to a unique opportunity in 2001-2 to embark upon some kind of reform programme, that condemned

---

18 "Political Purge in Uzbekistan indicates president is afraid of his own nation", *Eurasia Insight*, Eurasianet.org, 19 October 2006

the regime to its subsequent decline. However, the failure of the US to push harder on real rather than cosmetic reform; its willingness to allow the Uzbeks to believe that talk about human rights was just rhetoric; the divided messages from the State and Defense departments; the increasing domination of policy by the rhetoric of the war on terror; and the failure to grasp exactly what was happening in Uzbekistan and react accordingly—all these failures in intelligence, diplomacy and policy-making contributed to the failure of US engagement to have any positive impact.

It had been above all an intelligence failure, with not enough understanding of the reality of the regime or the potential for real reform. In 1995, according to the former CIA agent Robert Baer, the CIA did not possess a single intelligence "asset" in the whole of Central Asia. Not much seemed to have changed five years later. There was not enough good information on the internal politics and economics, and much too much reliance on official and semi-official accounts of political dynamics ("reformers" v. "conservatives", opposition to reform because of external security threats, and so forth). All these myths were soon exploded by investigation into the real politics of the country: the murky criminal links, the corrupt government ministers, the finances of the presidential family.

Secondly, there was a failure to distinguish between tactics and strategy, and between short-term security objectives and a broader geopolitical strategy. The short-term security objective probably only required the military base in Uzbekistan for six months to a year. It remained in place, partly because of traditional military inertia, but also because it served the idea of a growing band of strategists in the Pentagon to spread military bases and forward posts around the world, particularly Eurasia, in an attempt to establish an American security hegemony that would either preempt future crises or permit a rapid response. These strategists saw Uzbekistan as a useful forward base in a world in which both Iran and China seemed to pose potential future challenges to US hegemony in the region.

But this view of the world ignored all the nuances of international relations. Such simplistic military-led geopolitics underestimated the impact that any military presence has on bilateral relations with the host country, let alone with other regional powers. It undermined other strategic goals, such as promoting democracy and economic reform, and ensured that the US paid a heavy price in terms of reputation, not just in the region, but throughout the Muslim world. The relationship between Karimov and the US became a staple of propaganda by radical Muslim groups, such as Hizb ut-Tahrir, not just in Central Asia but globally, from Indonesia to central London.

The proponents of this type of forward-basing strategy ignored all the evidence from the past that suggested basing in non-democratic countries caused more problems than it solved. Previous experience in Franco's Spain, in Marcos' Philippines and in Saudi Arabia, to mention just three cases, suggested that such basing arrangements were unreliable in the long term and damaging to the reputation of the US in its broader policy goals.[19]

The search for a long-term basing arrangement, with poorly thought-through strategic goals, led to the third major problem in policy: the distinct stances taken by different US government departments and agencies. In theory, they should have been coordinated by the National Security Council, in coordination with the State Department, but in reality the Department of Defense was far too powerful to be overly worried by the State Department's occasional concerns about human rights. As a result, any emphasis on human rights, through the annual human rights report or through the efforts of the Assistant Secretary of State for Democracy, Human Rights and Labor, were not taken seriously by the Uzbek government, which viewed them as unlikely to damage the relationship with the Pentagon.

However, it would be wrong to characterise the embassy or the State Department as a hotbed of dissatisfaction with overall policy, stymied by the Department of Defense; they simply had a slightly more nuanced approach than the military. The belief of US diplomats in the potential for change by the regime was genuine, and they entered a kind of group-think that believed that things really were changing, partly because ministers in the government told them it

---

19 Alexander Cooley, 'Base Politics', *Foreign Affairs* (November-December 2005), pp. 79-92.

was so, and partly because they simply wanted to believe it. When the government failed to deliver, diplomats were surprised and often bitter. One senior US diplomat was particularly depressed by his experience: "He takes it personally you know," his colleague told me,. "He received personal promises that things would change, and he believed them."[20]

Many diplomats, although occasionally unhappy with the close relationship with Tashkent, suggested that there was simply no alternative, given the security needs of the US. This alleged dichotomy between close engagement and complete disengagement was disingenuous. The US was in a strong position in 2002: Uzbekistan needed the US in its struggle with the IMU; it had no desire to return to a humiliating relationship with the Russians—that was a last resort in 2005, forced on Karimov by the new political circumstances. The US should have issued a short time-frame for use of the base, perhaps two years, and suggested that any further relationship was dependent on fulfilment of the US-Uzbek agreement: failure to reform on the part of the Uzbeks would mean the closure of the base, and a cut-off of aid.

The other major problem was the inability of Western embassies to work together or develop a common line. In some cases this was the fault of the US, which was so intent on developing a bilateral relationship that it was unconcerned about wider, multilateral engagement. The Europeans were also to blame: the Italian and French embassies were sometimes so reluctant to engage on human rights issues that any EU action was difficult to organise, let alone wider engagement through the OSCE or other multilateral bodies that included the US. Once Craig Murray was dismissed from the UK embassy, British policy seemed to relapse into a strange inertia. And Germany was repeatedly anxious to undermine international criticism of the Uzbek regime, because of its commitment to the maintainance of its own military base in Termez.

The difficulty of establishing military-to-military relations with such regimes without undermining other policy goals has caused a

---

20 Personal communication, US diplomat, December 2004.

rethink among some military strategists. However, some suggest that the main problem with the US-Uzbek relationship was the extent to which cooperation became so public and attracted so much criticism. A new approach would see less emphasis on formal basing arrangements, and much more on small, light forward bases in "frontline" countries, partly replacing large, heavy deployments in Germany, Japan and South Korea.[21] This might seem a simple alternative with few political consequences, but any type of close military-military relationship of this type will in reality have enormous political impact, and will inevitably limit the ability of the US to maintain any kind of real critique of a host government. Long-term foreign policy goals, linked to values and political change, will always be thwarted by a desire to prioritise short-term security relations.

---

21 Kurt M. Campbell, Celeste Johnson Ward, "New Battle Stations?", *Foreign Affairs*, September/October 2003. See also Alexander Cooley, op.cit.

3

THE LIFE AND DEATH OF
TURKMENBASHI

The deeper your involvement here, the harsher your pain and suffering.

Abu Said, Turkmen Sufi poet, 10th century.

Russia's conquest of Central Asia in the 19th century, like all imperial conquests, was a brutal affair. But no battle was more bloody than the defeat of the warlike Turkmen tribes in 1881 at Goek-Tepe. Turkmen marauders had attacked caravan trades along the Silk Road for centuries, and they held out against Russian expansion longer than any other part of Central Asia. The Russian victory smashed the Turkmens' resistance and left them languishing as a Russian colony for the next century. The leader of the conquering force, General Mikhail Skobolev, claimed, "...the duration of the peace is in direct proportion to the slaughter you inflict on the enemy. The harder you hit them, the longer they remain quiet."[1]

Sometimes it seems as though the Turkmens are still recovering from Skobolev's massacre. Independence should have been a liberation from the traumatic legacy of both colonialism and the repressive Soviet state, but instead it has turned into another passage of suffering in a tragic history: Turkmenistan is now even more repressive than it was during the Soviet period; the population has less freedom, the education system and media are even more ide-

---

1   Cited in Peter Hopkirk, *The Great Game* (New York, 1992), p. 407.

ologised, while health and welfare systems are in crisis. Even after President Niyazov's timely death in 2006, there was little evidence that life was going to change significantly.

Before 1991 nobody had seriously imagined that an independent Turkmenistan would one day exist. There had never been a Turkmen state as such, only loose alliances of nomadic tribes, who had little time for borders or governments. Under Soviet rule, a new Turkmen republic was established, an educated Turkmen elite developed, and a certain sense of national identity developed.[2] However, there was only a limited pool of experienced Turkmen government officials: not surprisingly, those who headed the existing republican Communist Party quickly took over control of the new state. The Communist Party First Secretary, a wily political player called Saparmurat Niyazov, had little compunction about getting rid of any possible rivals.

On the surface, Niyazov was nothing out of the ordinary, just another slightly overweight Soviet bureaucrat, with a charming smile and a penchant for good cognac. Underneath this unprepossessing exterior, however, he was a complex psychological mix of megalomania and insecurity. His parents had died young, and he had been brought up in Soviet institutions from an early age. A psychiatrist would no doubt make much of his lack of close family in early life, and the subsequent cult of personality he devoted to his mother would seem evidence of an abnormal obsession with his absent parents. Orphans were frequently favoured by the Soviet authorities for political appointments, since they had few of the extensive kinship ties that the Soviets found difficulty in unravelling in the Asian republics. Turkmenistan had long been divided between rival tribes, and Soviet policy tried to overcome these internal rivalries, promoting instead a Soviet Turkmen identity. In this sense, Niyazov was an ideal candidate, who would be much more dependent on his Soviet upbringing than a more traditional Turkmen leader.

Niyazov did face a few democratic and nationalist opponents in the early years of his presidency, mostly members of a proto-party Ag-

---

2   On early Soviet history, see A.L. Edgar, *Tribal Nation: The Making of Soviet Turkmenistan* (Princeton University Press, 2004).

zybirlik, but this opposition from Ashgabad's small intelligentsia was almost totally suppressed by 1993. One of the most prominent critics of Niyazov, Avdy Kuliev, who was foreign minister of the new state for a short time after independence, was forced into exile in 1992, and thereafter led a lonely existence in Moscow and Oslo trying to attract the world's attention to the excesses of President Niyazov.

Niyazov did not even bother with much of a democratic façade. He "won" presidential elections in 1992, with 99.5 per cent of the vote; there were no other candidates. In 1994 he was even more popular, polling an unlikely 99.9 per cent of the vote (on a remarkable 99.9 per cent turnout) in a referendum to extend his period in office indefinitely. In 1999 the Halq Maslahaty (People's Council) requested him to stay as president for life, but Niyazov, modest as always, declared he would stay in office only until 2010. But nobody really believed that there would be a change in leadership while Niyazov was still alive.

Human rights abuses were appalling. Any dissent was met with brutal repression. A huge network of prisons was overcrowded, and marked by brutality, maltreatment and massive corruption. There were no independent media, and no political parties, except for Niyazov's Democratic Party of Turkmenistan. The population was restricted not only in leaving and entering the country, but in moving around within its borders. The judicial system was far worse than in any other post-Soviet state, with almost no real trials being held in political cases.

The lack of any political freedoms and the widespread abuses of civil rights attracted little international attention. The only international interest in this remote country in the 1990s was in its energy reserves, and particularly its vast resources of natural gas. Nobody was sure how much gas there really was. Official figures suggested that there were over 20 trillion cu metres, an astonishing figure that nobody took too seriously. More sober analysts suggested there was at least 2.9 trillion cu m, still a huge reserve, which if sold at 2007 world market prices would amount to nearly $700 billion, a massive resource for a country of just 5 million people. Even at relatively low production levels (some 60 billion cu m per year in the 1990s) and the extremely low prices agreed with Russia (Turkmenistan's only export route), this should have provided at least $ 2 billion in revenue per year for Turkmenistan.

However, little of this money reached the broader Turkmen population. In fact, almost none of it got even as far as the state budget. Instead it was channelled into opaque off-budget funds, such as the Foreign Exchange Reserve Fund and the Oil and Gas Development Fund, which were under Niyazov's personal control, and reportedly held in accounts in Frankfurt. Other hard-currency funds also went into these accounts, including the export earnings from Turkmenistan's major cash crop, cotton, cultivated, as in Uzbekistan, with the use of child labour.

Instead of channelling money into social services and development, Niyazov spent vast sums on building up an extraordinary cult of personality, and on megalomanic construction projects, built at huge expense by Turkish and French companies. These were not even useful contributions to infrastructure, but for the most part expressions of a growing cult of personality around Niyazov.

It was this bizarre architectural megalomania that first caught the eye of international journalists. A firm favourite among visitors was the 75-metre-high Arch of Neutrality in central Ashgabat, topped with a revolving gold statue of Niyazov, which followed the path of the sun. Local wits suggested the sun actually revolved around the statue. Turkish companies with good political contacts, such as Polimex and Çalyk holdings, won many contracts, but the biggest and most prestigious were won by the French construction company Bouygues, which perhaps not coincidentally was also involved in building projects for Saddam Hussein in Iraq in the late 1980s. The result was the usual array of overbearing dictatoresque architecture, not dissimilar to Baghdad: massive constructions with no obvious public function, but with gleaming surfaces covered with large amounts of expensive marble, gilt and precious stones.

It took some time for Niyazov's cult of personality to develop fully. At first Niyazov seemed to be just another post-Soviet dictator, with a peculiar taste for bad architecture. But gradually, whether for psychological or political reasons, his personal rule began to expand into all areas of life. It reached new heights at the tenth anniversary of Turkmen independence, in October 2001 (where the star exhibit was the world's largest handmade carpet, named "The 21st Century: The Epoch of the Great Saparmurat Turkmenbashi"). During the celebrations, Niyazov announced the publication of his first book, the *Ruhnama* or "Book of the Soul". Its promoters claimed that it contained answers to "all of life's questions", and it soon became required reading in all schools, universities and workplaces. A massive statue of the book was built in the centre of Ashgabad: electronic screens flashed up choice quotes. The evening television schedules were soon filled by whole programmes in which actors read out parts of the *Ruhnama* in dramatic form.

The Ruhnama *and the cult of personality*

The *Ruhnama* did not contain any specific political ideology or even a really coherent philosophy of life. Instead, it is a mixture of folk history, old wives' tales and rather conservative edicts on personal morals. It begins with an introduction to Turkmen history:

The Türkmen people has a great history which goes back to the Prophet Noah. Prophet Noah gave the Türkmen lands to his son Yafes and his descendants. Allah made the Türkmens prolific and their numbers greatly increased. God gave them two special qualities: spiritual richness and courage. As a light for their road, God also strengthened their spiritual and mental capacity with the ability to recognize the realities behind events.

This Turkmen-centric view of the world goes on for some 250 pages. It was treated as a joke by Ashgabad's more cynical residents, but it soon became clear that its impact was far more serious, as it quickly began to undermine the education system and mould a new generation of narrow-minded young people, force-fed a diet of Niyazov's ethnocentric prose. By the time a second volume of the *Ruhnama* was published, in 2004, the first volume had already had a profound and negative impact on the education system and on young people's knowledge of the world.

Soon bookshops stocked almost nothing except the *Ruhnama*. There had already been a vicious campaign against classical Turkmen literature, which had been removed from libraries during the 1990s and in some cases ceremoniously burnt. There was no hope of publishing anything new. Novelist Rahim Esenov was arrested in February 2004, and charged with smuggling his new novel into the country. He had only been able to publish it in Moscow: its historical theme was too sensitive for any local publication.

Once he began, Niyazov the writer found it difficult to stop: in 2002 the first of a series of poetry collections were published. Book after book of banal verse emerged from the presidential palace, and literary critics fell over themselves to describe each new offering as a masterpiece of Turkmen poesy. For those short of time, bookshops offered *The Source of Wisdom*, a handy schoolbook version of his poetic works, with readers' favourite excerpts from his verse. One extract is enough to give the flavour:

> *May my Turkmen people prosper*
> *May they live happily from century to century!*
> *May the flag fly like a green bird into the mists of time*
> *May every step of the people be sunny.*

This cult of personality was beginning to surpass even that of Stalin. From vodka to jeans, from asteroids to newly discovered plants, the name of Turkmenbashi was everywhere. Visitors arrived in the country on Turkmenbashi airlines, with a portrait of Niyazov in a gilded frame adorning the front cabin. They touched down at Turkmenbashi airport in Ashgabat. Oil executives often travelled on to the port town of Türkmenbashi (formerly Krasnovodsk). After the introduction of a new calendar in August 2002, if you arrived in January you were actually in the new month of Turkmenbashi. April was renamed after his mother, Gurbansoltan eje, while September would henceforth be known as Ruhnama.

There was almost no scope for popular dissent within this autocratic culture. But Niyazov's increasingly bizarre behaviour was also creating a climate of fear within the élite, as ministers and officials became potential targets of repression. As the cult of personality began to intensify, several leading government officials and diplomats fled the country, perhaps because they feared being dismissed and arrested, or because they could no longer square their consciences with what the government was doing. In November 2001 the foreign minister, Boris Shikhmuradov, defected to Russia, the highest ranking official to flee the country. He became a key figure in a divided and often incoherent opposition, mostly based in Moscow.

Old-time dissidents, such as Avdy Kuliev, who had opposed Niyazov for years and had a genuine commitment to democratic values and human rights, had little time for those who had spent 10 years in Niyazov's government. But the newcomers had financial backing and good contacts in Russia and elsewhere, and they seemed much more likely than the more idealistic dissidents to actually try and do something to end Niyazov's rule.

These "official dissidents" also had networks of influence back in Turkmenistan, extending to the security agencies, and their departure seems to have inspired another round of purges by Niyazov. In March 2002 he dismissed the head of the National Security Council, the defence minister and the commander of the border guards, claiming that they were involved in corruption and drug-smuggling. The purges spread wider into the prosecutor's office and civil ministries, as Niyazov denounced corruption, bribe-taking, drug-smuggling and brutality by security officers. Nobody took his strictures on moral behaviour very seriously; instead the purge was viewed as an attempt to forestall any possible opposition to Niyazov inside the security forces.[3]

Throughout 2002 groups of former Niyazov officials were regularly meeting in secret in Moscow and planning increasingly outlandish plans to get rid of the dictator. It was almost inevitable that this desperate group of exiles would attempt some kind of coup d'état against Niyazov. It seemed equally inevitable that any attempt would be a botched failure that would backfire badly on the perpetrators.

The failed coup: November 2002

When it came, the attempted coup was a disaster. The organisers had been supremely confident, so much so that Boris Shikhmuradov had

---

3   "Turkmenbashi's purge widens and deepens", *Jamestown Monitor*, Vol. 8, Issue 69 (9 April 2002), at www.jamestown.org.

smuggled himself back into the country ready to take over as soon as the president was dead. He seemed to have gained support from Uzbekistan, and possibly from some business groups in Russia. Certainly it was claimed that he reentered the country from Uzbekistan, and was apparently hiding in the Uzbek embassy in Ashgabad on the eve of the assassination attempt.

At 7.15 on the morning of 25 November 2002, the presidential motorcade was travelling, as usual, along Turkmenbashi street, towards the city centre. Seven cars, mostly Mercedes, reached the Archabil highway, and carried on, waved though by the ubiquitous traffic policemen. Sitting alone in a car by the roadside, a Mr Hatamov spoke into a mobile phone. "I am coming to work", he muttered. It was the codeword: the president was on his way. As the motorcade crossed Yashlar street, the cars came under attack from three directions from rifles and machine-guns. Somehow, the passengers survived and the attackers were arrested.

This at least is the official version. Not only was Niyazov unharmed, he somehow failed even to notice the attack, according to official accounts. Many of the government reports were contradictory: some suggested the motorcade was blocked by a truck; others suggested that bodyguards had been killed; but other official accounts maintained that only four traffic policemen had been wounded. Only hours after the "assassination attempt", Niyazov named all the alleged perpetrators on television, suggesting a hitherto unnoticed efficiency in Turkmen police operations. All this immediately provoked widespread cynicism among observers, who assumed that the "assassination attempt" was a stage-managed affair designed to justify a new round of repression.

In reality, there does seem to have been some sort of plan to oust Niyazov: Shikhmuradov's clandestine presence alone seems evidence that the opposition had a plan to overthrow the president, although his supporters claimed that he was planning peaceful demonstrations, not an armed attack. The most likely version suggests that the plotters had been infiltrated long before the incident, and that Niyazov had allowed part of the plot to go ahead before arresting the leaders. Either way, the attempted coup d'état was botched and disastrous.

It presaged a new era of even more repression inside the country and even greater isolation from the outside world.

The government immediately began arresting those accused of the attack, together with their relatives, friends and business partners. The government accused Shikhmuradov of masterminding the plot from abroad, in league with other exiled dissidents, such as the former head of the Central Bank, Khudaiberdy Orazov, and Saparmurat Yklymov, former first deputy Agriculture minister. Inside Turkmenistan the authorities claimed that it was a one-time friend of Shikhmuradov, the businessman Guvanch Djumaev, who had organised the attack on the ground. Djumaev and his relatives were the main targets in the repression that followed.

During December 2002 further arrests were made. First Batyr Berdiyev, another former foreign minister, was arrested and forced to confess to being involved in the plot. Then Tagandurdy Hallyyew, the chairman of the Mejlis (parliament), was arrested, for allegedly meeting the plotters and promising them the support of legislators. According to the official version, which was evolving all the time, Berdiyev had been preparing to represent the coup leaders to the outside world, while Hallyyew was ready to pass several laws legitimising their seizure of power.

Shikhmuradov, however, was still on the run. The security services in Ashgabad were in a frenzy, with even diplomatic cars liable to be stopped and searched. On 16 December Turkmen police forced their way into the Uzbekistan embassy, in violation of the Vienna Convention, and searched the premises, presumably looking for Shikhmuradov. The authorities claimed that he had been hiding in the Ambassador's residence. But the security forces drew another blank. It was not until 25 December that they finally arrested Shikhmuradov, apparently picking him up in an apartment in the city centre "with drugs in his pockets", as the police report commented.

On 29 December Shikhmuradov's gaunt face appeared on Turkmen television screens, with a one-word subtitle: "terrorist". He mumbled through a forced confession, eyes staring down at the paper in front of him. The former minister admitted he was guilty of the assassination attempt and also of other previous crimes (after he defected he had been charged with grand theft and larceny). In a low voice he added:

I and my allies... are not opposition members but ordinary criminals and drug addicts... there is not a single decent person among us; we are all thugs... I am not a man able to rule a state... I am a criminal able only to destroy the state.[4]

He concluded by calling on his associates to give themselves up, and proclaimed Niyazov as "a gift from above to the people of Turkmenistan". He was sentenced to 25 years in prison on the same day, without even the pretence of a trial. The next day his sentence was increased to life imprisonment.

In the 1990s Shikhmuradov would almost certainly have been shot, but Niyazov had abolished the death penalty in 1999, in an apparent concession to international concern.[5] In subsequent years prisoners were condemned instead to long periods of imprisonment, during which they frequently died of ill-treatment or lack of medical care, so the change made little real difference. The whole prison system was a hellish combination of corruption and brutality, with prisoners forced to pay guards even to open their cell doors during the burning heat of summer. Food was so inadequate that a former inmate claimed that a cat's corpse sold in prison for as much as $6.5.[6] A report by the OSCE concluded that "Only the strongest and the youngest detainees can hope to resist physically a detention period that would last as long as four years".[7]

By the end of 2002 the government claimed to have charged 23 people with involvement in the plot, although other sources suggested that over 100 people had been arrested. There were no proper trials, and there was no access to these prisoners for any independ-

---

4   Cited in Amnesty International, "Annual Report – Turkmenistan", 2003, accessed at http://web.amnesty.org/report2003/tkm-summary-eng.

5   In reality, the end of the death penalty seems to have only speeded up the demise of several hundred prisoners. In 1998 674 people were condemned to death, up from 400 the year before that.

6   Prof. Emmanuel Decaux, "OSCE Rapporteur's Report on Turkmenistan", 12 March 2003, p. 24.

7   Ibid., p. 28.

ent bodies, such as the International Committee of the Red Cross (ICRC). Niyazov also launched a further purge of the security forces. There had been rumours that dissatisfied security officials had also been involved in the alleged coup attempt, although it still remained unclear how much support the plotters had really enjoyed in the élite. There is little doubt, however, that the actions of the opposition increased Niyazov's paranoia to new levels, and encouraged him to repress even further any independent voices.

The repression continued unabated in 2004 and 2005, with even more pressure placed on non-governmental organisations and independent journalists or writers. Some of the last correspondents for international media, such as Radio Free Europe, fled the country. And dissidents, as in Soviet times, faced forcible incarceration in psychiatric hospitals. In 2004 Gurbandurdy Durdykuliyev was placed in a psychiatric hospital after he wrote to President Niyazov requesting permission for an anti-government demonstration in the town of Balkanabad.[8] Madness, indeed.

The few intellectuals left in Ashgabad were at constant risk of state repression, but at least they occasionally received international support. The punishments meted out to ordinary people went largely unnoticed. According to one report, in September 2004 Niyazov was flying over Turkmenistan in his specially constructed luxury Boeing airliner when his eye caught the small and rather poor settlement of Darvaz. The poverty of its dwellings was obvious even from high in the air, and he announced that he did not want to see it next time he flew over. On the ground, the police quickly moved in. Residents were given one hour to pack before the bulldozers started destroying their homes. Most ended up living in tents down the road, even poorer than they had been in their original hovels.[9] This kind of forced displacement was fairly common. In Ashgabad in particular, buildings were often demolished to make way for the latest new

---

8   Amnesty International, "Concerns in Europe and Central Asia, January-June 2004: Turkmenistan".

9   "Prinuditenoe pereselenie zhitelei Darvaza" [Forced resettlement of the residents of Darvaz], Memorial (Moscow), 24 September 2004.

grandiose construction by foreign companies. Their residents were seldom compensated: they simply were told to leave.[10] In rural areas, life for farmers was particularly grim. If there was a shortage of grain in the state coffers, soldiers were regularly used to seize grain from farmers, leaving them frequently destitute. Farmers were seldom paid for their work on cotton plantations, and schoolchildren were forced to work for almost nothing in shocking conditions.

Niyazov's increasingly bizarre decrees were frequently reported in the international media. In the month of August 2004, for example, he decreed that all learner drivers must pass a sixteen-hour course on the *Ruhnama* in order to gain a driving licence; later the same month he banned television presenters from wearing make-up; a few days later he outlawed *nas*, a popular form of chewing tobacco. And that was just one month. Other noteworthy bans announced included gold teeth, beards, miming to recorded music, and long hair for men. Some of these bans were never implemented seriously—overzealous officials simply implemented the likes and dislikes of their overbearing leader. But they made Niyazov a figure of fun, led observers to underestimate the real seriousness of the situation inside Turkmenistan, which stemmed not just from the appalling human rights situation, but from long-term policies of destructive social engineering.

Creating the New Turkmen

In their colony in the Congo, Belgium's brutal colonial rulers had a useful slogan: *pas d'élites, pas d'ennemis*—without educated elites, they understood, there would be no opposition to colonial rule. At the time of independence in 1960, only 17 Congolese youths had received a university education, one of the prime reasons for its subsequent collapse into a long and bloody civil war. The Belgian model remains a rarity: even the most odious dictatorships have tended to stress the need for education, at least in technical subjects, to help rule their empires. Turkmenistan is one of the few states in which a

---

10 See, *inter alia*, "Turkmenistan: The dirty secrets of urban renewal in Ashgabad", 30 April 2007, *Eurasia Insight*, at www.eurasianet.org.

deliberate policy of reducing education has been used to produce a politically compliant and educationally backward population.

Along with the rest of Central Asia, Turkmenistan had benefited enormously from the Soviet emphasis on education. True, much of it was ideological, and students spent long hours learning bits of Lenin off by rote. But many students also gained an effective classical education. Of course, it was colonial in essence, with students learning Pushkin and Lermontov, rather than the classics of Turkmen literature. And there was nothing in history lessons on the conquest of Turkmenistan by Russia or other controversial historical subjects: joining the Russian empire was interpreted as a voluntary move by the Turkmens, which represented a step forward from their own "backward" past.

Whatever its shortcomings, Russian education gave the Turkmens a relatively high literacy rate and a small educated elite, which had access to world literature and science through its command of Russian. When Niyazov first came to power, he was praised by some intellectuals for his attempts to revive the Turkmen language, and promote indigenous history. The revival of language had, after all, been the basis for many of the small nationalist groups that had emerged in the 1980s in Turkmenistan. And Turkmens had always had less inclination to learn or speak Russian than people had in some other republics.

In the early 1990s, promotion of Central Asian languages was viewed as a progressive step, allowing countries to emerge from the tyranny of Russian. In most cases, the reality has been different, as lack of Russian-language schooling has cut off Central Asians from international literature and press. Access to English-language education had been available only for a small elite.

The promotion of Turkmen contributed directly to Niyazov's policy of self-isolation. Russian almost disappeared from everyday life, with only one newspaper and one school remaining. All government work was to be conducted in Turkmen, along with all education, despite the lack of translated literature in many specialist subjects in the language. These difficulties of transition might have been overcome in time, with more publishing, and effective development of English and other alternative second languages. But Niyazov was not simply implementing a typical post-colonial policy of reasserting indigenous rights: he was going further, determined to produce a new generation of young people whose instinctive loyalty was to Niyazov and his ideals, spelt out in detail in the *Ruhnama*.

Niyazov began a reform of the education system in 2001 that cut the length of school education by one year, and reduced higher education from five years to just two years of study. The number of schools dropped from 1,800 to 1,705, but the number of pupils rose from 700,000 to one million. The Academy of Sciences was abolished, and several of its research institutes were shut down.[11] The impact was most damaging for children trying to get a university education. The number of university students in 2006 was one-sixth of the number in 1993.[12] A university degree from Turkmenistan became effectively worthless and was no longer recognised by other countries. And the shortened school education programme ensured that Turkmen schoolchildren were not adequately prepared to enter degree programmes anywhere else. The lack of schooling was compounded by the widespread use of child labour to pick cotton, ensuring that they lost up to three months of schooling during the year, further reducing their chances of actually learning anything in the classroom.

The changes were disastrous for parents seeking a modern education for their children, but would also have a major impact on the future potential of the country. With few technocrats able to run the country or engage in international business, long-term prospects for political and economic development were seriously damaged. The only options left to parents were a network of Turkish schools and one Russian-language school in Ashgabad. These were also subject to the restricted education period, and also taught compulsory lessons of the *Ruhnama*, but alongside it, teachers gave

---

11 Burt Herman, "President puts his stamp on Turkmenistan; education policy is seen strengthening leader's grip", *The Washington Post*, 22 June 2003.

12 Turkmen Initiative for Human Rights, "Education in Turkmenistan", November 2006, is a comprehensive analysis of this issue.

children a reasonable education in essential subjects that allowed them to enter university afterwards.

Those who could not get access to the Turkish or Russian schools were left to try and cope without much help; some parents tried to give their children extracurricular lessons, using private tutors, but this was relatively expensive. Those with money tried to get their children out of the country to study abroad, primarily to Kyrgyzstan, Russia, Ukraine and other CIS countries. However, in an effort to stem this outflow of students, in 2004 Niyazov declared that no degrees awarded by foreign universities would be recognised by state institutions in Turkmenistan; this effectively meant that any student with a foreign degree would be unable to get a job in Turkmenistan.

Not only were children spending less time in school, but the content of their lessons had been reduced to little more than nationalistic brain-washing. Niyazov's writings became the basic textbooks for millions of schoolchildren, who were forced to learn much of the *Ruhnama* off by heart. In schools and colleges more than half of all teaching hours were devoted to various types of ideological instruction. In one fairly typical vocational college, the Lyceum No.22 in Ashgabad, the weekly curriculum included 10 hours of instruction on the students' real subject, while the rest of the time was taken up with:

Ruhnama—six hours;
Politics of independence of Saparmurat Turkmenbashi the Great—six hours;
History of neutral Turkmenistan—three hours; and
Teachings of Saparmurat Turkmenbashi —two hours.[13]

Even the 10 hours or so of real instruction was not immune to the cult of personality of Niyazov, or the Great Serdar (leader) as he was also known. A mathematics textbook included the following problem:

---

13 Cited in Turkmenistan Helsinki Initiative, "Education in Turkmenistan", p. 5.

Begench has read nine poems from the Great Serdar [Niyazov] while Arslan has read four times as many. How many poems of the Great Serdar has Arslan read?[14]

International cultural initiatives were not immune to this kind of political interference. The British Council tried to develop an English-language textbook for Turkmen schoolchildren. They were prepared to compromise with the obligatory portrait of Niyazov inside the front cover, but when the authorities insisted that most of the book should consist of quotes from English translations of Niyazov's writings, the project had to be abandoned.

Some Westerners argued that Niyazov's education policy was simply a typical nation-building exercise, similar to the kind of reforms that had been introduced in Turkey in the 1920s under Kemal Atatürk. In reality, it was very different. Successful nation-building policies have often been brutal with old traditions and often nationalistic to the exclusion of ethnic minorities. But they have almost always focused on the development of a new highly educated generation, which could take part in the modernisation of the country. The real political aim of the Turkmen education reform was to produce a generation of unquestioning young people who would have automatic loyalty to Niyazov and his cult of personality, regardless of their inability to function properly in a modern, globalising world. Sadly, the policy seemed to be working.

A new generational divide was opening up. In one telling incident, older Turkmen students at a university in Bishkek in Kyrgyzstan designed a poster caricaturing Niyazov: younger students were outraged by this lack of respect for their president, and pulled it down. Inside Turkmenistan, similar anecdotal evidence suggested that the new generation was much more inclined to believe the edicts of the president and much more likely to subscribe to nationalistic views, at the expense of Uzbeks, Armenians or other minorities.

Niyazov's death in 2006 raised hopes of some change in the education system. It could not have come too soon. For some in

---

14 Ibid., p. 4.

the present generation of young Turkmens, the only book they may have read is the *Ruhnama*. In April 2005 Niyazov ordered the closure of all libraries in the country, except for one state library in Ashgabad, noting that everybody should already have the books they really need—i.e. his own *Ruhnama*—at home.

State television and other media were also completely controlled by the regime, and reminiscent of the worst years of Soviet propaganda. The only escape for most people from this barrage of falsehoods was satellite television, where Hollywood movies or Brazilian soap operas offered some respite. There is little coverage of Turkmenistan on international news, partly because the government seldom grants visas to journalists and restricts their research if they do get inside the country. Russian channels tend to be very cautious in their coverage, since the Turkmen authorities complain bitterly at any reports that are less than hagiographic. There are internet sites that provide some coverage of events in Turkmenistan, but the internet has not been widely available, and where it can be accessed, users are under close scrutiny. Turkmen Telecom, the state-owned communications provider, monopolises all access and bans access to all opposition sites, as well as many Russian-language news sites that provide coverage of Turkmenistan.

The result of this oppression has been an increasingly ill-educated population and a rise in narrow-minded, nationalist thinking. Not only has this new generation been brought up to worship the president and his writings, it has also been reared in a spirit of increasing ethnocentrism that continually lauds the great achievements of the Turkmen people, and by implication denigrates its neighbours, particularly the Uzbeks. It is not uncommon to hear derogatory remarks about Uzbeks among young people, something that seems to have increased as a result of this top-down nationalism. These views seem bound to influence foreign policy in the future, but they are already having an impact on ethnic minorities within the country, who are the targets of overt, government-sponsored racism in favour of ethnic Turkmens, and against other minorities, notably Uzbeks, Russians and Armenians.

"Purifying the Turkmen": the plight of ethnic minorities

A casual visitor to Ashgabad might easily presume that Turkmen society is largely homogeneous: there is little visible sign of any ethnic symbolism or dress other than that of the Turkmens. In fact, there is a sizeable ethnic Uzbek minority, living primarily in the northeast of the country, and smaller communities of ethnic Russians, Armenians and others, mostly living in Ashgabad. Nobody knows how many non-Turkmens there really are, because in recent years the government has blatantly falsified the figures.

According to the 1995 census non-Turkmens made up 23 per cent of the population, but by 2005, according to government figures, that figure had dropped to only 5.3 per cent, a remarkable change that cannot entirely be accounted for by migration (although many Russians have left the country) or by minorities claiming Turkmen ethnicity for political reasons. In reality, much of this statistical transformation must be the result of deliberate government under-reporting. In 1995 10 per cent of the total population of 6.5 million claimed to be ethnic Uzbeks, 7 per cent were ethnic Russians, while other nationalities made up 6 per cent of the population. By 2005 the government asserted that the proportion of Uzbeks in the population had dropped to just 2 per cent, Russians made up just 1.8 per cent, and others had fallen to 1.5 per cent.[15]

The government discriminated overtly against non-Turkmens in every sphere of life. As a result, many parents give their children Turkmen-sounding names in the hope that they will at least be able to pass examinations or get employment. In this way, ethnic Uzbeks and other smaller nationalities are becoming increasingly assimilated: once children go to school, all lessons are in Turkmen, they are forced to wear Turkmen national costume to school, and they learn exclusively Turkmen history and literature. On finishing school, any Uzbek trying to get a state job or to enter university faces serious

---

15 See International League for Human Rights, "Alternative Report to the UN Committee on the Elimination of Racial Discrimination (UN CERD)", 3 August 2005. Available at www.ilhr.org/ilhr/regional/centasia/protests/ILHR-Turkmenistan-Report-August-3-2005.pdf.

problems. In some cases, simply an Uzbek name on an examination paper has been enough to ensure the rejection of a candidate.

Russians and other minorities face the same problems. Applicants for jobs are required to fill out a form, called a *maglumat*, in which they list their parents, siblings and grandparents. The form is frequently used to deny employment to those who have anything except pure Turkmen ethnicity for the past three generations. It also serves to exclude anybody who has relatives with any political convictions, a practice common in the Stalinist period also. One Russian kindergarten worker told DeutscheWelle radio:

It has become very tough for Russian speakers. Anyone who was financially secure and had relatives in Russia has already left. Those left behind are the helpless and the old. They're living in misery now. Russian schools have almost all been shut down—there are one or two classes where Russian is still taught, though the students are still obliged to converse in Turkmen. The situation is, you could say, catastrophic. The children are not being educated; they just get sent off to the cotton fields. There are no Russian teachers, just Turkmens. Children are beaten at school, and the schools operate in appalling conditions.[16]

During the Soviet period, although Russian was the dominant education medium, and all children had to learn the language, there were also schools which gave some instruction in minority languages, including Uzbek and Armenian, and helped keep these languages alive in public life. There are no longer any schools in Turkmenistan designed for ethnic minorities, with the exception of the sole remaining Russian school in Ashgabad. The absence of such minority-language schools is particularly felt by minority peoples in Turkmenistan because the alternative—Turkmen schools—are so dominated by the titular language and culture.

Most ethnic minorities would probably prefer schooling in Russian to either Turkmen schooling or schools in their own language. Russian is seen as a passport to better job opportunities and study or work abroad. So the closure of so many Russian-language schools does not just damage the educational prospects of ethnic Russians,

---

16 Deutschewelle, Russian service, 5 December 2005, accessed at www.dw-world.de/dw/article/0,2144,1803356,00.html.

but those of many other ethnic minorities as well. As a result, ethnic minorities have faced a stark choice—assimilation or exile—with many choosing the latter. There are a few non-Turkmens who find a niche for themselves in the state, despite this overt discrimination. Mostly, they are specialists in the oil and gas sector, whose skills are indispensable, or they are engaged in private business or trade, where their business talent or international networks overcome their nationality.

It was not only in the education system that Russian and other cultures and languages were being suppressed. Turkmen culture and arts also dominated to the exclusion of all else. The centres of all provincial Soviet cities were usually designed around a rather grand theatre for opera and ballet; in areas where non-Russians lived there was usually also a national theatre, in which emasculated local cultural events were held, and there was often a Russian drama theatre, to which schoolchildren were taken to experience the Russian classics. These cultural institutions were an important instrument in Russian colonial policy, marking the difference between "backward" local cultures and "progressive" Russian culture: the true Soviet Turkmen was supposed to aspire to the great cultural achievements of the Russians, and not remain enmired in the old feudal culture of his forebears.

In September 2001 Niyazov ordered the closure of several Russian-language theatres, and banned shows of opera or ballet at the main theatres. These were now viewed as foreign imports, and therefore suspect: "Who needs *Tosca* or *La Traviata* any more?" Niyazov was reported as saying.[17] Instead of opera classics, theatre-goers would now be subjected to long evenings of Turkmen historical epics. In post-colonial terms it was an understandable rejection of a dominant culture that had marked Turkmen culture as second-best. But the real result was to isolate Turkmens from broader cultural experiences and lock them in a narrow version of their own history, which was interpreted by the country's only acknowledged intellectual, Mr Niyazov himself.

---

17   Nazik Ataev, "Ballet Offends Turkmenbashi", Institute for War And Peace Reporting (IWPR), *Reporting Central Asia,* No. 70, 21 September 2001.

For Russians, these attacks on European cultural institutions were a blatant form of discrimination. In March 2004 the government announced the closure of the last Russian-language cultural institution in the country, the Pushkin Drama Theatre, reportedly because President Niyazov planned to build another huge fountain on the site of the theatre. For once, the plans provoked outrage from cultural figures in Russia itself; such was the criticism that the authorities promised that the Pushkin Theatre would be given another building in which to operate. However, there was no real change of heart. In January 2006 Niyazov appointed a new director of the Russian theatre; members of the theatre were surprised to discover that he spoke no Russian.

In the media too there was overt discrimination against minorities, with only one official newspaper published in Russian, and no newspapers in any other languages used in the country. In 2004 the last Russian-language broadcasting, of Moscow-based Radio Mayak, was closed down. The impact of this attack on the Russian-language media was partially lessened by the wide range of Russian-language programming available on satellite television. There were occasional rumours that Niyazov would ban satellite television, but he never dared to move against one of the last entertainments for most of the population.

This discrimination against ethnic minorities was not simply a post-colonial linguistic policy or a reaction against cultural imperialism in the past. In its totality, the whole policy constituted a state-level official policy of racial purity, and effective ethnic cleansing, gradually forcing more and more non-Turkmens to leave the country. Niyazov frequently made speeches emphasising the need to purge "impure" applicants from state jobs, stressing that key officials should be appointed after they have been checked for their Turkmen origins over at least three generations. In 2002 he said:

In order to weaken the Turkmen, the blood of the Turkmen was diluted in the past. When the righteous blood of our ancestors was diluted by other blood our national spirit was low... Everybody has to have a clean origin. Because of that it is necessary to check the origin up to the third generation.[18]

This emphasis on racial purity reached extremes after the 2002 alleged coup, when some of the coup plotters were condemned for having "mixed blood", usually a reference to Boris Shikhmuradov's mixed parentage—his mother was an Armenian, an ethnic group frequently unpopular in the Turkic world. A dangerous correlation was advanced between political reliability and racial purity, with Niyazov advancing the notion that only "pure" Turkmens could be depended on for political loyalty.

These xenophobic notions reached ridiculous extremes. Under a much-derided law any foreigner wishing to marry a Turkmen woman was required to pay the state $50,000. This particularly affected ethnic Uzbeks in border areas, who had often married across the frontier; most ignored the decree, but it made it difficult for girls to get any personal documents—in several cases young wives living in Uzbekistan had no personal documents at all attesting to their marriage or citizenship. Finally, the law was abandoned in 2005, but it was a clear demonstration of the regime's rejection of all things foreign.

The uses and abuses of neutrality

Every year on 12 December Turkmenistan celebrates Neutrality Day, a national holiday celebrating the UN recognition of its adoption of "permanent neutrality" as the basis of its foreign policy. A move initially welcomed by the West, as a sign that Turkmenistan was moving out of the orbit of Moscow, "neutrality" has become a useful disguise for a policy of isolation from the rest of the world, and a rejection of international norms on human rights and every other part of international law.

The adoption of neutrality by Turkmenistan was a largely meaningless statement in terms of international law, since neutrality can only be "recognised" during a state of war, but the Turkmens used it as a way of first escaping from the influence of Russian-domi-

---

18 See International League for Human Rights, op.cit.

nated security structures, and latterly as a partial excuse for ignoring other international conventions that it had signed. Turkmenistan is a member of the OSCE, and a signatory to many UN conventions on human rights, but it has rejected all strictures and criticisms made by international organisations.

Like everything else, foreign policy was personally controlled by Niyazov, and showed his erratic and unpredictable style. In the main, policy was shaped around key economic issues—the export of gas, the division of the Caspian Sea—and informed by certain personality-driven disputes, such as the difficult relationship with Uzbekistan's President Karimov. Security concerns also informed policy towards the south, where fear of instability creeping over the border from either Afghanistan or Iran forced Niyazov to adopt a conciliatory attitude towards both countries' regimes. Turkmenistan was one of only very few states to develop diplomatic relations with the Taliban. It opened a consulate in Mazar-e-Sharif, which was later alleged to be involved in drugs smuggling. Some reports even suggested that Taliban leaders had escaped the US attacks on Afghanistan through the Afghan-Turkmen border.[19]

Other foreign relations were dominated by business and energy issues. A gas export pipeline to Iran was constructed in the mid-1990s—too small to be of major commercial value, but symbolic of good political relations between the two states. But interaction was limited: Iranian businessmen occasionally ventured northwards, attracted as much by Ashgabad's more liberal nightlife as by any real business opportunities. In most cases, in business deals, the Iranians were squeezed out by the Turks. One Turkish businessman in particular, Ahmed Çalyk, head of the construction-to-textiles conglomerate Çalyk Holdings, had adopted Turkmen citizenship and was a key adviser to Niyazov.

With other Turkic states, relations were less than smooth. With Azerbaijan, on the opposite coast to Turkmenistan across the Cas-

---

19 See International Crisis Group, "Cracks in the Marble: Turkmenistan's Failing Dictatorship", Asia Report No. 44, 17 January 2003, at www.crisisgroup.org.

pian, relations were particularly frosty, soured by disputes over the division of the Caspian Sea and particularly the fate of two offshore oilfields, which BP had begun to explore, but which were still claimed by Turkmenistan. The collapse of the Transcaspian pipeline project, which would have taken gas across the floor of the Caspian to Azerbaijan and on to Turkey, also damaged relations: Niyazov blamed the Azeris for not cooperating; everybody else blamed Niyazov.

But the worst relations were with Uzbekistan. The two presidents, Niyazov and Karimov, were reputed to hate each other, and disputes over borders and water made relations difficult. Turkmenistan's treatment of ethnic Uzbeks provoked some disquiet among Uzbeks, although it never emerged as a key issue on the state level: Karimov had never cared much about the fate of Uzbeks outside Uzbekistan's borders, viewing them more as a threat than as a target of state assistance. The real issues revolved around convoluted disputes over resources, borders, land, and above all water.

In Central Asia control over scarce water supplies has always been associated with power. Control over water supplies ensures control over irrigation systems, and thus the power of life or death over the mass of the rural population. This prosaic reality is expressed in a banal symbolism that links water with political authority. Presidential palaces and city centres abound with fountains, none more so than Ashgabad, which boasts more fountains, according to tourist guides, than any other city in the world. It is easy to believe—right along the main strip of Turkmenbashi Prospect high fountains pump out gallons of water every second. No major building is complete without its over-sized water feature, and Ashgabad reputedly hosts the world's largest fountain, an oversized wedding-cake of marble with streams of water flowing down its overpriced sides.

This astonishing wastage of water contrasts with the reality of life for many residents of the city, let alone the countryside, who do not enjoy constant access to running water. Agriculture is highly dependent on irrigation, but lack of water has led to falling harvests since the early 1990s. Much of the cultivation is of cotton, which requires artificial irrigation in Turkmenistan's hot climate. The only source of water for the country is the Amu-Darya river, which feeds the massive Soviet-era Kara-Kum canal. But the canal has hardly been maintained since independence, more through lack of government will and the outflow of specialists than through lack of funds. Turkmenistan and Uzbekistan both compete for use of the Amu-Darya's water, and mutual charges of overuse are frequent. Turkmenistan's grandiose plans to construct a "Golden Lake", a massive $9-billion reservoir covering 1,000 square miles of desert, did little to assuage Uzbek fears of water wastage. The Turkmen government claimed the lake would be filled by rainfall and groundwater, but most experts believed it would only increase the drain on the Amu-Darya. High levels of evaporation meant that any such reservoir would be highly inefficient as a water storage facility, and while huge funds were being diverted to its construction, the critical Kara-Kum canal was hardly maintained at all.

Conflict over water between the two countries was exacerbated by conflict over border demarcation. At least once in the 1990s both countries mobilised military forces as border disputes threatened to escalate. In 2003 a final demarcation of the borders was agreed, but border management remained a significant problem. There were frequent clashes between border guards and the local population, whose main occupation, in the absence of any other empoyment in either country, was smuggling subsidised petrol from Turkmenistan, where it cost less than bottled water, to Uzbekistan, where it could be sold at a high mark-up. Border crossings became more difficult, with locals having to pay an official fee of $6 to cross the border, a huge sum in such a poor region.

Relations went further downhill after Turkmenistan accused the Uzbeks of involvement in the assassination attempt on Niyazov in November 2002, and cooled almost to freezing after Turkmen security forces raided the Uzbek embassy in December 2002, but Tashkent, perhaps fearing that its involvement could embarrass it internationally, eventually offered some concessions to the Turkmens. In 2004 the two leaders began to patch up some of their quarrels. Both were increasingly ostracised by the international community, and seemed to find they had some common ground after all, at least in their rejection of Western influence in their respective countries.

In November 2004 they met in Bukhara, their first meeting for years, and announced that they had resolved all problems between the two countries. In reality, nothing much changed in substance, either for local border populations or on water use issues, but the meeting was nevertheless a breakthrough in their personal relations.

All these regional relations were nothing like as significant as ties with Russia, which was vital to the Turkmen regime's survival, since the only significant gas export pipeline went to Russia. From the very beginning, Niyazov moved quickly away from Russian security and political influence: He requested Russian forces to leave, and developed his own military structures, albeit initially with the help of many Russian officers. He used his self-declared "neutrality" to avoid involvement in post-Soviet security structures, such as the Commonwealth of Independent States Common Security Pact. But economically Russia continued to treat the Turkmens as if their country was still a Soviet republic, buying their gas at ridiculously low prices. It seemed Turkmenistan had little leverage against Russia, but in 1996, after yet another bout of fraught price negotiations, Niyazov simply turned off the gas. This was disastrous for the economy, but after more than a year it brought Russia back to the negotiating table with a much improved contract.

Since then Russia has taken a different approach to Turkmenistan: a series of Russian ambassadors were notable for their obsequious approach to Niyazov, with bilateral relations completely dominated by price negotiations over gas, first with Itera, a Gazprom subsidiary, and later with Gazprom itself. Turkmenistan's discrimination against Russian-speakers, had almost no impact on this relationship, despite a media campaign in Russia itself and some strong statements against Niyazov from Russian parliamentarians. The power of the gas lobby was overwhelming, although some more broad-minded officials in security structures were thinking ahead about possible post-Niyazov scenarios. But for most of the Russian establishment, as long as the gas kept flowing, there was no need to rock the boat.

Turkmenistan and the West

Russia's only real concern was that Niyazov might agree a deal for an alternative export pipeline, ending the lucrative Russian monopsony on Turkmen gas. Turkmenistan's relations with the West initially centred on discussion of these alternative pipeline routes, and on possible investments in the hydrocarbon sector. Gradually, human rights issues also came to the fore, although never to such a degree as to hinder potential business links. Following 9/11, with a new focus on the region, Turkmenistan suddenly emerged as a potentially key strategic partner for the US-led coalition in Afghanistan. The initial approaches were all linked to humanitarian aid and the need for transit through Turkmen territory. Unlike Uzbekistan, which initially resisted any attempt to open its border, Turkmenistan was quick to see the political benefits from cooperation with the West.

Turkmenistan became a key transit point for the aid, mostly food, and was second only to Pakistan in terms of volume of aid taken in to feed Afghans. Its assistance brought quick political dividends: a congressional delegation arrived in January 2002 to thank the government for its assistance. In April the US Defense Secretary, Donald Rumsfeld, met Niyazov in the port city of Turkmenbashi to discuss regional security issues; a State Department official, Lynn Pascoe, visited in July, and Commander-in-Chief Tommy Franks stopped by in August. US aid doubled, albeit only to $18.1 million, although for the first time a considerable percentage of that figure ($8 million) went to security and law enforcement.

The tone of this warming relationship changed in November 2002, after the assassination attempt on Niyazov, when reports of mass arrests started reaching diplomats. A US statement questioned the rationale for the mass arrests, and the embassy was also concerned that one US citizen, Leonid Komarovsky, a friend of Guvanch Djumaev, had been caught up in the arrests and was being held incommunicado. By the end of 2002, with Komarovsky still in prison and consular officials denied access to him, the State Department was becoming "deeply concerned". European states were also following the wave

103

of arrests closely, as well as reports of torture of those detained and abuses committed against relatives of the accused.

In response to this new upsurge in repression, 10 members of the Organisation for Cooperation and Security in Europe (OSCE) launched the so-called Moscow mechanism to investigate the repression after the assassination attempt. The Moscow mechanism was an almost forgotten paragraph in the OSCE treaties, which had not been used since the early 1990s. In effect, if 10 member states agreed, they could force an investigation of the human rights situation in any other OSCE member state. A French professor, Emmanuel Decaux, was asked to write the investigative report. He was refused a visa to enter Turkmenistan and proceeded to gather as much information as he could among exiles and from diplomatic sources.

The failure of Turkmenistan to cooperate with Decaux did not prevent him from producing a widely praised report.[20] But as so often with the OSCE, that was where the action stopped. There was no part of the Moscow mechanism that indicated what should happen next or how Decaux's findings could be enforced. The only real possibility—the suspension of Turkmenistan's membership in the OSCE—was not popular among senior OSCE staff, since it would cut off all potential dialogue for the future. In any case, Russia would be expected to veto any such move.

Lacking any consensus on how to follow up on the Moscow mechanism, the OSCE went back to business as usual. By June 2004 the organisation's Special Envoy to Central Asia, the ubiquitous former president of Finland, Martti Ahtisaari, was in Ashgabad, thanking the Turkmen government for "opening up to different international organizations, [such as] ICRC, the attitude of the government also vis-a-vis religious organizations". When asked if there were any differences with Niyazov, Ahtisaari explained that there were "slightly different nuances in views".[21] There was no mention of the Moscow

---

20 Emmanuel Decaux, "OSCE Rapporteur's Report on Turkmenistan", 12 March 2003.

21 "Martti Ahtisaari Upbeat on OSCE-Turkmenistan Relations", www. NewsCentralAsia.com, 16 June 2004.

mechanism, no mention of human rights, no mention of political prisoners, and no mention of the destructive ideological campaign against education. OSCE officials in Turkmenistan were unhappy, complaining that their speaking points for Ahtisaari had been ignored.[22] Subsequently, the Turkmen authorities refused the local head of the OSCE in Ashgabad, Ambassador Badescu, an extension to her visa. She was forced to leave the country, an action that raised no protest at all from OSCE headquarters in Vienna. It was this kind of diplomatic inconsistency that made it almost impossible to put real pressure on the regime.

In April 2003 Komarovsky was released, but a spat over US embassy premises with the government, and US support for a UN resolution on human rights abuses in Turkmenistan in November, kept US-Turkmen cooperation at a fairly low level. Relations with the US gradually improved in 2004, with a visit by the US Central Command chief, General John B. Abizaid, in August. There was a new emphasis on cooperation against drug trafficking, despite the overwhelming evidence that drug transit through the country was conducted largely by government officials. In July the customs service received 40 jeeps from the US embassy, this in a country where the government ordered 40 top-specification limousines every year for its own officials; it had long been Daimler-Chrysler's best sales country in Central Asia. In August 2004 Turkmenistan received a visit from three Native American trackers, apparently nicknamed the "Shadow Wolves", to train customs officers in counter-narcotics tracking. Most of the programmes of this sort were at best a waste of US taxpayers' money. The only possible argument for them was that they allowed US officials to glean a little information on the existing border regime.

In reality, there was good evidence that the regime was deeply involved in drugs-trafficking, with heroin crossing the border in growing quantities. It seems likely that it was the Turkish mafia that first began using Turkmenistan as a staging post for heroin-smuggling: a well-known Turkish drugs king is rumoured to have built up a

---

22 Personal interviews, OSCE officials, October 2004.

drugs-to-casinos network in Turkmenistan before his death in 1995. Thereafter, state officials seem to have taken control; reports by exiled officials suggest that drugs were even stored in the presidential palace and in the vaults of the national bank. It did not pay to know too much. In 1997 one patriotic officer, Major Vitaly Usachev, reportedly discovered 400 kg of heroin in a plane at Ashgabat airport, en route from Afghanistan. Rather naively he reported his concerns to the authorities. He was immediately charged with drug-smuggling and executed. Officials now in opposition tell many similar stories.[23]

Turkmenistan was the only Central Asian country that did not cooperate with the UNODC (UN Office on Drugs and Crime), which had wide-ranging anti-narcotics programmes in Tajikistan and Kyrgyzstan. There seemed to be a short breakthrough in 2004, when some meetings did eventually take place and a conference was organised in Ashgabat. But in 2005 UN officials admitted that there was still very limited cooperation with UN bodies.[24]

The evidence of state-sponsored drug smuggling, the gross infringements of human rights, the overwhelming cult of personality, the growing poverty in the countryside, and the virtual destruction of the education system elicited merely occasional quiet protests from the international community. Partly this was due to commercial interests: France was particularly active in the construction business, and oil majors were still interested in the potential for investment. Partly it was geopolitical: the US viewed Turkmenistan as an important strategic location, both for the conflict in Afghanistan, and for any future conflict involving Iran. But for the most part international silence could be put down to indifference. There was not even the usual excuse that Turkmenistan faced a potential threat from Islamist extremism.

In Turkmenistan, unlike Uzbekistan, all the well known opponents of the regime were committed to secular politics. The Turkmens were perhaps the least religious of the Central Asian peoples;

---

23 See International Crisis Group, op. cit.
24 "Turkmenistan: INCB calls for greater drug control compliance", 30 November 2005, IRIN, at www.irinnews.org.

they were largely indifferent to organised religion, and few visited the grandiose mosques that Niyazov had built in Ashgabad. Instead, their version of Islam was limited to traditional rituals and pilgrimages to shrines. There were occasional reports of Islamic groups recruiting members in prisons, but there was never any real sign of a growth in interest in radical Islam. There were some small Christian communities, and even smaller Jehovah's Witness groups, and fringe religions such as the Hare Krishna movement, but these were frequent targets of government harassment and repression.

In theory, only two religions were legal: Sunni Islam and Orthodox Christianity. Every other worshipper operated in a legal grey zone, subject to frequent harassment and sometimes arrest. Despite the restrictions on religious freedom, the US did not use its legislation to declare Turkmenistan a "Country of Particular Concern" under the 1998 International Religious Freedom Act, which could have triggered a series of sanctions. However, the threat of such designation does seem to have prompted an announcement by Niyazov in March 2004 that registration of religious groups would be liberalised. After a period of some relaxation, by the end of 2005 things were back to normal, with the government refusing to allow Asma Jahangir, the UN special rapporteur on freedom of religion and belief, into the country. Nevertheless, in its 2005 report the US noted "significant improvements" in religious freedom, something denied by every other organisation involved in monitoring the situation.[25]

Control over religion was matched by increased pressure on the already very small number of independent non-governmental organisations (NGOs). Setting up and running NGOs had always been difficult in Turkmenistan, although a few activists had managed to develop some activities in areas seen as relatively neutral, such as ecology and the environment. Others had run charities or youth groups without official registration. A new law introduced in November 2003 made registration of NGOs much more difficult,

---

25 Robert McMahon, "Central Asia: Rights Monitor Slams US Religious Freedom Report On Uzbekistan, Turkmenistan", *RFERL*, 16 November 2005.

while criminalising any independent NGO activity without formal registration. This latter provision was later rescinded, but the law as a whole effectively ended most remaining NGO activity, and thus the programmes of many international donors in the country.

The crackdown on NGOs and the difficult human rights situation made any significant improvement in US-Turkmen relations difficult. Nevertheless, following the Andijan massacre in May 2005 and the subsequent expulsion of US troops from their base in Karshi, there was much discussion of alternative US basing opportunities in the region. A visit by General John Abizaid to Ashgabat in August 2005 reinforced Russian suspicions that the large military airport at Mary might be an alternative for the US military. Both the Turkmen government and the US military denied any such agreement. However, there were signs that the Turkmen government seemed to have moved slightly further out of the Russian orbit, announcing that henceforth it would only be an associate and not a full member of the Russian-dominated Commonwealth of Independent States.

The US relationship with Turkmenistan was not close, but it was still probably softer on human rights in Turkmenistan than towards any comparable dictatorship around the world. It was not alone, however. Officials at the UN Department of Political Affairs were particularly enthusiastic about Turkmenistan's development, and sought to engage with Niyazov as closely as possible.[26] Disaffected diplomats in Ashgabat recalled senior UN envoys making long obsequious toasts to Niyazov at government banquets.[27]

The European Union did no better. Apart from rhetorical support for the OSCE Moscow mechanism, the EU did little to censor Turkmenistan's growing abuses of human rights, let alone call for democratisation. True, a Partnership and Cooperation Agreement (PCA) with Turkmenistan was never ratified, unlike those with other Central Asian states: it was finalised in 1998 but several member-states indicated that their legislatures would be unlikely to approve the accord. However Turkmenistan had a trade and cooperation

---

26 Personal communication, senior official, UN DPA, October 2004.

27 Personal communication, December 2004.

agreement, which among other concessions gave it a quota-free export line to the EU for textiles—important for its Turkish and other joint-venture companies.

Between 1999 and 2004 relations seemed to be largely frozen, but talks began again, inexplicably, in early 2004. EU officials became strangely upbeat about the relationship with Turkmenistan. In attempts to help European companies win contracts in Turkmenistan, EU officials creatively used quotations from the *Ruhnama* in their diplomatic letters to bolster support for investors.[28] Despite evidence that the human rights situation was actually worsening, the EU announced that aid to Turkmenistan would almost double from €2.8 million to €4 million in 2004-9. The amounts were small, but the symbolism was important.

Other institutions also had inglorious track records in Turkmenistan. The European Bank for Reconstruction and Development (EBRD) was supposed to invest in countries committed to democratic values and the market economy. Yet it invested over 117 million euros in Turkmenistan, including sectors that directly benefited President Niyazov and his close advisors, such as oil extraction and the garment industry.[29] It seemed astonishing that the EBRD could operate in Turkmenistan while the World Bank (which has no political restriction in its mandate) had found itself unable to fund any significant projects.[30]

The West was by turns too naïve, too greedy and too easily manipulated in Turkmenistan. Few, however, matched the levels of corporate greed and cynicism displayed by the French conglomerate Bouygues, which built an array of grandiose palaces and monuments for Niyazov. In October 2006, in one of the most shameful moments of international involvement in Turkmenistan, the government unveiled a $17 million headquarters for journalists, named, with no

---

28 Personal communication, EC official, Brussels, 2004.

29 The 2004 EBRD strategy at last recognised some of the inconsistencies of its approach, but its lending was still poorly conceived until the 2006 country strategy. See www.ebrd.com for the EBRD strategies on Turkmenistan.

30 World Bank information on Turkmenistan available at www.worldbank.org.

apparent irony, the House of Free Creativity. The company behind this Orwellian fantasy? As usual, Bouygues. According to Global Witness, an NGO, construction projects of this type netted just two companies $3.5 billion over 15 years.[31]

Bouygues was not alone. Western banks were happy to accept the funds that Niyazov alloted himself from the sale of gas and cotton exports. A former central bank official suggested that at least $1.8 billion had been accumulated in one account under Niyazov's personal control by 2003. He referred to it as Niyazov's "personal pocket money". Another $1-billion account was apparently held in Switzerland.[32]

No humiliation was too low for these companies in their efforts to gain a share of Niyazov's riches. Daimler-Chrysler, in an attempt to ingratiate itself even further with Niyazov, sponsored the German translation of the *Ruhnama* in 2003. Another German company, Zeppelin Baumaschinen, stepped in to translate the second volume.[33]

Corporate greed made it easier for Niyazov to manipulate international opinion. He would cleverly play off different parties against each other, now encouraging the Russians with a new gas deal, now nodding towards the Americans with some meaningless concession on human rights. When he was having difficulties with both, he would give an inconsequential EU envoy an audience. But the rhetorical principles expressed by organisations such as the OSCE or the UN were left at the door of the court of Turkmenbashi.

The last days of Turkmenbashi

During the first decade of Niyazov's rule, there seemed to have been a certain acceptance among at least part of the population of a Soviet-style social contract. A one-sided contract to be sure, but in exchange for severe limitations on political and civil rights, the state

---

31 "It's a gas – funny business in the Turkmen-Ukraine Gas Trade", Global Witness, April 2006, p. 14

32 Khudaiberdy Orazov, cited in op. cit. p. 17

33 Peter Finn, "A Turkmen Tome Gets Foreign Aid", *Washington Post*, 23 February 2005, p. A15.

guaranteed the continuation of some Soviet-era welfare benefits, together with a huge subsidy regime that offered cheap fuel and food. After 2000 this rather limited contract began to break down badly. Niyazov became increasingly paranoid about his position, and his personal enrichment began to have a serious impact on the ability of the state to fund even a minimal welfare safety net.

Health care had always been a fundamental element of Soviet rule, particularly in Soviet Asia, where European medicine was part of the great Soviet battle with the "vestiges of the feudal past". Free health care was a substantive part of the Soviet social contract, but in Turkmenistan healthcare "reforms" and budget cutbacks brought the system to the brink of disintegration.

With the budget in crisis, as a result of Niyazov's massive embezzlement of state funds, the government ordered a part-privatisation of the health service in December 2004, whereby patients would henceforth have to pay 50 per cent of health costs themselves. Niyazov dismissed 15,000 medical personnel in March 2004, replacing them with conscript soldiers in an effort to save money. And in 2005 he announced that all district hospitals would be closed, forcing patients to travel to regional centres or to Ashgabad for treatment.

Medical officials and doctors were banned from discussing any infectious diseases: when an outbreak of plague killed several people in eastern Turkmenistan in June 2004, the government responded by declaring the word "plague" illegal. Doctors were ordered to disguise the cause of death in their records. Statistics were routinely falsified: while official life expectancy was proclaimed to be 69 years, the World Health Organisation estimated life expectancy at just 62, the lowest anywhere in the former Soviet Union.[34]

The dismissals of experienced staff were compounded by the lack of new medical professionals emerging from Turkmenistan's failing education system. And even the Hippocratic oath was not immune

---

34 On the health crisis, see Rechel B McKee, "Human rights and health in Turkmenistan", London School of Hygiene and Tropical Medicine, April 2005 (http://www.lshtm.ac.uk/ecohost/projects/health-turkmen.htm) ; M. Sian Glaessner, "Grim Reality of Turkmen Health Care", BBC Online, at news.bbc.co.uk/2/hi/programmes/crossing_continents/4440148.stm.

to the cult of personality. It was replaced in October 2005 by an oath of allegiance:

Having received the high rank of doctor and starting on my professional career, I solemnly swear:

To observe the Constitution of Turkmenistan and laws of Turkmenistan;

To be to true to the precepts of Saparmurat Turkmenbashi the Great and to the high ideals of the sacred Ruhnama—vessel of knowledge, wisdom and sound thought, created by the great genius Serdar [Niyazov]; ...

... I will pay a worthy tribute of respect to the invaluable and wise legacy of the Seit Ismail Gurgenly, Mohammed Gaimaz, and other well-known Turkmen healers who have left an indelible trace on the science of medicine, and I will continue their glorious traditions.[35]

Niyazov himself—and his loyal elite—did not suffer any hardship. Niyazov was treated by German doctors, and had his own special medical centre built in Ashgabad. But the gradual destruction of the national health system made life even more miserable for the majority of the population, without the money or connections to get private treatment in the capital or abroad.

The constant pressure on the budget that was destroying the health service was also causing serious poverty in many areas of the country. In 2006 Niyazov announced that certain categories of pensioner would not henceforth be eligible for pension payments, although for many this was the only source of income they had. The repercussions for some were so dire that there were even reports of small protests by pensioners, almost unheard of in this repressive system. The pension crisis was part of a broader economic crisis, with state institutions paying the price for Niyazov's multimillion-dollar extravagance on grandiose projects, the latest of which was a huge investment in satellite television, broadcasting the *Ruhnama* in six languages to a non-existent global audience.

This hollowing-out of the state had wider repercussions for the future. State institutions were effectively emptied of all independent

---

35 See "Hypocritical Oath", at http://turkmenistan.net/?p=36.

power through Niyazov's cult of personality. Niyazov had forced the majority of competent officials into exile; the exceptions were mostly in prison. Hospitals, universities and schools had all been losing funding and professional staff, and were all now in some disarray. The country was also losing doctors, teachers, technicians: Niyazov was singlehandedly destroying its already small scientific and cultural elite.

By 2005 Niyazov's paranoia was out of control. A new wave of arrests began right at the top, with the detention in May 2005 of the long-time oil and gas supremo and deputy prime minister, Yolly Gurbanmuradov. He was later charged with embezzling hundreds of millions of dollars, presumably to fund the extravagant lifestyle the government accused him of indulging, with his many luxury cars and his three wives. Gurbanmuradov was one of the few remaining officials who could seriously damage Niyazov: he knew many of the details of the president's financial machinations, and if he decided to go into exile he would be a formidable opponent to the president.

A few weeks later, Gurbanmuradov's main rival for power, Redjep Saparov, was sentenced to twenty years in prison, having been found guilty of "bribery, embezzlement, appropriation of entrusted property, illegal acquisition and storage of guns, ammunition, explosives and explosive device, abuse of office, and exceeding authority", according to the official report.[36]

This scale of mass corruption is familiar from the tales of former officials. The system was corrupt from top to bottom. In almost every case of political repression, corruption was used against officials as an excuse to arrest and charge them. The corruption was unofficially sanctioned by Niyazov and was already well known when these officials were occupying high-level posts. Indeed, the corruption in the system was advantageous to the president: it ensured that everybody was breaking the rules, and so everybody was vulnerable to criminal prosecution should the need arise.

With Saparov and Gurbanmuradov out of the way, there were few powerful independent political figures remaining in the elite.

---

36 "Criminal gets his deserts [sic]", Turkmen State News Service, 28 July 2005.

The close circle of officials who remained were highly dependent on Niyazov for their positions, and were seen as instinctive, narrow-minded Niyazov loyalists. Key among them was Niyazov's former chief bodyguard, Akmurad Rejepov, a former KGB agent who had few qualifications as a government minister, except for the most critical one: the trust of Niyazov.

Being a government minister in Turkmenistan under Niyazov was a dangerous affair. According to one source, since independence 80 deputy cabinet chairmen, 130 ministers, and almost 50 regional and city leaders had been dismissed.[37] Many of them ended up in prison, or sentenced to internal exile. Sometimes they came back to office after a period of penance. Others were not so fortunate. Niyazov often presided over the dismissal of ministers publicly on television, where he liked to upbraid them publicly for their misdemeanours, and the public no doubt enjoyed watching them shake with fear before the all-mighty leader.

Niyazov's paranoia extended beyond his immediate official circle. In June 2006, in an uncanny echo of Stalin's last months in power, Niyazov announced that he had uncovered a major spy ring, which included the French embassy and the OSCE office in Ashgabad. Three journalists and human rights workers, who had been helping a group of French journalists, were arrested. One of them, Ogulsapar Muradova, a correspondent for Radio Free Europe, was reportedly tortured to death by the security forces in September 2006.

Possibly Niyazov's paranoia was becoming a serious concern even to his most loyal followers. The economy was in a disastrous situation, and socio-economic conditions were causing widespread discontent. Russia—and particularly Gazprom and members of the intelligence services—had been concerned about the succession issue for some years.[38] Rumours that his son Murat might have been preparing to succeed him could also have concerned his inner circle. Niyazov also

---

37 "Dirty Business", 3 November 2005, at http://turkmenistan.neweurasia.net/?p=22.

38 Personal communication, Russian government official, Moscow, June 2002.

had a daughter, but neither lived in Turkmenistan, and his relations with them seemed distant. There were signs that Murat might be beginning a more active role in government in July 2006, when for the first time he represented Turkmenistan in some negotiations with the United Arab Emirates.

Saparmurat Niyazov died of heart failure on 21 December 2006. There were immediately rumours that his death had not been entirely due to natural causes; he had suffered from heart problems for some years, but his German doctors had given him a clean bill of health just two months before he died. And it was a convenient death for many, both inside and outside Turkmenistan. Some reports suggested that even if it were a natural death, there had been a gap between the death and the announcement, giving time for the potential successors to decide on their next steps.[39]

In theory, the chairman of parliament, Ovezgeldi Atayev, should have taken over as acting president until elections were held. However, within hours of Niyazov's reported death, Atayev was arrested and the constitution amended to appoint the deputy chairman of the council of ministers, Gurbanguly Berdimuhammedov, a dentist turned Health minister, as acting president. Alongside him was the regime's key strongman, General Akmurat Rejepov, a former KGB agent and head of the presidential guard, who had developed control over other branches of the security forces, including the much-feared ministry of national security. This small cabal of Niyazov loyalists quickly asserted their control over government, with no time for other potential challengers to emerge.

Niyazov's funeral was a fittingly bizarre finale to his disastrous rule. Thousands filed past his coffin, guarded by soldiers, in an almost parodic version of a Soviet leader's funeral. His coffin was driven through the streets to his extravagant family mausoleum at Kipchak on an old trailer, covered in flowers, pulled by an armoured personnel carrier. State delegations turned up, not to mourn, but to catch

---

39 Slavimir Horak, "Turkmenistan's Succession: Welcome to Berdymuhammedov's World", *Central Asia-Caucasus Analyst*, 10 January 2007, available at www.cacianalyst.org.

a glimpse of the new rulers, and above all to talk of oil, gas and pipelines. Diplomats carefully eyed the funeral organising committee, much as they had done in Soviet times, to try and understand who was in and who was out in the new regime.

There was little hope that Berdimuhameddov would have any yearning for democratic transformation. He and Rejepov had been the most loyal of henchmen to Niyazov. The most that could be expected was that the worst excesses of the Niyazov regime might be ended. Certainly the cult of personality would decline, and already some of the ubiquitous images of the late president were beginning to disappear in early 2007. Berdimuhameddov laid out a fairly promising array of promises ahead of a presidential election in February 2007, including internet access for all, a review of the pension system, the return of 10-year schooling and an expansion of higher education. But there were no promises of more liberal governance, measures to tackle growing poverty, or respect for human rights, let alone democratic elections.

The presidential elections that ushered Berdimuhammedov into power are hardly worth describing. Five fictional candidates stood in addition to the preordained winner. 99 per cent of eligible voters apparently went to the polls, and 89 per cent voted for their new leader, something of a drop from Niyazov's regular 99 per cent approval rating, perhaps demonstrating Berdimuhammedov's desire to start improving relations with the West.

He was subsequently unanimously proclaimed chairman of the 2,504-member Halk Maslahaty (the Assembly of the People's Council), which was constitutionally the most important legislative body, after Niyazov amended the constitution to downgrade the already weak parliament. In reality, the Halk Maslahaty had no power—it mets only once a year to unanimously applaud the president's initiatives.

Niyazov's death was reminiscent of Stalin's demise. And the semi-collective leadership that emerged awoke hope of a Khrushchevian spring. But early indications indicated little movement towards immediate liberalisation; instead the new leader focused on consolidating his political position, as Khruschev had done many years earlier, by easing out the security chief who had supported his rise to power.

In May 2007 he dismissed Rejepov, in a move that surprised many observers, who assumed that Rejepov was the real power behind the president. That may have been the case, but Berdimuhammedov clearly felt strong enough to move against his potential rival. Rejepov was subsequently arrested.

Berdimuhammedov may have been boosted by apparent support from Russia. Since the death of Niyazov, there had been renewed interest in Turkmenistan's potential as an energy exporter. Western diplomats unfolded dusty plans for the Transcaspian pipeline, energy experts booked tickets to Ashgabad, Russian diplomats cajoled and flattered the new leader, hoping to tie up its lucrative gas deals and exclude Western interests from the country. Matt Bryza, US Deputy Assistant Secretary of State, accused Russia of "playing Monopoly" in Central Asia, and called for a new chapter in US-Turkmen relations.[40]

On 12 May Russia, Kazakhstan and Turkmenistan agreed to a new Turkmenistan-Russia pipeline, running along the Kazakh coast of the Caspian Sea, apparently precluding any pro-Western pipeline in the future. But contrary to Russian claims, Berdymukhammedov indicated that the Transcaspian route was still under consideration. Niyazov was dead, but the "Great Game" was back in play.

[...Berdymukhammedov indicated that the Transcaspian route was still under consideration] and he continued to discuss pipeline options with foreign oil companies and Western politicians. He made several important overseas visits, and relations with both the US and with the EU improved considerably. The new leadership prioritised better relations with Turkmenistan's neighbours, Kazakhstan and Uzbekistan, and even began improving ties with Azerbaijan. In a significant break with Niyazov's policy of self-isolation, the new president began to take a more active role in regional organisations.

This gradual re-engagement with the outside world offered some hope for more reform in the future, but in domestic policy change was very slow. The full authoritarian structure of Niyazov's totalitar-

---

40 Stephen Castle, "Gazprom lambasted by US over monopolistic intentions in Europe", *The Independent*, 18 April 2007.

ian state remained in place, and promises of more media freedom and political pluralism did not produce any significant results. Reforms were announced in the education and health systems, but it would take years to overcome Niyazov's destructive policies in these areas. Turkmenistan had achieved a relatively smooth political succession from the nightmare of Niyazov's megalomania, but he had left a legacy that would trouble the country for many years to come.

4
DABBLING WITH DEMOCRACY: KYRGYZSTAN'S UNCERTAIN REVOLUTION

Where is this civil society that we worked on for so long? It simply doesn't exist, it turns out.[1]

Kyrgyz civil society activist, during the Kyrgyz revolution.

In 2001, after a decade of independence, it was tempting to view the political landscape in Central Asia as essentially unchanging. Since 1991 there had been no change in leaderships—except in ill-fated Tajikistan—and it seemed possible that these old Communist leaders could hang on for another decade. None of them showed any intention of leaving power voluntarily, and most outsiders viewed Central Asian peoples as somehow politically "passive" and unlikely to mount a serious challenge to the regimes. And in most cases, there was no serious pressure from external powers for any kind of change.

But gradually this Brezhnevite stasis started to crumble. Firstly, the US intervention in Iraq reminded Central Asian leaders that former friends of the US were not guaranteed friendship for life. The parallels between the regimes of Saddam Hussein, Islam Karimov and Saparmurat Niyazov were uncannily close. Pictures of the US takeover of Baghdad initially sent shivers around the presidential palaces of Central Asia. Subsequently the disastrous chaos of Iraq would

---

1   Personal comunication, February 2005.

have other, much more negative consequences for Western influence in Central Asia, but at first it seemed to prove both the magnitude of US power and the tendency of US leaders to turn against former allies in the most profound way.

This suspicion of US motives became reality in November 2003, when another former American ally, President Eduard Sheverdnadze, was ousted by popular protests after a falsified election. Sheverdnadze pointed to his former US ally as the cause of his downfall: "I have serious... suspicions that this situation that happened in Tbilisi is an exact repetition of the events in Yugoslavia," he said. "Someone had a plan."[2] Shevardnadze was referring to the ousting of Serbian president Slobodan Milosevic in 2000, which many Russians had claimed was the result of an alliance of international NGOs and the US government, together with the student movement Otpor.

Central Asian leaders began to view the US with a much more jaundiced eye. Following the events in Georgia, there was increasing suspicion in Central Asian capitals of a range of US-backed NGOs, like the National Democratic Institute (NDI), the International Republican Institute (IRI) and Freedom House, which had all opened offices in Bishkek and Tashkent, alongside some more technical groups, such as IFES, which concentrated on elections. These groups were partly funded by the State Department, as well as other US donors. The Soros Foundation, funded primarily by billionaire George Soros through his Open Society Institute, had also been the target of accusations of involvement in the Georgian events. It had offices in four of the five Central Asian states.

Central Asia's leaders became even more nervous after the political events in Ukraine in December 2004. By an odd coincidence, John Herbst, who had so strongly supported Karimov as US Ambassador in Tashkent, was now operating in a somewhat more revolutionary mode as US Ambassador in Kiev, criticising the apparent fraud in the November presidential election, which had ensured a victory for the Russian-backed candidate Viktor Yanukovich. The pro-Western

---

2   "Shevardnadze says US betrayed him", BBC world online, at news.bbc.co.uk/1/hi/world/europe/3242652.stm.

candidate, Viktor Yushchenko, persuaded thousands of young activists to protest on the streets, eventually forcing a rerun of the election, which he won. Again, Western-funded organisations and media were involved; again Russia accused the US of funding a "political coup", although Russia itself was reported to have underwritten its candidate's campaign with millions of dollars of assistance.

In all these events—what came to be known as the "colour revolutions" (in Georgia it had been the "rose revolution"; in Ukraine the protestors wore orange)—there was widespread misrepresentation of what Western-funded organisations actually did. Mostly the funding went to NGOs, which were not directly supporting a candidate but were campaigning against electoral fraud or supporting independent media or democratic campaign groups. Almost by definition such groups tended to be emotionally in the opposition camp, opposed as they were to the existing regimes, with their heavy control of state media and their intolerance of any opposition. But in each case it was only an environment of deep popular dissatisfaction with each regime, where there was a possibility to mobilise large numbers of activists, that gave the opportunity for independent NGOs or media outlets to have any impact.

The lessons from the "colour revolutions" for any post-Soviet dictator should have been to avoid falsification of elections, tackle corruption, and open up the political system and media enough to provide a safety valve for simmering discontent. Central Asian leaders drew different concusions. Karimov and other Central Asian leaders pointed to the relative liberalism of figures such as Shevardnadze and Kuchma as causing their downfall. Their unwillingness to use force to defend their regimes was viewed as weakness, and their willingness to permit Western-funded NGOs and independent media to function relatively freely was seen as a key mistake in their survival strategies. Central Asian leaders were determined not to follow their example, and clamped down even more on opposition figures and critical media outlets, and began viewing relations with the US in a different light. With Russian encouragement, even pro-Western politicians such as the Kyrgyz president Askar Akaev began to believe that the overthrow of Kuchma and Shevardnadze had been planned and executed in Washington, and had nothing to do with the nature of their regimes.

Although it was wrong to see the "colour revolutions" as the result of some far-reaching, secretive plot dreamed up in Washington, they did fit neatly into a broadening US geopolitical agenda. A neo-conservative consensus, supported by liberal humanitarians, began to put more emphasis on democratisation as a tool of US foreign policy. Partly this was a response to the failure of other justifications for the Iraq campaign—with no weapons of mass destruction discovered, only the argument for regime change and democratisation was left. Partly it was a broader idea of a "war on tyranny" that saw regime change as the first necessary step towards long-term stability in the Middle East. And to a certain extent it was a significant element in American nationalism that believed in the export of the American way of life, and justified it by universalising its content.

The political environment in Central Asia was hardly ripe for "democratisation". Weak states, kleptocratic elites, repressive security forces, and widespread poverty were a difficult starting point for a stable transition to democracy. In any case, many Central Asians were anyhow wary of the term "democracy", which in the popular consciousness of many was associated with the violence in Tajikistan in the early 1990s, or the rapacious privatisations of "shock therapy" in Russia. After 2003 the US policy of "democratisation" was inextricably linked in many minds with the bloody chaos of Iraq. Moreover, it was mostly seen, rightly or wrongly, as a cynical tool of US foreign policy rather than as a common public good.

On the other hand, there was no easy way for Central Asian states to develop succesfully without introducing at least some element of political pluralism and rule of law. And it was clear that there would be no significant economic reform in, say, Uzbekistan while Karimov maintained a complete monopoly of political power. But the problem with many Western democratisation programmes was that they attacked the symptoms of the problem, rather than the systemic weaknesses that made political leaders unwilling to reform. All these contradictory tendencies came to rest in what was to be a case-study of democratic experimentation, Kyrgyzstan. This most liberal of

Central Asia's regimes was also the first to see real political change. When it came, it unnerved Central Asia's dictators even more.

Kyrgyzstan: prelude to revolution

At independence the mountainous country of Kyrgyzstan, with its five million-strong population of former nomads, was hardly prepared for an unexpected adventure in state-building. It had little industrial infrastructure, with most of the population engaged in agriculture, and some 70 per cent of the local budget came from Moscow. When the new Kyrgyz Republic was established in 1991, the money from Moscow disappeared, and the population was plunged into a precipitous economic decline. Even ten years later, in 2001, some 60 per cent of the population survived under an already low official poverty line. The republic's economy was dependent on one single gold mine. GDP figures mostly reflected the ups and downs of production at the mine, while most of the population scraped by on subsistence farming or trading at bazaars.

Struggling with this economy in freefall was a former physicist, Askar Akaev. Viewed as a new, democratic type of leader, he was the only Central Asian president who had not moved seamlessly from heading the local Communist Party. Although a Communist Party member, he had grown up in the more liberal environment of natural sciences, an arena where many independent thinkers (the Russian dissident Andrei Sakharov being the most famous) had developed their careers in the Soviet era. He seemed an ideal choice to lead the Kyrgyz nation into a new era of independence. He launched economic reforms in coordination with international economic institutions, and won wide respect for his rhetorical commitment to democracy and economic liberalism. His speeches were no longer laced with quotations of Lenin; instead glowing references to World Bank Chairman James Wolfensohn were more common.

But the "island of democracy", as Kyrgyzstan came to be labelled, did not stay democratic for very long. Akaev gradually assumed more and more powers for the presidency at the expense of parliament, in a series of bruising political battles. Akaev argued that he needed more power to conduct reforms, and indeed faced an often recalcitrant parliamentary body. And he was under constant pressure from the more repressive regimes surrounding Kyrgyzstan.

However, more political powers did not always help him enact reforms, let alone undermine the widespread corruption that blighted the economy. Organised crime—including narcotics trafficking—flourished, and poverty remained endemic. At the same time, the involvement of the international community encouraged the development of a kind of virtual Kyrgyzstan, with some sort of democratic norms, and reforms promulgated and enacted, while international assistance played a key role in raising national living standards.

The reality was somewhat different—much of this international interaction had little impact on most people's lives. Reform programmes were launched in a flurry of excitement, only to disappear from memory as the money was spent and the initiative lost. Many of the ideas were good on paper: a World Bank Comprehensive Development Framework (CDF), for example, offered complex and often unworkable policy options, divorced from the political reality of Akaev's Kyrgyzstan. In reality, most people carried on with relatively simple ways of making money: growing fruit and vegetables, trading in cheap Chinese goods, and where possible promoting relatives into state service to glean some pickings from the already slim state budget.

The poorest areas were in the south, a region cut off from the capital, Bishkek, by a tortuous road through dramatic mountain scenery. In spring in particular the road became dangerous, with frequent landslides often blocking all traffic between north and south, and avalanches sometimes burying a convoy of the old Soviet trucks and Lada cars that ferried back and forth. The largest town in the south was Osh, an ancient stopping-point on the old Silk Route from China that was gradually regaining its historic place in east-west trade. Chinese goods from Kashgar and Urumchi flowed into its markets, most ending up at a huge trading estate on the nearby Uzbek border at Kara-suu. Controlling the market was about the most lucrative thing you could do in Osh, and it was the frequent object of tussles between different criminal groups.

Osh was about equally divided between ethnic Kyrgyz and ethnic Uzbeks, and interethnic resentment had boiled over into violence in 1990, leaving scores of local people dead. The situation had calmed considerably, but underlying tensions remained. More significant, perhaps, in domestic politics was a growing north-south divide, which reflected real differences in historical experience between the northern clans, who had traditionally been closer to the Kazakhs and had come earlier under Russian influence, and the southern clans, who were closer to the culture and history of the Fergana valley and its dominant Uzbek population. Northern Kyrgyz tended to be Russian-speaking, less religious, and better educated than their southern counterparts. Southerners viewed the northerners as too Russified and irreligious, and unwilling to share the relative riches of Bishkek with southern elites. This resentment among the southern Kyrgyz at the dominance of northern clans was an important dynamic in politics. Akaev came from the north, and many southern elites felt excluded from political power and more important, from financial flows. Money came to Bishkek, and stayed there, despite frequent government promises that there would be more aid for the poorer south.

Akaev in power

By the time of parliamentary and presidential elections in 2000 there was already serious opposition to Akaev, not just in the south of the country, but also among some of his former allies in the north, most notably Feliks Kulov, a former vice-president who had fallen out of favour with Akaev and joined the opposition. However, the opposition was poorly coordinated and divided, and Akaev's mastery of the political process ensured that most opponents were either cleverly co-opted into the system or effectively sidelined through political pressure on their businesses or their families. Kulov was disqualified from the 2000 parliamentary elections, and subsequently imprisoned on politically-motivated corruption charges. Akaev won the subsequent presidential election fairly easily, though not without some serious malpractice at the polls.[3]

Following the 2000 elections, the Akaev family consolidated its control, with both the elder son, Aidar, and the daughter, Bermet, beginning to play important roles in both business and politics. Akaev's wife, Mairam, was particularly unpopular among many in the political elite because of her alleged interference in appointments and domestic politics. Nevertheless, the political and economic environment in Bishkek was far freer than in any other Central Asian state. There were some opposition newspapers, occasional protests, and some form of political activity permitted. Economically, there were serious problems, but some reforms had progressed at least on paper. In practice, bureaucracy and corruption made investment difficult.

The hopes of the opposition and NGOs were raised in 2001, when they expected greater international attention as a result of a US-Kyrgyzstan basing agreement. President Akaev allowed the US-led coalition in Afghanistan to construct an air base at Manas civilian airport in Bishkek. His decision was partly influenced by the fees the US offered for use of the Manas runway, although the prospect of US political support was also an obvious factor. Fuel deliveries and other businesses related to the base came to be controlled by members of the presidential family, which added to the allure of the agreement.[4] Both Russia and China were clearly unsettled by Akaev's decision, but in the political atmosphere of 2001 there was little they could do to prevent Akaev from proceeding. If nothing else, the base added a cosmopolitan edge to Bishkek's rather staid nightlife, with contingents of Italians, Spaniards, Danes and French soldiers all passing through the capital's nightclubs and casinos. American forces, however, were restricted to one beer a week, and were mostly locked away in their tents at the air base.

---

3   On the presidential election, see "Presidential Elections: Kyrgyz Republic, 2 October 2000. OSCE/ODIHR Final Report", at http://194.8.63.155/documents/odihr/2001/01/1383_en.pdf.

4   David Stern,. "Kyrgyz President Admits Relative Sells to US Base," *Financial Times*, 22 July 2002.

Trouble in the south: Aksy

Despite his increasing dominance of the political process, Akaev's position always looked fragile. In 2002 an apparently minor event triggered a crisis that almost led to his downfall. In the distant region of Aksy, in the south of the country, the local parliamentary deputy Azimbek Beknazarov was arrested on dubious charges relating to an affray several years before. As with all arrests of political figures in Kyrgyzstan, the real reason for his detention was entirely different. Beknazarov had been involved in a campaign to oppose the transfer of some remote territory in eastern Kyrgyzstan to China, an agreement reached after several years of negotiation between the two sides. The area was uninhabited and had long been in dispute, but the opposition—which tended to be more nationalist than the government—seized on this "betrayal" and attempted to initiate measures in parliament to impeach Akaev. This was never likely to succeed, and if the government had ignored Beknazarov and his followers, the dispute would have faded away. Instead, Akaev panicked and ordered Beknazarov's arrest.

The ham-fisted attempt to arrest Beknazarov led to protests from his supporters. From around the region protestors began to converge on Kerben, the main town in the region. The chain of command in what happened next was long in dispute, but an order of sorts to "stop" the demonstrators seems to have gone out from Bishkek. One group, on the way to join other protestors in Kerben, was halted by police and local officials in a hamlet called Bospiek. Demonstrators started throwing stones at the police, who opened fire into the crowd, killing five of the unarmed demonstrators and injuring many more. As the news of the deaths spread to Kerben, a riot broke out, in which the police station was set on fire, and a further protestor was killed in the unrest.

A conciliatory response from Akaev could still have stopped the protests. "If only he had come himself to talk to us", protestors kept saying. Instead, the government tried to cover up what had happened, and began a media campaign to discredit the demonstrators. The government claimed that they were being paid to protest, that they were all drunks, or that they were only protesting because they were being coerced into it. The relentless propaganda on state television incensed the demonstrators, and one television crew narrowly escaped a beating.

In reality, Beknazarov's supporters were quietly impressive. Most of them were his close or distant relatives, or at least from the same remote region. The majority were poorly educated, and often unemployed. I watched them set off on a long protest march from the town of Tash-Kumyr, a depressing straggle of rickety houses strung out along the cliffs above the Karasu river, where some local women made ends meet by digging coal out of disused mines by hand. Usually young boys stood by the side of the road, selling third-rate coal to passers-by. But there was no trading this week. Beknazarov's supporters had blocked the road, the only route between Bishkek and Osh. Some drivers remonstrated angrily with the protestors, but most sat patiently, resigned to wait.

Slowly the protestors organised themselves, with remarkable discipline, into ranks, five abreast. They marched off, seemingly oblivious to the hundreds of miles they still had to cover to reach Osh, their destination. It was fiercely hot, and they were afraid of being attacked by the police in the night, but they seemed resolute, singing songs and holding up banners, calling for justice for their dead comrades, and berating Akaev for his cowardice. Along the road, sympathisers gave them food, but few of the curious onlookers joined in. This was not a national protest, but a huge act of solidarity for one man: Azimbek Beknazarov.

At this time Beknazarov was hardly known in most of the country. A local prosecutor, who had managed to get into parliament in a remote part of the country, he was a political nonentity before the Aksy shootings. Persecution by the government was a certain way of winning notoriety and even popularity, and Beknazarov was learning how to use his local support for national gain. Other opposition leaders also gave their backing. No public meeting was complete without the rousing speeches of Adahan Madumarov, a parliamentarian, who was one of the few Kyrgyz politicians able to stand on a makeshift tribune in a town square and stir up a crowd with his oratory.

Hundreds of protestors finally completed their "long march", arriving on the outskirts of Osh, where the police were on edge and the bazaar was full of rumours. The authorities were worried that any unrest could lead to clashes between Uzbeks and Kyrgyz. The raw memories of inter-ethnic killings in 1990 were still fresh. After long negotiations with the local governor, Naken Kasiev, over copious bowls of *plov*, the protestors agreed to turn back, to avoid a dangerous confrontation. But they did not give up. Marches and protests dragged on throughout the summer of 2002. Finally, in September, with none of their demands met, several hundred of the protestors began a march on Bishkek. But once they reached the edge of the city, the fight seemed to go out of them, and they meekly agreed to a secretive agreement between Beknazarov and the government that ended their protest. With little resistance, they were bundled into buses and taken back home to Aksy.

Some felt betrayed by the opposition leadership that had stepped back from its increasingly radical demands; other vowed to fight on. But for now the protests were over. The government claimed a victory, but its weakness had been starkly illuminated. The regime was brought almost to its knees by a few hundred demonstrators in a remote southern region. Its inability to negotiate with the demonstrators, and the collapse of state authority whenever it met this kind of concerted opposition, boded ill for the future of the regime. The killings at Aksy also led to disaffection within the police, who felt they had been used by political leaders, and then left to face the wrath of the population. Many would be far more reluctant to use arms to defend the government in the future.

In an apparent concession to the opposition, Akaev agreed to convene a Constitutional Council in Bishkek, which would examine the balance of power in the political system, and take away some of the overreaching powers of the presidency. The opposition were invited to join in the Council, the government seemed conciliatory, and several workable drafts were put together of a series of constitutional changes. At the last minute, however, in a move typical of Akaev's political tactics, a special commission came up with a final document which was almost totally at odds with everything that had been agreed at the Council.

These constitutional changes were immediately adopted by the government, which announced a snap referendum for February 2003, at which voters would also be asked to approve the constitutional changes, and to decide whether Akaev should serve out his constitutional term in office until 2005. The opposition was wrong-footed, and the subsequent referendum left them demoralised and despairing. The local authorities did everything to ensure that voters turned out and voted in the right way. If there were not enough voters, they filled the ballot boxes anyway. Akaev won a comfortable majority in the poll, and claimed this dubious exercise as a vote of confidence in his leadership. In reality, the referendum only further disillusioned voters.

While Akaev worked to bolster his political position, his family worked hard at their economic portfolios. Aidar Akaev had become a high-profile figure in Bishkek, often seen out drinking at the city's nightclubs, and causing increasing resentment among competitors, who alleged that he was rapidly expanding his control over the business world. Many businessmen complained that they faced predatory attempts at takeovers by the family, either from Aidar Akaev or from the president's son-in-law, Adil Toigonbaev, the husband of Bermet Akaeva, the president's eldest daughter, and one of Akaev's closest confidantes. Bermet was increasingly seen as a more reliable "gatekeeper" to the president for investors than her brother or leading government members. One foreign diplomat, seeking to sort out a dispute involving a foreign investor, asked a government minister in formal control of foreign investments for assistance. "What can I do?" shrugged the minister. "Go and see Bermet, she's your only chance."[5]

Bermet saw herself as the strategist in the family, and was keen to build her own political future. She was young, smart, and Westernised, but she did not seem able to escape her own particular personal history and mindset, and had little understanding of ordinary Kyrgyz and their views of the presidential family. Her husband Toigonbaev

---

5   Personal communication, Western diplomat, Bishkek, December 2004.

was a Kazakh businessman, who used his financial weight and political connections to take over media outlets, including the main Bishkek newspaper, *Vechernii Bishkek*. Bermet also set up her own political vehicle, the Alga Kyrgyzstan party. Although some of its founders saw it as a potential platform for the more reform-minded young businesspeople who gathered around Bermet, as soon as the party began to function in the regions it quickly turned into what the Russians called a "party of power", packed with functionaries loyal to the presidential family. It offered no more policy ideas than any other of Kyrgyzstan's weak political parties, and had no real popular support.

The actions of the "family" infuriated many in the elite. Gradually, one-time supporters of Akaev began to drift, if not into outright opposition, at least towards sufficient frustration with the family's interference to make them ready to switch sides if and when the time came. There were still a few hardline supporters of the president. The ubiquitous Bolot Januzakov, a diminutive ex-KGB officer, who delighted in the epithet of "grey cardinal", was always ready to defend the president's line. The state secretary, Osmonakun Ibraimov, a man so unpopular with diplomats that one foreign ambassador claimed he found it impossible to shake his hand, was also available to offer support at any moment. But there were few other die-hard supporters. This motley collection of on-the-make bureaucrats did not give the kind of support that Akaev really needed, but other figures in the elite were increasingly staking out a more independent position. Competent officials, such as the Osh governor Naken Kasiev, were sidelined, often because of some petty conflict with other members of the family, and Akaev was left with an entourage whom nobody respected. Even Bermet Akaeva called them "dinosaurs", officials who had hardly changed their office furniture, let alone their thinking, since Soviet times.

Meanwhile, a few officials had gone over completely to the opposition, notably Kurmanbek Bakiev, a former prime minister who resigned after the Aksy shootings, and was now tipped as a potential opposition candidate for the next presidential elections, due in 2005. The opposition remained diverse and divided. Bakiev was a southerner, but was mistrusted by some other southern politicians, such as the long-time opposition parliamentarian Omurbek Tekebaev. Northern opposition figures were also suspicious of their southern allies: the political prisoner Feliks Kulov was popular in Bishkek and among the Russian-speaking population, but his imprisonment kept him out of active politics, although it did seem to give him time for reflection, and he claimed to have discovered an affinity with democratic values that had been less apparent while he was in government.

The most active part of the opposition was a collection of NGO leaders and human rights activists who took part in small demonstrations and protests in Bishkek, but had little in the way of wider popular support. These were the figures who appeared at international conferences, and survived largely on Western grants. Even when united, they did not look like much of a threat. They could gather easily around the kitchen table of Zamira Sadykova, editor of the independent newspaper *Respublika* and the informal leader of many of the NGO activists and journalists. These were people who had opposed the government for many years, whereas Bakiev and others were seen as latecomers in their recognition of the necessity for change. Many observers dismissed this opposition as incapable of posing a real challenge to the government; indeed they were frequently involved in squabbles amongst themselves.

However, in late 2004, they began to attract greater support from among one-time government officials. As well as Bakiev, the former education minister Ishenbul Boljurova joined the opposition, while the former foreign minister Roza Otunbaeva returned from working with the UN in Georgia to take part in domestic politics again. Otunbaeva was a long-time opponent of Akaev, who had been "exiled" to London as ambassador, one of many foreign affairs specialists who had fallen out with the administration and had been sent abroad. At times, the Ministry of Foreign Affairs seemed to be an outpost of the opposition, rather than the government's representatives abroad.

The opposition made several attempts to create a united slate of candidates for the parliamentary elections, scheduled for February 2005. However, the Kyrgyz political system did not really encourage a national opposition based on ideas rather than personality. Politics revolved around regional and personal networks. Sometimes it was based on traditional clan networks, particularly in the south, or on regional networks, but there were also new networks based on business, criminal links, and political expediency that were just as effective.

Politics was personal, and at least part of the opposition to Akaev was based on personal slights or grudges: former officials who had been dismissed or not promoted, or who had somehow fallen out of favour with the presidential family. The broad opposition was united in their discontent with the ruling presidential family, but could not coalesce around any particular platform or ideology. Nevertheless, a rough-and-ready coalition of northern and southern opposition politicians announced that they would run in the parliamentary elections. Nobody gave them much chance of getting elected. Otunbaeva announced that the opposition hoped to win one-third of seats in the new parliament, but it was not clear that they even had that many candidates.

The February 2005 parliamentary elections were critical for Akaev. He needed a resounding majority to provide him with political options ahead of presidential elections in October of that year. According to the constitution, Akaev had to step down in October, having served for two terms, but with a strong parliamentary majority he had the chance to change the constitution, either leaving himself in control or changing the political system to allow a prime minister (perhaps his son or daughter) to take over most executive functions.

Elections and unrest

Even his opponents admired Akaev's mastery of the political game, but ahead of the parliamentary elections, Akaev began making uncharacteristic tactical mistakes. Firstly, he had agreed to a disastrous reform of the electoral system. Two chambers of parliament were to be reduced to one, ensuring that some powerful figures would not get a seat in the new legislature. This was already cause for concern, but other reforms made things even worse. Previous elections included a party-list system—people voted for a list of candidates belonging to nationwide political parties. Under the new system, 75 parliamentary deputies were to be elected in local constituencies. This was designed to get Akaev a pliable parliament consisting mainly of local business-people, who had the money and connections to bribe, cajole and pressure their way into parliament. In reality, it produced hard-fought local contests in which candidates could mobilise their supporters to protest against any infringements in the elections. It was almost designed to create unrest. An additional side-effect was that local criminal authorities—who had the money, and often genuine popular support—were among the best-placed candidates to get elected.

The second mistake was to try and get his own relatives elected. This was a move away from his usual tactic of compromise and coop-tion of elites, and towards a narrower ruling gr, dominated by the family. Akaev's son Aidar and his daughter Bermet both announced they would be running for parliament. At one point seven of Akaev's relatives were thought to be contesting the poll, although several pulled out once their unpopularity became clear. But the decision of the two elder children to contest the elections caused discontent among the broader population and also in the elite.

In mid-February, with just two weeks to go to polling day, these two tactical errors started to cause serious problems. Traditionally, the south of the country had been the hotbed of protest, particu-larly since the Aksy shootings. Now protests suddenly erupted in the usually politically quiet areas around Lake Issyk-kul to the east of Bishkek, and in a remote village, Kochkor, on the road to China in the east, after candidates were unexpectedly disbarred from running in the election.

In Kochkor Akylbek Japarov was disqualified from the poll on a technicality. In reality he was forced out because he seemed likely to defeat Turdakun Usubaliev, the 88-year-old former Communist Party chief, who had a long-standing belief in his god-given right to remain in parliament for ever. Under the old electoral system they would both have been elected; now, with fewer parliamentary seats available, a conflict was inevitable.

Japarov's supporters quickly staged a protest against the disqualifi-cation of their candidate. His followers in Kochkor blocked the main road to China, putting up felt yurts (traditional tents) on the road, making it impossible to pass. A confused Scandinavian election observer from the OSCE argued in vain to let his car through: the old women in charge of the blockade were in no mood for compromise. Further on, at the approach to the village itself, dozens of trucks were backed up, blocked by the protestors from proceeding on their long journey from Kashgar to Bishkek. Their drivers looked resigned, sitting around, waiting for something to happen. Young men galloped up on horses, latter-day nomads for democracy. As in some vignette from a Russian revolutionary propaganda film, the local town mayor was standing on the back of a cart, while local activists stood around him discussing whether to try him at a "people's tribunal". Angry women—who were at the forefront of most protests in Kyrgyzstan— were forming an unlikely lynch mob around the cart.

Kochkor was the first sign of how weak the state really was. The regional governor ran away, chased over a fence by enthusiastic youngsters. "He was too fast for us—he's a good athlete" the boys told us apologetically. The police were nowhere in evidence; the local government building was almost empty. One lonely election official remained in his office: "I told them [Bishkek] not to interfere", he sighed. Everybody else had fled, and for a short time there was a power vacuum in these villages that would soon be repeated around the country.

Eventually, after negotiations in Bishkek, Akylbek Japarov came back to Kochkor and persuaded his followers to disperse. Instead of continuing the protest, he urged them to use the option of voting against all candidates on the ballot paper in an attempt to get the vote declared void.

Similar protests around Issyk-kul also dispersed after candidates were reinstated, but unrest was gathering elsewhere. Ravshan Jeenbekov was a one-time ally of the Akaevs, a smooth young politician who had been a major player in the regime. He was running for election in the remote northern region of Talas, but was now shifting towards the opposition after the authorities tried to oust him from the electoral race. His supporters came out on the streets, and only their protests prevented the local court from disqualifying him from the poll on flimsy accusations. The result of these essentially local disputes was a big shift in opinion among otherwise loyal officials of the old regime: more and more were shifting their stance and talking to the opposition. Not only had they seen how easy it was to mobilise public protest against the regime, but the lack of response from the state persuaded many that the government was weak and out of touch. Outside Bishkek, the mood was changing fast.

In the capital, however, there were few signs of potential upheaval at first. Many figures in the elite were dissatisfied with Akaev, but were too afraid to come out in overt opposition to him. But on the eve of the election one of Kyrgyzstan's best-known figures, the controversial psychiatrist Jenishbek Nazaraliev, published an open letter to Akaev. The letter was uncompromising, criticising Akaev in blunt language, and concluding with an open challenge: "Either Akaev leaves the country or I do." Nazaraliev was a highly unusual personality. He had started the first private medical clinic in the Soviet Union, which offered treatment for Russia's most universal complaint, alcoholism. A couple of column inches in a Moscow newspaper in the late 1980s produced thousands of applicants for his unusual courses of treatment. Later he began treating drug addicts, with a unique approach that involved techniques closer to shamanism than to modern medicine, including a six-day walk up his own private mountain with a rock on one's back.

Nazaraliev's open rebellion was an important step in the distancing of the elites from Akaev. Nazaraliev came out against Akaev partly for personal reasons: a lack of recognition of his achievements, and a real sense of betrayal by this upstart presidential family. But his open rebellion had an important multiplier effect: other members of the elite were now wondering whether it was wise to support Akaev too wholeheartedly.

Akaev meanwhile had launched a new campaign, accusing the US embassy, NDI and other NGOs of planning a revolution against him. In truth, most diplomats and international organisations expected nothing to happen. Indeed, from Bishkek everything appeared to be relatively calm. Only outside the capital was the level of potential unrest becoming clear. The opposition leader Roza Otunbaeva was running around Bishkek, trying to gain support for her opposition coalition, but complaining that international organisations were doing nothing to help.

On election day, 14 February 2005, everything seemed to be going according to plan. Voters filed into the local schools and universities that were used as polling stations. Overseeing the process was usually the director of the school, who was aware that a successful vote (high turnout and the right candidate elected) meant financial reward for him and for his school; a bad performance probably meant losing his job. In the university district in Bishkek, students filed in to vote, their reluctant faces suggesting they were not all there by choice. Most voted dutifully for the president's daughter, Bermet, filling out their ballot papers underneath a huge portrait of the president himself.

At times there seemed to be more election observers than voters. The most professional group was from the Organisation for Security and Cooperation in Europe (OSCE), with hundreds of observers strung out around the country. The OSCE's role had been sharply criticised by Russia during the Georgian and Ukrainian elections, largely because their reports detailing errors in the electoral process had partly fuelled subsequent protests against electoral fraud. Russia had developed its own observer team, the CIS observers, who were guaranteed to echo the government line that the elections were free, fair and entirely legitimate. Alongside them were an array of bizarre pro-government observer teams: two slightly bemused Chinese diplomats were in the odd position of having to judge the legitimacy of the kind of elections their own country had never experienced. Others came from spurious-sounding Western human rights groups. In the evening after the vote, some of them were displayed on state television to show "foreign approval" of the elections. But few people believed what Kyrgyz state television told them; instead they gleaned their information from independent broadcasts by Radio Free Europe and the BBC.

The government had learned lessons from Georgia and Ukraine, where independent media had played a key role in mobilising support for the opposition. Prior to the elections it ended Radio Free Europe's broadcast licence prematurely, thus cutting off much of the country from its programming, and also cut off electricity supply to a US-financed printing press, which published the opposition newspaper MSN. The information blockade had some effect. In Kochkor nobody knew what was happening in Bishkek. In Bishkek few people knew what was going on in Talas. And the south was largely cut off from news from the capital. But the old network of whispers and rumours at the bazaar still played its part, and for the first time mobile telephones, which now had coverage in many urban areas outside Bishkek, started to play a role.

The OSCE, the UNDP, the US embassy and others had tried to improve some of the technical aspects of the election. Transparent ballot boxes were introduced, designed to make ballot-rigging more difficult, although they were so transparent that it was easy to see which way some people had voted. In one instance, a voter in Naryn was reportedly beaten up by one election official after he saw that he had voted "the wrong way" after happily accepting the usual payment to vote for another candidate. The technical improvements and the presence of so many observers at polling stations meant that on the day itself there was less scope for the authorities to interfere in the electoral process. Most of the damage was done in the run-up to the poll: hundreds of thousands of dollars were pumped into the electoral process by rich businesspeople, some of it spent on improving roads or housing for voters before the election, some paid directly to voters or authoritative figures within communities to get them to vote for them.

To win in the first round of voting, a candidate needed to get 50 per cent of the votes cast, otherwise the top two candidates fought a second round of polling. In one of the first shocks of the election, Bermet Akaeva, running in Bishkek, did not win on the first round, gaining only 45 per cent of the vote, despite enormous pressure on students to vote for her and restrictions on the campaigns of her opponents. The family parliament was looking a little less likely, although Aidar Akaev got through easily in his home town of Kemin. In Kochkor, in an unprecedented vote, most people voted against all candidates on the ballot paper, a humiliation for the unpopular figure of Usubaliev. In the south few opposition politicians had got through in the first round. Only in Aksy, where Beknazarov won with over 50 per cent of the vote, did a major opposition leader win a seat on the first round. Most constituencies would be contesting a second round.

As soon as the election results were announced, a series of protests broke out in the south, where there were many contested results. Candidates accused each other of malpractice and brought their supporters out onto the streets. In most cases this was nothing to do with the government-opposition dynamic; these were conflicts between different powerful authority figures, each seeking to use their relatives and their money to put pressure on electoral commissions and courts to massage the result in their direction. Far from being an election process totally controlled by the government, in many places the voting had slipped completely out of central control.

Nevertheless, opposition figures complained of massive interference in the electoral process, and now began to protest at the results being announced by the Central Electoral Commission. On 4 March 2005 around 1,000 supporters of Jusupbek Bakiev, the brother of the opposition leader Kurmanbek Bakiev, seized control of the regional administration building in the south's second city, Jalalabad. Jusupbek had lost in his constituency, gaining only 26 per cent of the vote, and claimed it was the result of electoral fraud. His brother, Kurmanbek, was still in the race: his election, along with many other undecided first-round votes, would have to be repeated in two weeks' time.

The seizure by Bakiev supporters of the Jalalabad regional administration was a turning-point in the election. It was a direct threat to the state, and demonstrated, as in Kochkor, how weak the state had become. Protestors camped out in the building and there seemed to be little the police could or would do about it, beyond complaining about poor sanitation among the protestors. "They could at least go home and wash", complained the police. Similar events elsewhere led to talk among the opposition of developing parallel power structures, electing "people's governors" and taking over local authority. The government ignored these developments, assuming they would fade away once the second-round results had come in. Previous elections had also provoked small local protests, but usually the authorities had managed to use a mixture of pressure and persuasion to prevent them getting out of control.

However, far from clarifying the situation, the second round of voting on 13 March only deepened the growing sense of crisis around the elections. Rather short-sightedly, most observers, from the OSCE and other organisations, had left after the first round, leaving much more scope for traditional ballot-rigging and general chaos at the polls two weeks later. Predictably, as the results came in during the night, the street protests began. First to spark demonstrations was Adahan Madumarov, the charismatic opposition candidate in Uzgen. His fight against a local bazaar owner—who had support from the government—had come down to a few votes' difference, and the electoral authority initially ruled that Madumarov had lost. With thousands of his supporters chanting in the streets, they were forced to reverse their decision, and declare Madumarov the victor, but this only provoked rival demonstrations by his opponent. Elsewhere, Kurmanbek Bakiev lost in his constituency, in a major blow to the opposition. He complained of constant interference by the authorities, at one point alleging that they had deliberately provoked a snow avalanche to block his campaign tour. Ravshan Jeenbekov also lost, in an ugly campaign in his Talas constituency. The next day Jeenbekov's supporters came out on the streets, seized government buildings and briefly took some officials hostage. The situation was threatening to slip out of control.

For once the opposition put on a united front. On 15 March the Bakiev brothers, Roza Otunbaeva, and other opposition leaders gathered in Jalalabad, where protestors still retained control of the administration building. Behind the scenes more shadowy figures, notably Bayaman Erkinbaev, a well-known local businessman widely suspected of involvement in drug-smuggling, were offering the opposition their support. On 18 March opposition demonstrators seized government buildings in Osh, and appointed Anvar Artykov as "people's governor". Artykov was an ethnic Uzbek, and his appointment went some way to assuaging Uzbek fears that protests of the (mainly Kyrgyz) opposition might lead to interethnic tensions. Uzbeks had generally supported pro-Akaev candidates in Jalalabad, Uzgen and Osh, and they were wary of the nationalism of the Kyrgyz opposition, particularly among its southern representatives.

The end of the affair

Early in the morning of 19 March special forces stormed the government headquarters in both Osh and Jalalabad, expelling the protestors with some ease and with only limited casualties. But this was the last throw of a failing regime. Hours later over 10,000 people gathered in the square in front of the administration in Jalalabad. This was a key moment of truth: in Uzbekistan 14 months later, a similar confrontation would end in a massacre. But in Kyrgyzstan, much to Akaev's credit, the security forces had orders not to shoot, and soon they were chased out of the building, and the protestors were back in charge.

The streets were now full of young men wielding Molotov cocktails, the police station was soon ablaze, and protestors moved quickly to seize the airport to prevent any new troops from being flown in. Not long afterwards, a similar revolutionary scene was played out in Osh, as protestors took back control of government buildings, and also moved to the outskirts of town to take control of the airport, leaving the whole of the south effectively in opposition hands. For the first time, there was a sense of something new and much more dangerous developing: the protestors were young men, some of them drunk, some with blood-shot eyes; all were worryingly unpredictable. Many seemed to be loyal to dubious authority figures, such as the drug lord Erkinbaev, rather than the formal opposition. Indeed, opposition leaders seemed almost as surprised as government officials by what was going on. Events were taking a dangerous course.

In the capital there was a sense of unreality about the events unfolding in the south. Osh and Jalalabad always seemed a very distant reality for most Bishkek residents. And with little news coverage of the protests in the south, the capital was relying on rumour and conjecture for much of the time. There were small demonstrations in the capital but nothing on the scale of the southern protests. On 23 March about 500 people gathered in the city centre to protest against the election results. Police arrested several activists and the crowd dispersed. Akaev appointed a new interior minister—the hardline Bishkek police chief Keneshbek Dushebaev. Encouraged by his children and advisers, Akaev attempted to clamp down. But it was already far too late.

With the opposition largely based in the south, the authorities could have blocked any attempt to move north to the capital, but they failed to do so. On the morning of 24 March opposition leaders began to arrive in Bishkek, bringing with them as many supporters from their regions as possible, in convoys of buses and cars. The opposition began planning a major demonstration on the city's central square later in the day. Almaz Atambaev, the leader of the Social-Democratic Party and a well-known Bishkek businessman, was one of the key organisers. Prickly and driven, Atambaev was one of the few opposition leaders who had real support among young people in the north, and he now gathered some 5,000 supporters, who began marching towards the central square. From the other direction, a more diverse group, a mixture of southerners from the bazaar, idealistic young students from democratic groups such as Kel-Kel, and ordinary Bishkek residents, gathered at Nazaraliev's medical clinic. They reached the square first, brushing aside police attempts to block the route. Atambaev's group arrived later, but by 1 pm there were perhaps as many as 10,000 demonstrators in the square, only 100 metres from the presidential administration, housed on the seventh floor of what locals called the "White House", a modernist brute of late Soviet architecture.

Moderate political figures were now desperate to avoid bloodshed. Several intermediaries had tried to talk to Akaev to arrange some compromise. The head of the Constitutional Court, Cholpon Baekova, had spent two days pleading with his entourage to allow her to talk to him, but they refused.[6] It still seemed possible for Akaev to remain in power if he jettisoned some of his more odious advisers and promised new elections. But President Akaev was increasingly out of touch with reality. His advisers were simply unable to comprehend the reality of what was going on. The arrogance of power had blinded them to their own fate.

---

6   Personal communication, Bishkek, April 2005.

Police were strung around the White House, and in the basement of the building troops from the National Guard were armed and waiting. Opposition leaders began making speeches, but at the edges of the crowd clashes began between demonstrators and groups of young men in baseball caps, *provocateurs* previously used by supporters of the president to provoke violence at opposition rallies. Fights broke out, but eventually the baseball-capped thugs fled, fought off by aggressive young men on the opposition side. The speeches continued but somehow the attention of the crowd was wandering. Youths were hyped up by the outbreaks of violence, and ready for more action. The intellectuals in the crowd had hoped for a Ukraine-style revolution: forcing the government to capitulate after days or even weeks of student-led occupation of the square. They saw a protest as a kind of intensive course in democracy. But this was not mainly a crowd of young students anxious about the democratic process; the motives were mixed, but for many it was a pent-up feeling of rage and a thirst for revenge.

A huge cheer went up in the crowd as a column of protestors from Osh arrived at the square, many of them apparently followers of Bayaman Erkinbaev. Without stopping to hear the speeches, they marched on towards the White House, and were joined by other young men from the crowd. Twice the riot police pushed them back, and again they surged forward. The police had been ordered not to use firearms, and there was no shooting. As the pressure of the crowd got too much for the outnumbered police, they suddenly gave way and began to run. The crowd swept past into the grounds of the White House itself, and finally smashed through its big double doors into the supposedly well protected headquarters of the state. The National Guard was armed and might have used force, but its commander, General Abdykul Chotpaev, understood the game was up. His soldiers were escorted away by young activists, and the crowd rampaged up the stairs to the holy of holies of the Kyrgyz state, the rather vulgar offices of the presidential administration.

Akaev had left the building long before, and was visiting the Japanese Ambassador during the afternoon, perhaps oblivious to what was going on. The state secretary, Osmonakun Ibraimov, had

143

resigned and fled the building half an hour before the crowds reached his office. Only the old loyalist Bolot Januzakov remained in his office. A crowd of youths captured him; hotheads wanted to pull him apart, literally, but two journalists intervened and took him out of the building, his head covered in a blanket, badly injured but alive. Meanwhile, protestors rampaged through the building, papers flew from windows, chairs smashed down onto the forecourt below. The White House was being looted.

Bakiev did his best to try and calm the crowd, and gradually some order was restored inside the White House, but youths now spread out round the city and began looting stores. The Narodny chain of supermarkets, thought to be owned by Aidar Akaev, was a particular target. The Turkish-owned Beta Stores was also set alight and looted: some of the looters were the young men from the protest, but others were simply local residents lifting televisions and refrigerators from the wrecked buildings. Much of this was evidently planned, with thugs in jeeps pointing out which stores to attack and which to leave alone. By nightfall several buildings were on fire, and a pall of smoke coagulated over the city.

During the day a group of protestors had gone to the prison where Feliks Kulov was being held, and released him from prison. His appearance on the streets calmed some of the protestors and encouraged some of the police to come back on duty. Kulov stopped an attempt to loot the big Tsum store in the centre of town, and gradually the police, and a quickly formed people's militia, started gaining ground against the looters.

As soon as the news of the capture of the White House reached him, Akaev had fled, with his family, apparently spirited out of the country first to Kazakhstan and then to Russia, where he insistently claimed that he was still the legitimate president. Meanwhile, in Bishkek the opposition was trying to form a government. Huddled in the offices of the National Security Service, fearing revenge attacks by government supporters and the uncontrollable crowds in equal measure, Bakiev initially seemed paralysed by the ease with which power had slipped into his hands.

For several days the situation remained tense. Supporters of Akaev threatened to march on Bishkek from Kemin, his home town, but they had little popular support. Akaev had lost much support even before the uprising, and his last remaining backers were switching sides as fast as possible once they heard he had left the country. His panicked flight lost him any last vestiges of respect among elites. Januzakov was in hospital apparently fighting for his life, and the prime minister Nikolai Tanaev had also left the country, after being tracked down and forced to sign a letter of resignation.

The new authorities faced difficult choices. The first problem was that there were two parliaments competing for power. The initial protests had been sparked by unfair elections, and some members of the old parliament claimed that the newly elected legislature was illegitimate. In any case, many constituencies had still to declare a winner, and some races would remain disputed for weeks. The more radical members of the opposition wanted to sweep away the new parliament and keep the old one until new elections could be staged. But any such wholesale attack on the new legislature was neither constitutional nor politically expedient. The new parliament included some of the most powerful political figures in the country, who were unlikely to accept the dissolution of a legislature after they had spent so much time (and huge amounts of money) getting elected to the new body. Sensibly, the new leaders did a deal with the parliament. The opposition would accept its legitimacy if the parliament agreed to the appointment of Kurmanbek Bakiev as prime minister and act-ing president. This sidestepped some constitutional niceties, notably the fact that Akaev still considered himself (and in constitutional terms still was) the president, but it gave an air of legitimacy to the hurried seizure of power by a few thousand protestors in Bishkek.

After the revolution

There was some jubilation in Bishkek as the White House fell, but it was tempered by the fear of instability: Bishkek residents were shocked by the scale of the looting and disorder that had accom-panied the overthrow of the government. In the capital many were

145

fearful of a new order, which seemed to be dominated by southern politicians and supported by their rural backers, young, rough men who had little in common with the more middle-class residents of Bishkek. This north-south divide would remain a fundamental dynamic as the political scene settled down.

Other long-term social divisions also came to the fore. Bishkek had long experienced in-migration from rural areas, particularly, but not only, from the south. Villagers who could not survive on small patches of land in remote rural areas flocked to Bishkek to work in the bazaars or in construction, living sometimes several families to a couple of rooms. Increasingly, their children were seen begging on the streets, or working. The government had largely ignored these migrants, and did little to try and find them homes, land or official registration in the capital.

Many of them had participated in the revolution. They had been part of the crowd that protested, and had risked their lives to oust Akaev and usher in a new government. Now they wanted some payback, and they occupied land around Bishkek and dared the government to throw them out. Some of this land was rented by local farmers, some of it was designated parkland. Protestors pointed to the luxury villas that were sprouting on this supposedly protected land, and asked why they could not also build there. At times they came into conflict with local residents, who urged the police to intervene and oust the migrants from lands that they used for growing crops; several times the two sides nearly came to violence.

The government was slow to respond, but gradually a land registry commission, some intervention from the police, and the clear reluctance of the government to meet the land squatters' demands dampened their enthusiasm; the bulk of the land squatters filtered back to their cramped apartments and self-built hovels, waiting for another day, another revolution. A few carried on the fight, trying to persuade the authorities to make good on their social promises. But the government was too divided and too short of resources to resolve all the country's problems immediately. There were many vague promises but little action.

The revolutionary fervour unleashed by the March unrest carried on for months. There were frequent attempts by supporters of this or that candidate to storm the Supreme Court, where various electoral contests were still being settled. Occasionally protestors occupied other government buildings; it was not always clear why—sometimes it seemed to have become a hard-to-break habit. The revolutionary spirit was alive and well, but it was unclear what else could be revolted against. The problems in the country were not easily solved, requiring better administration, less corruption, and more economic growth. None of this long-term state-building could be ushered in through protests and sit-ins. And the elite no longer wanted upheaval. The uncertainty in the country still threatened serious instability, and most political figures were keen to move forward to presidential elections as fast as possible to ensure some legitimacy for the new regime.

Feliks Kulov had been appointed coordinator of the security forces in the immediate aftermath of the storming of the White House, and he had played an important role in bringing calm back to the streets. Kulov retained a good deal of respect among the police, and his intervention encouraged them to protect law and order in Bishkek. But as soon as a tentative peace reigned on the streets of Bishkek Kulov resigned, arguing that his job had been done. He was not very welcome in the new regime: Bakiev and Kulov hardly talked to each other, and saw each other as rivals not partners. Kulov was a northerner, most respected in Bishkek, and particularly popular among Russian-speakers, who shared his demand for law and order and his suspicion of southern politicians. Bakiev was the cleverer politician, knowing the Kyrgyz system of government inside out.

Bakiev saw off several potential rivals. The maverick Adahan Madumarov was persuaded to give up his challenge for the presidency with the offer of a government post. Other powerful leaders also got new posts: the mayor of Bishkek, Medetbek Kerimkulov, hardly an outspoken opponent of Akaev, became First Deputy Prime Minister. The new head of the National Security Service (NSS), Tashtemir Aitbaev, was part of the old Soviet elite that had lost power under

Akaev, and a relative by marriage of Bakiev. All these new appointments made some wonder what had changed. "Why did we make this revolution?" asked one of the more cynical activists. "So that Bakiev could get his friends and relatives in power?"[7]

All this infighting was to be expected in a situation of virtual state collapse. Moderates were now seriously concerned about instability and were pushing for the two main contenders for power, Kulov and Bakiev, to come to an agreement and run in tandem for the presidency. Many feared that if the two ran against each other, the whole north-south divide would be represented in the presidential race, which would almost certainly provoke civil unrest. After many weeks of sparring, the two men finally agreed that Bakiev would run for president, while Kulov was promised the post of prime minister.

The agreement made the presidential election something of a formality, since no other political figure could hope to compete against these two figures. But one or two were still willing to try to upset this smooth transition process. In June 2005 thousands of people again stormed the White House. This time they were supporters of a political movement called Mekenim Kyrgyzstan (My Homeland—Kyrgyzstan), led by a little known would-be presidential candidate Urmat Baryktabasov, a wealthy businessman who had spent years in Dubai and Kazakhstan. He had considerable resources and plenty of ambition, but almost no comprehension of politics. Police used tear gas and batons to disperse the demonstrators, and government officials blamed the Akaev family in exile for trying to support a counter-revolution, although there was no direct evidence of the Akaevs' involvement.

The election itself, held on 10 July 2005, was something of an anticlimax. As predicted, Bakiev won a landslide victory, gaining 89 per cent of the vote. Nobody else got more than five per cent, with the Ombudsman Tursunbai Bakir-uul trailing on four per cent, and Akaev loyalist Keneshbek Dushebaev on less than one per cent. The OSCE reported "tangible progress towards meeting…. international commitments for democratic elections", but noted a "a small number

---

7   Personal communication, NGO activist, March 2006.

of serious irregularities" including some ballot-stuffing and problems with the count in some polling stations. The turnout of 74 per cent was questioned by some cynics, since there were reports of widespread apathy among voters in Bishkek and elsewhere in the north. But there was more enthusiasm in the south, with over 80 per cent of voters reportedly turning up to cast their ballots.[8]

Bakiev, continually doubted even by many of his supporters, had played a clever political game from the very beginning. He was not a natural opposition leader, and was happiest when devising some new bureaucratic reform or playing the informal games of smoking-room politics. He was led initially in a more radical direction by opposition leaders such as Roza Otunbaeva and Beknazarov. Subsequently, his natural inclination towards consolidation ended these alliances and he found common ground with former bureaucrats such as Medetbek Kerimkulov and other Akaev-era officials. By September both Beknazarov and Otunbaeva were out of office, having been increasingly sidelined by Bakiev and his allies, particularly Usen Sydykov, the unpopular head of the presidential administration and a key player in the new regime. Prime Minister Kulov was also sidelined by the new leadership, with the presidential administration taking over many of the government's functions, and tension between the two men was palpable. The "tandem" was tested time and again, not least over the relationship between the regime and organised crime.

The criminal world

Bakiev hoped that the election would end any questions about his legitimacy, but it turned out to be merely the beginning of an even more turbulent period of politics. Alternative centres of power, particularly criminal authorities, began to challenge the dominance of the government. Under Akaev the family had developed a rather symbiotic relationship with these mafia groups, giving them space to operate relatively freely as long as they did not interfere with family business or politics. With a vacuum opening up in the political

---

8 OSCE Press Release, "Kyrgyzstan makes tangible progress", 11 July 2005, accessed at www.osce.org/item/15624.html.

leadership, powerful criminal figures rushed to fill the gap. Like everything else in the country, they divided roughly into two groups, southern and northern.

The most powerful of the northern groups was led by Ryspek Akmatbaev, who had been on the run for years over suspicion of involvement in a murder. Such was his influence that the police made no serious attempt to arrest him. His brother Tynychbek Akmatbaev (who had been arrested, although later freed without charge, in relation to a contract killing in 2004) was elected to the new parliament in 2005. His subsequent election as head of the parliamentary committee on law and order was met with hollow laughter. Kyrgyz politics looked more and more like a theatre of the absurd.

Parliamentary deputies claimed that there were at least seven serious criminals sitting in the new parliament. One of them was Bayaman Erkinbaev, who had come to the fore during the parliamentary elections and the overthrow of Akaev. He strenuously denied any criminal activity, but police sources linked him to illegal machinations around the Kara-Suu bazaar and involvement in drug-smuggling. He had never been sentenced on any of the charges brought against him. When he was charged with electoral malpractice during the 2000 elections, he simply marched into the courtroom and beat up the judge. The case was dropped.

After the March events, in which he and his supporters played a leading role in support of the opposition, he seemed to be expanding his authority in the south. He had been reelected as parliamentary deputy with a record 95 per cent of the vote, but his rapid expansion of influence gained him some serious enemies. In April he appeared on television claiming to have been the victim of an assassination attempt, with a bloodied bandage over his nose, where he had apparently been shot. In September, in a scene resembling an all too predictable gangster movie, Bayaman Erkinbaev was shot dead outside his house in Bishkek.

He was not the first victim of a contract killing after the revolution. In June gunmen shot dead parliamentary deputy Jyrgalbek Surabaldiev, also reputed to be a mafia leader, in Bishkek. Rumours swirled around the parliament, with deputies claiming that there was a "black list" of figures destined to be assassinated. Bakiev lashed out at parliamentarians and the police, claiming:

The fact that criminal elements have merged with law enforcement agencies is not news to anybody. You all know this perfectly well, too. Among those sitting here are people who know perfectly well about it, who know who is connected to whom and how they are connected.[9]

Bakiev's opponents responded with allegations of links between members of the presidential administration and criminal leaders. Either way, it was clear that the weakness of the state was making it vulnerable to increased influence from criminal and semi-criminal groups.

Nobody expected Erkinbaev to be the last victim of a contract killing. But the next murder sparked off an even more serious crisis. It began with a prison riot, in October 2005, at prison No. 31 near Bishkek. In these prisons nothing much had changed since Soviet times. Conditions were grim for prisoners, with tuberculosis rife and food inadequate. Most only survived because their relatives brought them food and bribed the guards to ensure better treatment. In many cases, the guards only controlled the situation in coordination with criminal authority figures who were also incarcerated. These "thieves-in-law", as they were called in Soviet times, ensured order inside the prison, and in exchange had considerable freedom and often excellent accommodation and unlimited access to luxuries. In prison no. 31 Aziz Batukaev, a Chechen criminal authority, was incarcerated in rather more luxurious conditions than his fellow prisoners, occupying 16 rooms in the prison, including a billiard room and a sauna, and even a small herd of goats and three mares; he used their milk to treat a stomach ulcer, apparently.[10]

During the October prison riot a parliamentary deputy, Tynychbek Akmatbaev, went to try and mediate, but events took a fatal turn.

---

9   Bruce Pannier, "Kyrgzstan: Lawmaker Murdered In Apparent Mafia-Related Shooting", RFE/RL, 22 September 2005.

10 On the appalling state of prisons, see International Crisis Group, "Kyrgyzstan's Prison System Nightmare", Asia Report, No. 118, 16 August 2006.

During a meeting Akmatbaev was shot dead, provoking a furious response from his brother, Ryspek, who accused the government and its allies of orchestrating the killing. Ryspek organised a mass protest on the main square of Bishkek, attended by hundreds of his supporters. Ministers and parliamentary deputies queued up to visit him on the square, where he presided over proceedings like a monarch-in-waiting. Ryspek had already held what his detractors called a "coronation" in his homeland in the Issyk-Kul lake area in August 2005, an event attended by almost the entire political establishment, although some went with more secrecy than others. Ryspek represented a new type of political figure, combining strong Kyrgyz nationalism with traditional concepts of honour, kinship and social protection through mafia-like structures. His success in gaining such authority was a direct result of the lack of respect for formal political figures, and a frustration with the whole post-March political settlement.

Although Ryspek's protest was eventually dispersed without violence, the government remained unable or unwilling to assert its control over such figures. Diplomatic sources suggested that narcotics continued to transit Kyrgyzstan with few obstacles, and that some leading political-business figures had already visited Afghanistan after March 2005 to rearrange control of transit routes.[11] The government did almost nothing to try and limit the drug problem, but it seemed clear that many of the contract killings and the constant battles around control of the security services were linked directly to this most lucrative business.

Politics as usual: Bakiev vs Kulov

Bakiev was a smart political tactician, but he had no idea what he wanted to do once he achieved power. His economic policies were vague, centring on unreal plans to build factories and create Soviet-style industry. He did nothing to tackle governance problems, and constantly backtracked on promises for constitutional reforms that would have limited presidential power. By March 2006 there was an uncanny sense of *déjà vu* hanging over Bishkek. Businessmen

---

11 Personal communication, Western diplomat, January 2006.

complained that the president's son Maksim was following in the footsteps of Akaev's children. Corruption and bribery seemed to be at an all-time high. The economy had shrunk by 0.3 per cent in 2005. Foreign investment had slowed to a trickle, after the government revoked the licence of Oxus, a British company, to develop the Jeeroy gold mine. A representative of Oxus was shot in Bishkek in July 2006, and the government took over control of the mine in September. Rumours of massive corruption surrounded the presidential administration. Akaev had gone, but almost everything else remained the same.

There was growing opposition to Bakiev from among some of his erstwhile supporters, and in parliament. In April 2006 an opposition coalition, called "For Reforms!", led protests in Bishkek, calling for constitutional reforms and the resignation of the more odious of Bakiev's allies. "For Reforms!" was led by a number of parliamentarians, notably Omurbek Tekebaev, who had resigned as parliamentary speaker after an ill-mannered spat with Bakiev in February 2006. Other perennial opposition figures, such as Roza Otunbaeva and an NGO leader, Edil Baisalov, were also in the movement.

Bakiev made some concessions to the opposition, dismissing the unpopular head of the presidential administration, Usen Sydykov, together with his state secretary and the head of the National Security Service (NSS). On 10 May, in another widely predicted moment, Ryspek was shot dead in Bishkek. The timing of his killing was too fortuitous not to arouse suspicions that it was politically motivated.

These moves seemed to have calmed the oppostion, but an unlikely scandal involving a matrioskha doll again seriously undermined Bakiev's hold on power. On 6 September opposition leader Tekebaev was detained at Warsaw airport. Customs officers searched his luggage and discovered a matrioshka doll (a wooden Russian doll, popular as a souvenir) containing heroin. It was immediately clear that he had been framed, and the most obvious suspect, Bakiev's brother Janysh, who was deputy head of the NSS, resigned, although he denied any knowledge of the affair. The NSS chief, Busurmankul Tabaldiev, followed suit.

The Tekebaev affair gave fresh momentum to the oppostion, which initiated talks with Bakiev to try and convince him to offer constitutional reforms. By early November, it was clear that the talks had failed, and Bishkek's central square was again filled with protestors. More than 10,000 gathered in front of the White House, demanding Bakiev's resignation. For several days the protestors remained camped on the square, but on 7 November there were clashes between pro- and anti-Bakiev supporters, and there were serious fears of civil conflict ensuing. These clashes seemed to have prompted a renewed effort to find a compromise, and on 9 November Bakiev signed a new compromise constitution, which limited his powers slightly.

This was only a temporary setback for Bakiev. At the end of December he managed to force parliament—under threat of dissolution—to pass new constitutional amendments returning some of the power he had lost in November. But the new constitution merely guaranteed a return to the confrontations of 2006. Although the anti-Bakiev forces posed their demands in terms of constitutional change, there was increasing opposition to Bakiev himself, rather than just the institution of president. Many of those who had supported Bakiev in 2005 felt betrayed by his refusal to implement any reforms, and by his repeating of the worst excesses of the Akaev regime.

In early 2007 the Bakiev-Kulov tandem finally came to an end. The only surprising thing was how long it had lasted. Kulov resigned in December, after constant wrangling with the parliament. Bakiev proposed him again as prime minister, but he was then rejected by parliament, and finally resigned in February. He immediately moved easily into opposition to Bakiev, claiming that corruption was reminiscent of Akaev's time, and that there was increasing government control over the media.[12] Kulov was a controversial figure, however, and his resignation from government effectively split the opposition. He established a new movement, "The United Front for a Worthy Future for Kyrgyzstan", while many of the leaders of the previous year's protests set up a rival grouping, "For a United Kyrgyzstan".

---

12 Taalai Amanov, "Kulov may unite opposition", *Reporting Central Asia*, IWPR, 23 February 2007, at www.iwpr.net.

The threat of protests by the United Front prompted Bakiev to appoint a moderate opposition leader, Almaz Atambaev, as prime minister, but many United Front leaders were now pushing only for Bakiev's resignation. However, most of the Kyrgyz public were tired of the constant rallies and protests, which had been continuing at regular intervals since the overthrow of Akaev in March 2005. A further rally held in early April by Kulov's United Front called for Bakiev's resignation and early presidential elections, but ended in some disarray. Again demonstrators had occupied the square, and camped out in the now traditional revolutionary yurts. This time, however, after nine days of protest, the police moved in, dispersed the crowd and arrested some of the ringleaders.

Increasingly, the discussion was not about reform but about the two political leaders, Kulov and Bakiev. Their rivalry was worsening regional divisions, with Kulov representing the north and the Russian-speaking population, while Bakiev (although opposed by some southerners) was still the south's representative in the political arena. The north-south divide, which had always existed cultural and historically, was increasingly being used as a tool by political leaders to mobilise support. In so doing, they further exacerbated regional divides, and made future consolidation of political forces much more difficult.

The revolution in retrospect: reflections on democratisation

The chaos and violence which followed the March revolution provided the perfect argument for those who argued that democratisation was a mistake in Central Asia, and that it would lead to more instability, not less. It was an argument relayed almost constantly on Kazakh television, for example, to dissuade its citizens from any similar attempt to protest against the government. However, whatever the difficulties faced by Kyrgyzstan after the March events, and however divorced the revolution was from a real democratic change of government, the upheavals had produced the first peaceful change of government in Central Asia's history since 1991. That simple fact was the greatest threat to the other leaders in the region, and they sought security in the kind of repression and isolation that Akaev, to his credit, had always rejected. From his hideaway in Moscow, President Akaev was probably smiling in self justification as he saw the new regime struggle to cope with the reality of everyday politics. However, it was in large part the failings of his regime that had ensured that any subsequent leader would face almost insurmountable problems.

Nevertheless, the instability in Kyrgyzstan—and the fear that it would descend into serious civil conflict—gave pause for thought to those organisations and state that had long pushed for more democratisation in Central Asia. After the March revolution in Kyrgyzstan, its opponents blamed the West for the upheavals, claiming that Western-funded NGOs and US support for the opposition had been the key elements that had led to Akaev's overthrow. Some supporters of the change in regime also believed that years of support for NGOs and democracy programmes had finally borne fruit. In reality, the regime change in Kyrgyzstan had little to do with Western NGOs or alleged American machinations. It was a revolt of elites against an overbearing presidential family, supported by a large part of the population who had simply had enough of poverty and corruption. The greedy and narrow-minded Akaev family had lost the support of the people. The people threw them out. In the end, it was almost that simple.

Even in early 2005 few people in the international community really believed that there would be any kind of regime change in Kyrgyzstan. The opposition was viewed as weak and divided, and the population was considered too apathetic to take to the streets against the government. Many in the opposition did not really believe in a world without Akaev either. Some almost seemed to be going through the motions of opposition, hardly daring to expect that they would be successful. There were small groups of student activists in Bishkek, such as Kel-Kel, which was partly modelled on the Yugoslav and Georgian examples of student political movements. However, they could never mobilise large numbers of young people. Most of the youth on the streets in March were of a very different type. Poorly educated, loyal only to their local leaders, without any overarching ideas, they were hardly the Western-educated stormtroopers of colour revolutions elsewhere. The ability of their leaders to mobilise these crowds owed much to traditional links of kinship and fellow-feeling, rather than some common democratic ideals.

There was certainly no funding from Western sources for what happened in March 2005. One leading participant claimed that the "revolution" cost just $25,000, most of it spent on transporting demonstrators from the south of the country.[13] Compared with the money that was spent on candidates' electoral campaigns, sometimes reaching hundreds of thousands of dollars, this was cheap indeed. True, Western-funded NGOs and media had run a long campaign of criticism against the presidential family. Western-funded election monitors and technical assistance made it easier to point up electoral malpractice, but this had little real impact. International projects to mark voters' hands with ink to prevent multiple voting, or to conduct exit polls, had no discernible impact on the outcome.

The US embassy did maintain a strong barrage of complaints to the government about the election process. This caused considerable resentment in the government, mostly because the regime did not want to correct these irregularities, but also because of the way some US officials went about their job. US Ambassador Steven Young, sitting in a meeting with the head of the Electoral Commission, Sulayman Imanbaev, started slow-clapping Imanbaev's speech claiming the elections would be free and fair: "You're so Soviet", Young interrupted Imanbaev rudely.[14] His frustration was understandable: Imanbaev was a past expert in electoral machinations, and the authorities were intent on controlling this poll as well. But other participants in the meeting looked embarrassed: this kind of intervention smacked all too much of some kind of latter-day colonialism.

Far from ushering in a new era of pro-Western policies in Kyrgyzstan, the new regime was if anything far more suspicious of Western approaches than the previous government. Many were simply tired of being lectured on their shortcomings. Bakiev, in particular, was very resistant to meetings with delegations of critical Westerners. Foreign diplomats found it far harder to get meetings

---

13 Personal communication, Bishkek, April 2005.

14 Personal observation, Bishkek, February 2005.

with the new president than with his predeccessor. Others, such as Roza Otunbaeva, were disappointed by the lack of support they had received before the March events, and she studiously avoided meeting some Western NGOs during her short period in office. There was also much less respect for the usual demands of the IMF and the World Bank, who were quietly concerned by the new government's attitude to macroeconomic stability. And in 2007 the government rejected the controversial Heavily Indebted Poor Countries (HIPC) programme, which would have written off some debts in exchange for economic reforms, claiming that the programme would undermine the country's sovereignty.

The unrest and political chaos gave heart to those who argued that Central Asia was not ready for democracy. At times, it seemed as if Kyrgyzstan could break down into civil conflict or war, north against south, clan against clan. The economy was badly affected, and most of the population yearned for some stability and an end to the criminal and political killings. However, there were some pluses. Compared with, say, Uzbekistan, the Kyrgyz retained a remarkable level of political pluralism and civic freedoms, and an ongoing debate about what a Kyrgyz state could or should be. It was messy, and sometimes violent, but it still offered some hope of change for the better.

The one lesson that Kyrgyz revolutionaries quickly learned, was that the overthrow of bad government was much easier than creating a credible new order. Democratic change and reform inevitably undermines stability in the short term. This is even more so when the state is weak, the rule of law is almost absent, and much of the population lives in poverty. Personalised rule, as practiced by Akaev, created a vacuum where the state should be: instead of developing viable institutions that would survive regime change, the president did his best to ensure that stability was encapsulated only in himself. This was an obvious trap for any political leader. Developing sound political institutions and an effective state was difficult and posed potential challenges to a leader's political survival. In all cases, Central Asian leaders instead chose to personify the state, building up patriomonial rule and dependent business and political elites. This worked in the short term, but when they left power, much of the state disappeared too.

5

STATE-BUILDING:
THE FEUDAL APPROACH

'Mustaqilik [Independence]? Who needs it? I need a job.'

Casual labourer, Tashkent, August 2004.

Much of the Western critique of Central Asian states and governments focused on the overwhelming state bureaucracies that were
seen as a leftover from the Soviet past and an obstacle to development. However, although ministries and bureaucracies were often
overstaffed and overpowerful at the micro-level, these states were
actually very weak. Their legitimacy was faltering: they failed to pre-
serve the social contract of the Soviet period, but could not replace
it with a new, popular legitimacy based on an effective state. Only in
Kazakhstan, by the beginning of the 21st century, was there a sign of
an effective, sustainable state-building project, and even there much
remained to be done.

State-building was difficult, partly because these states had little
concept of nation to support them. Nation-building in the Soviet
period had gone some way to overcome localism, but there was still
much attachment to alternative sub-state and superstate identities,
from tribal and clan loyalties to transnational identities such as Islam.
Many people remained nostalgic for the old Soviet Union; others
saw Russia or one of the other republics as their homeland. A large

minority saw their only hope of self-fulfilment in escape; for most that meant leaving by one method or another to get to the West.

Ineffective states could be buttressed by appeals to nationalism, but this often produced contradictory impulses. To develop some kind of national feeling, leaders emphasised the history of the main ethnic group. Kyrgyz leaders liked to laud the *Manas*, the great Kyrgyz oral epic poem, but this offered little attraction for ethnic minorities inside Kyrgyzstan; Uzbeks in the south had ambivalent loyalties—many still looked towards Tashkent, at least until the economic and political situation in Uzbekistan deteriorated sharply. But Akaev also developed the idea of "Kyrgyzstan—Our Common Home", an inclusive view of civic nationalism that sat uneasily with the alternative *Manas* view of a Kyrgyz state.

In Uzbekistan, historical despots such as Tamerlane were feted as national heroes, but the instrumental use of Uzbek nationalism did little to create a real sense of nationhood. By 2005 it was common to hear Uzbeks decrying the constant government refrain of "*mustaqilik*" (independence), and asserting that independent statehood had merely brought economic failure and political repression in its wake. Again, ethnic minorities, such as Tajiks, Kazakhs or Russians, often felt excluded from the state's attempt to build up a sense of Uzbek nationhood.

In each country the leader used his own image as a paternal national figure to try and build up legitimacy. In Turkmenistan the Niyazov project was initially seen by many Turkmens as a valid approach to nation-building, overcoming centuries-old tribal divisions and the legacy of colonialism, until his ideology descended into a narrow cult of personality. Karimov also burnished his image as "father of the nation" and published dozens of unread tomes of his thoughts and ideas. Askar Akaev was less prone to a personality cult, but he too sometimes seemed to spend more time writing books on Kyrgyz history than on running the country.

The failure to develop nation-state loyalty was one of the reasons for the emergence of personalised neo-patrimonial regimes. Without an effective state ideology, or loyalty to an overarching national identity, leaders sought to ensure their political legitimacy among the population through personal forms of rule. In the political culture of Central Asia, this had some success, at least initially, and was a useful way for leaders to deflect popular discontent onto subordinates. Niyazov's televised scolding of government officials was only the most bizarre example of this practice, which was designed to ensure that the leader remained untainted by the failure of the state to deliver on its promises. In Uzbekistan, the families of prisoners often wrote letters to President Karimov, apparently assuming that he would end the repression of their loved ones if only he was informed of their plight. Similar attitudes were common in Stalinist Russia.

But personalised rule and the rapid rotation of elites had negative long-term consequences. In most cases they merely accentuated the weakness of the state, as it became increasingly subordinate to the wishes of the leader and his family, and it failed to produce the kind of consolidated elite necessary for long-term political development. This was most extreme in Turkmenistan, where no independent state institutions survived the depredations of Niyazov. But even in Kyrgyzstan, the personification of the state in Akaev weakened its ability to cope with regime change: there were no neutral state institutions that were not viewed as under the control of one or other political group. And in all cases patrimonial rule undermined the rule of law, with court favourites and ruling families exempt from censure. Inevitably this also led to rampant corruption in the ruling elite, which in turn led to a decline in legitimacy for the ruling family.

The lack of an effective state had important implications for political and economic development. People had little trust in state institutions, and subverted them to their own ends, by using kinship networks and contacts with friends in high places as an alternative to ordinary state processes. This was most obvious in attitudes to law enforcement agencies and the justice system. Nobody expected impartial treatment by such bodies. Just as Russian families used to give up a son to the Church, so many Uzbek families would encourage a family member to join the police or the prosecutor's office; this kind of personal link was assumed to produce a reliable form of protection for other members of the family engaged in business. But this "state capture" further undermined the Weberian ideal of an impartial

163

state bureaucracy, and the result was a vicious circle of weakness and corruption. States became incapable of dealing with regime change, and leaders asserted that without their personal rule, their countries would face chaos and violence. And by their actions, they accelerated the likelihood of this happening. Meanwhile, corruption and injustice were fertile soil for radical Islamist groups, whose calls for the overthrow of these states met with at least some sympathy from parts of the population.

These neo-patrimonial states had some advantages. Their methods of governing ensured a fragile stability, as long as they did not face serious challenges from outside. At their best, they were sometimes good at co-opting potential opponents, ruling by compromise among clan leaders rather than simply relying on repression. In most cases, they allowed for some freedom for businesspeople, as long as they paid homage (and more importantly taxes) to the leading families. But they discouraged the rise of a middle class, which would undermine the feudal structure of the state, and they feared powerful independent businesspeople, who would inevitably threaten the leaders' monopoly of economic power. Above all, they were unable to contemplate any prospect of a change in leadership. Changing the leadership did not necessarily mean any change in ideology or policy, but it collapsed a whole pyramid of mutually advantageous financial and criminal linkages, inevitably leading to a period of chaos and redivision of property.

For the first decade of independence, the Central Asian states managed to avoid many of the pessimistic prognoses that accompanied their creation. But by the end of the 20th century the most immobile of them, Uzbekistan and Turkmenistan, were facing political and economic crises as the limitations of the neo-patrimonial state order became clear. In Kyrgyzstan the neo-patrimonial system collapsed in 2005, and to the horror of many neighbouring states, as the personal pyramid of power crumbled, the state crumbled with it. This problem of state-building, and the two answers—the old patrimonial system, or a step into the unknown of democracy and political inclusion—were present in all the Central Asian countries. But they were seen particularly clearly in the most remote and poorest of the Central Asian states, Tajikistan.

Tajikistan: on the edge

A parade of limousines drives up to the front gate of President Rahmonov's palace complex in central Dushanbe, and are waved through into a different world. Luxury mansions are set out in a green park, watered daily, despite the lack of clean water in the rest of the city. It is the fifth anniversary of the Tajik peace process, bringing together UN diplomats, ambassadors, and the two sides of the peace process: President Rahmonov and his one-time adversary, the Islamic Party leader, the late Said Abdullo Nuri. It should be a place of reconciliation and celebration: the creation of a democratic, modern state on the ruins of war and conflict.

The reality is rather different. Nuri soon slinks away from the celebrations, and the vodka begins to flow. Dull diplomatic speeches are dispensed with, and the dancing girls appear on stage. Rahmonov begins to show who is really boss. He advances onto the dance floor, and threatens some bemused Swedish diplomats that "either you will all dance, or I will sing". It is not an empty threat. Soon he is behind the microphone, and even the most staid UN officials are dancing with his scantily clad court of singers and dancers. The foreign minister looks worried. Rahmonov exclaims loudly, "I am Rahmonov, and I will always be Rahmonov, I don't care whether you like it or not."

The evening encapsulates much of the real nature of the Tajik state. The UN-sponsored peace talks and political compromise that ended the civil war in the mid-1990s were mostly on paper. There was no real compromise at the end of the civil war: there was a victory for Rahmonov and his acolytes, who proceeded to build a state in which the façade of UN-sponsored democracy was as thin as rice-paper. Real politics went on in the court of Rahmonov, a succession of court favourites joined in banquets with the president. It was not modernising authoritarianism, but a kind of modern-day feudalism.

This remote state, in which Rahmonov was king, often felt like the edge of the world, especially on a cold winter's day, with snow falling fast on Tajikistan's capital city, Dushanbe. One unmade road which connected the central regions of Tajikistan with the northern Leninobod region around Khujand was closed all winter, and only opened in May, once the snow had melted. Even then it was a back-crunching 12-hour drive on a rough track over 4,000-metre passes. An even longer road to the eastern Badakhshan region was equally uncomfortable, and was frequently closed due to bad weather. The only all-year international road links went to Uzbekistan, but they were often closed for political reasons. Most Tajiks could not get an Uzbek visa anyway. Tajikistan's geography made its residents highly dependent on the pilots of Tajik Air, who performed frequent miracles in getting their ageing fleet off the ground and, more important, back down again.

Tajikistan is geographically-challenged. Its remoteness and its lack of transport infrastructure made its very existence as an independent state precarious. Created by the Soviets, but without the two main Tajik cities of Samarkand and Bukhara, it faced a daunting task of uniting a group of regions with little in common other than a national flag. The one-time garrison of Dushanbe—little more than a village in the 1920s—became the republic's capital. The new republic embraced a challenging terrain, from the inhospitable Badakhshan region in the east, dominated by the towering plateau of the Pamir mountains and inhabited by Tajiks of the Ismaili faith, to the almost desert plains of the south, running down to the Afghan border, the great line in Asia drawn between the British and Russian empires along the Amu-Darya river.

Tajiks lived on both sides of the Amu-Darya, but the USSR gradually built up border controls along the river, cutting off Soviet Tajiks from their compatriots and relatives on the other side of the water. Until the Soviet invasion of Afghanistan, contact across the frontier was minimal, but Soviet forces began to use their own Tajiks as interpreters after the Soviet intervention in Afghanistan, and news and ideas spread back across the border, the most significant of them being a radical version of Islam that was previously unknown in Soviet Tajikistan.

The challenges of state-building in this complex political and geographical terrain became clear when Tajikistan declared independence in 1991. The existing Communist government was ousted by a coalition of opposition groups, the result being protests, confrontation and finally violent clashes. The civil war that ensued left at least 50,000 dead, and shocked a region that had not known widespread conflict since the time of the 1917 revolution. Much of the animosity was based on regional differences: southern Kulobis fought against eastern Gharmis, bringing to life tensions that had been simmering for years. It was not just regional animosity that sparked the violence, but also a clash between more secular ex-Communist leaders, new political groups that promoted an Islamist ideology, and a small intelligentsia seeking democratic change. The latter two groups, united in the United Tajik Opposition (UTO), spanned everything from the drug-runners/Islamists of the Islamic Movement of Uzbekistan to fairly secular groups fighting for autonomy for Badakhshan.

The fighting was fierce, with once peaceful neighbours in the same village turning on each other in a vicious foretaste of future conflicts in the Balkans and elsewhere. In 1994 the UN began talks aimed at a compromise peace, and negotiations began between the two sides, spread out over meetings in Teheran, Ashgabad and Moscow. Finally, a grudging compromise was hammered out, with the ex-communist President Imomali Rahmonov—from the southern Kulob region—making some concessions to the Islamist and democratic opposition, mostly from Gharm and Badakhshan. The strongest part of the opposition was represented by the Islamic Renaissance Party of Tajikistan, at one time a fairly radical proponent of Islamist ideas. Its enthusiasm for the idea of an Islamic state was partly tempered by time spent in exile in Afghanistan, where its members saw the Taliban in action.[1] When they returned to Tajikistan in the late 1990s under the peace deal, they seemed much more concerned with making sure the peace deal did not collapse than with building the ideal Islamic society.

---

1   Personal communication, IRPT members, Dushanbe, July 2003.

To the international community, the Tajik peace deal was a triumph. Not only had the violence been halted, but secular and Islamist groups had been forced together into a coalition, with the opposition taking in theory at least 30 per cent of the seats in government. Several key opposition leaders did take up government positions, but they soon found that they had little control over policy. Some were seduced by the financial advantages political office provided, others were simply sidelined into irrelevance as decisions bypassed their offices. Nevertheless, the façade was intact, and Rahmonov continued playing his careful game of compromise.

Rahmonov and 9/11

Rahmonov's world changed in September 2001. On 9 September two Arab journalists inveigled their way into the headquarters of the charismatic Ahmed Shah Massoud, head of the Northern Alliance—the Tajik-dominated opposition to the Taliban—and blew themselves up, killing Massoud. The Northern Alliance had long been ignored by the world: Iran and Russia had occasionally sent arms or assistance through Tajikistan to the only real opponents of the Taliban, but the rest of the world had little interest in a small group of fighters in a remote valley in northern Afghanistan. Massoud's death seemed to threaten the end of the Northern Alliance, and the frightening prospect of the Taliban advancing up to the Tajik frontier. But two days later came the suicide attacks on New York's World Trade Centre. With thousands dead in the twin towers attack, the equation changed again. There was no doubting the link between the two attacks, and suddenly world attention scurried across the globe in the direction of this remote part of Inner Asia. Now, as the US began moves to invade Afghanistan, journalists pored over maps and rang embassies: the closest access was through Dushanbe.

In 2001 it was hard to imagine a city less well-prepared to receive this influx of foreigners. Resident aid workers and UN officials still observed a curfew at night; dozens of rebels had died in outbreaks of fighting earlier in the year, and UN workers had been kidnapped in the lawless regions east of Dushanbe. There were only two Soviet-era hotels. The water was the colour of mud. There was no internet, and it remained one of the few parts of the world where mobile phones still did not work.

Rahmonov became the centre of international attention. His calls over the years for more help for the Northern Alliance had fallen on deaf ears. Now Rahmonov started getting calls from the world's leaders and, more importantly, political support and economic aid. In 2002 the security situation gradually improved, and the economy began to pick up. Without the threat of instability from the other side of the Afghan frontier, and without interference from the Islamic Movement of Uzbekistan (which had occupied a base in Eastern Tajikistan in the late 1990s), the Tajik government began to develop better control of its territory.

Rahmonov was a colourful personality, and much more open to dialogue than his Uzbek and Turkmen counterparts. But the dialogue was very much on his terms, and diplomats found evenings with the president an exhausting and memorable experience. Rahmonov was not a Soviet intellectual like Akaev, nor a thoroughbred Communist Party bureaucrat like Nazarbaev. He had gone from running a collective farm in Kulob to being president of an independent state, but his behaviour had changed little. This endeared him to many people, who found him relatively approachable, but his presidency also attracted many people around him who were even less enamoured of intellectual debate or diplomatic protocol.

The civil war had cut swathes through the Tajik intelligentsia; hundreds of thousands of the best educated had fled the country, mainly to Russia. Ethnic minorities, notably Russian-speakers, had also left in huge numbers: almost the only Russians left were elderly women begging on the streets to supplement their miserly pensions of $2 per month. Dushanbe was transformed in the 1990s: in the place of urbanised Tajiks and ethnic Russians and Caucasians, provincial Tajiks, many from the south, moved into the city. Those urban Tajiks who remained were scornful of the new arrivals: "the village has come to the city", many complained, and they were even more disdainful of many of Rahmonov's government appointments,

169

which tended to promote poorly qualified officials from his home town of Dangara.

The result was a government that for the most part lacked serious technocratic thinkers, and was mired in high-level corruption. The security services were brutal and notoriously close to organised crime; the press was mostly under government control, with the exception of a couple of brave independent newspapers. Although the economy picked up slightly in 2002 and 2003, most of the money was coming not from a growth in employment inside Tajikistan, but from remittances from the millions of Tajiks who regularly travelled to Russia to work.

This huge migration of workers to the north was probably the main factor in preventing the country from collapsing again after 1997. Not only did the flow of money from migrants give an important boost to the economy, and keep many families from starving, it also removed the most potentially troublesome elements in the population; young, unemployed men, many from areas of traditional opposition to Dushanbe, were employed on construction sites and oilfields in some of the most inhospitable parts of Russia.

The lives of these migrants were miserable in the extreme. Those who could not afford the air fare travelled to Russia by train or bus, meeting humiliation and extortion at the hands of border guards in Kazakhstan, Kyrgyzstan and Uzbekistan along the way. Once they reached Russia, they were easy targets for the rapacious Russian police, and were also the victims of violent attacks by neo-fascist groups. Tajiks were second only to Chechens in the list of racist stereotypes promulgated in the Russian media, where they were portrayed as drug runners and Islamic extremists. Even when they survived the depredations of border officials and the Russian police, their work was often dirty and dangerous. Hundreds died on building sites and oilfields where health and safety regulations were seldom observed. They lived in miserable dormitory blocks, and were often subject to gang masters, who held them in virtual slavery until they had completed their contracts.

Despite all this, the flow of migrants did not slow. Salaries in Tajikistan were simply impossible to live on. The minimum wage was around $2-3 a month, and many rural workers were not paid at all. Women worked four or five months in the burning heat on cotton fields, but rarely received wages. The most they could hope for was to gather the dried stems of the cotton plant that were left behind after harvest: a good season's collection of these sticks would provide firewood for the winter.

For the educated and the young, there were very few opportunities outside the collection of embassies, international organisations and NGOs, whose employees drove around town in their white Landcruisers. Other talented young people left the country. A friend got a good job in the Ministry of Foreign Affairs, but his salary of 12 somoni a month (US$4) did not even cover the bus fare to work and back. There was a serious lack of qualified medical staff, but with starting salaries for doctors just six somoni (US$2) a month, there were few takers.

Not surprisingly most officials supplemented their tiny incomes with bribes. Corruption began at the top and flowed downwards, with every official doing his best to supplement his income somehow. Their attempts were aided by a mass of Soviet-era laws, almost designed to make business difficult. Any businessman with good contacts and a willingness to pay off the right people could cut through some of this bureaucracy, but it made business expensive and investment insecure.

Not surprisingly, there were no serious foreign investors. Even Russian companies talked of Tajikistan as a black hole, into which money disappeared never to be seen again. Aid agencies, and multilateral institutions such as the World Bank, were frequently stymied by government corruption. Insiders at lending institutions reckoned that maybe $100 million had gone missing from international loans.[2] Most of this money ended up in the pockets of government officials, but the international community was slow to accept that it had to make corruption a central issue in its dealings with the government. Staff in many institutions were judged mainly by whether they disbursed their budget, not by the probity or efficacy of their transac-

---

2   Personal communication, World Bank official, 2004.

tions. Other international bodies were sympathetic to the problems of governance, because Tajikistan was still viewed as a post-conflict environment. Nobody wanted to rock the boat too much.

This corrupt form of feudalism was kept afloat by international aid, drug money and the mass migration of the potentially politically active population. But popular discontent with the economic situation and with corruption was never far below the surface. There were huge discrepancies in wealth; the rich lived in astonishingly expensive palaces, while much of the population survived on less than $1 a day. Rahmonov's position was relatively secure, however, because his demise seemed likely to reignite the violent tensions of the past, and nobody could see any advantage in a renewal of civil conflict. When opponents did appear on the political arena, Rahmonov dealt with them initially through cooption—by bringing them into the government in some capacity, or through economic means, giving them the green light for some business opportunity. He gave them something, to make sure they had something to lose.

Rahmonov and his enemies

International support after 9/11 gave Rahmonov a new sense of confidence, both on the international arena and in his dealings with internal enemies. But there were still other powerful political figures to contend with. Particular respect was reserved for Mahmadsaid Ubaidulloyev, the Mayor of Dushanbe, a powerful, thick-set man, who enjoyed philosophising about world peace and had even ordered a statue of Gandhi to be built in Dushanbe. But there was always a shadow of fear on the hard faces of the black-suited men who scurried around him. His relationship with Rahmonov was believed to be strained, but nobody ever really knew what made this dynamic between the two work. Nevertheless, as Rahmonov grew in confidence in 2002 and 2003, Ubaidulloyev faded away as a potential challenger.

There were plenty of other potential challengers still around. Many of Rahmonov's former allies—brutal warlords from the south—were at best an embarrassment, and frequently seemed potential opponents for the future. He tolerated many of them, apparently afraid of their ability to use semi-private militias against him, but their power was dissipating as memories of the war slowly faded and Rahmonov grew in strength. In 2004 Rahmonov began to purge some of these old allies from his government, and at the same time started to move against the formal opposition, who he feared might yet pose a challenge to his position, particularly with parliamentary elections due in February 2005 and presidential elections to be held in 2006.

The purges of the old guard, a mixture of drug-traffickers and thugs who had led much of the fighting in the civil war, had begun in 2002-3. The notorious Cholov brothers, who had ruled as virtual feudal lords in Kulob, were gradually ousted from power, with one of them arrested and jailed. Other less powerful warlords were also gradually sidelined or forced into exile. In January 2004 Rahmonov challenged one of the most powerful of the remaining warlords, General Ghaffor Mirzoyev (nicknamed Sedoi [grey]). Mirzoyev had been head of the presidential guard since 1995, in charge of an elite military unit charged with protecting the president and suppressing anti-government revolts. Mirzoyev was dismissed and for 24 hours the capital was awash with talk of an attempted military coup. Rumours suggested that 200 members of the presidential guard threatened to resign. Security forces flooded the capital. Talks between the two men seemed to defuse the tense situation, and Mirzoyev was sidelined to head the Drug Control Agency, a UN-run body designed to tackle the massive narcotics problem. His appointment was hardly welcomed by the UN. In August Mirzoyev was arrested and sentenced to life imprisonment, charged with an attempted coup; 15 other officers were sentenced with him.

Once Mirzoyev was dealt with, Rahmonov moved against another old enemy, Yaqob Salimov. Another former Kulobi warlord, he was notorious for his brutality during the civil war, but was implicated in a mutiny in 1997 and fled the country, ending up in Russia, where Tajikistan sought his extradition in 2003. In early 2004, in an apparent political deal, Russia sent him to Dushanbe, where he was quickly imprisoned.

The third enemy to be targeted was Mahmadruzi Iskandarov, a former opposition field commander, and a native of the Gharm region. Iskandarov joined the peace talks and was given a role in government, running the national gas utilities agency. He was a small, rather well-spoken official, who also was head of the Democratic Party. He was one of only a few members of the government and opposition who seemed to think seriously about the country's future. During 2003 he had become increasingly outspoken in his criticism of the regime.

In November 2003 he was dismissed from his post in the gas industry, and he moved out of the capital to his native region of Rasht, apparently fearing for his safety in Dushanbe. Immediately rumours began that he and another commander, Salamsho Muhabbatov, were gathering their former comrades-in-arms in expectation of an attempt to arrest him. Iskandarov dismissed allegations that he was planning any military action, and in October 2004 he thought he had reached a compromise with Rahmonov. He was wrong. In December he was charged with conspiring to overthrow the government, but he had already fled to Russia. Initially, Russia refused to extradite him to Tajikistan, but he later turned up in a cell in the ministry of security in Dushanbe, apparently kidnapped in Russia by Tajik security forces. He was subsequently sentenced to 23 years in prison on dubious charges of terrorism.

The kidnap and imprisonment of Iskandarov marked a new low in Tajikistan's political development, but it was a logical continuation of the personal politics that determined the future of the state. Rahmonov thrived on his dominance of the feudal pyramid, but he did little to develop effective state institutions or pluralistic political mechanisms. Elections had always been something of a farce in Tajikistan. Although opposition groups won a few seats in parliamentary polls in 2000, they believed they were unfairly denied many more. The three main opposition parties—the Democrats, the Social-Democratic Party and the Islamic Renaissance Party—were given little opportunity to build up a bigger popular base. Local authorities were firmly on the side of the ruling presidential party, the People's

Democratic Party, which was essentially the old Communist Party renamed.

Ahead of parliamentary elections in 2005 the government was concerned by the unrest that accompanied Kyrgyz elections held at the same time. They began to put more pressure on foreign-funded NGOs, and there was suspicion of US aid programmes with any political bent. In reality, there was very little political work being done, whether by small US-funded NGOs or by the UN or the OSCE. The elections passed off in traditional manner, with the PDP sweeping almost all the seats in the new parliament. But for most of the population, the election was merely an empty exercise; for most people there was no democratic choice and they were powerless against the frequent malpractice of the local authorities. The Tajik state was fragile. The authorities tried to strengthen it by resisting any attempts to democratise its structures. In the short-term it worked, because the government removed any serious opposition to Rahmonov. But political power remained highly personalised, corruption was rampant, and the criminalisation of state structures remained a major long-term problem that seemed impossible to overcome.

The UN believed it had achieved a democratic basis for a new Tajik state to emerge from the civil war. Rahmonov undermined that political settlement little by little, each time pleading for support for his attempts to develop political stability. Each time, the UN, and the international community, held back from criticising too strongly, fearing that the conflict could erupt again. As a result, by 2007 Rahmonov had turned into a smaller, and still slightly more liberal, version of his difficult neighbour Islam Karimov. The pluralism of the UN peace agreement was forgotten. Rahmonov had build a new state, but as in Turkmenistan and Uzbekistan, it was a personal political project, designed to suit the leader, not to develop an effective and sustainable state.

More than any other state, perhaps, in the region, Tajikistan's state-building was undermined by criminalisation of state structures. At first, it was the former warlords that had challenged the state at every turn; by 2005 most of them had been jailed or forced into exile. Only the fantastically wealthy Suhrob Qosimov remained, heading what was euphemistically called the Interior Ministry Rapid Reaction Force, but looked much more like a private army. He eventually resigned in March 2007, to "spend more time at the Football Federation". As the influence of the warlords faded, criminal groups were merging more closely with the state, with high-ranking security officers frequently accused of involvement in the country's most lucrative business: drugs trafficking.

Tajikistan and the drug trade

For a region as poor as Afghanistan and Central Asia, the discovery that the dried milk of a poppy flower could be exported, and earn billions of dollars a year for traders and farmers, should have been a godsend. Instead, this mild-sounding plant extract has caused political upheaval, violence and misery. For the dried milk of the opium poppy contains two simple painkillers, codeine and morphine, and with a simple laboratory process the morphine can be converted into the drug of choice of Europe's underclass, a pure white powder that doctors call diamorphine, and everybody else calls heroin.

The heroin trade threatened to undermine all attempts to develop a modern state in Tajikistan, but, as one international drug specialist liked to joke, "The only thing worse than a Tajikistan awash with drugs, is a Tajikistan with no drugs." Drugs meant money, and money, even if much of it left the country, or was wasted on opulent mansions, meant jobs and a slight dent in the poverty figures. In the long term, however, the drugs trade had a corrosive effect on the state: criminal groups merged with state officials, who used their control of state institutions to permit the trade to continue almost unhindered. This in turn undermined the capacity and willingness of the state to embrace other types of reform that would have enabled other sectors of the economy to flourish. And any attempt by political forces to clean up the state or seriously tackle interdiction of the trade seemed likely to lead to serious violence or even war.

Although there were occasional rumours of attempts to begin growing opium poppies in Tajikistan, for the most part it was a transit zone: a key state in a route that stretched from northern Afghanistan through the Central Asian states and on to Russia or Turkey, and finally to its most lucrative markets in Western Europe. There were other routes of course, through Pakistan to the south and to Iran to the west, although the latter had become much more difficult after the Iranian authorities clamped down. Turkmenistan was also growing fast as a transit country, with the overt connivance of the government, and Uzbekistan was a direct as well as indirect transit route; again senior officials were very much involved.

Tajikistan had been a favoured transit route since the early 1990s: poor border management, the country's remote location, high levels of corruption and the general poverty, particularly in border communities, all contributed to the trade. One of the major routes in the mid-1990s ran through the eastern town of Khorog, through Badakhshan and round on the Pamir highway to Osh in Kyrgyzstan. There were various attempts to tackle this route, all of them failures, until the Aga Khan stepped in and by all accounts declared that humanitarian aid to the Badakhshan region—the only thing that kept the population from starvation—would be ended unless the drug traffic was halted. Although this did not completely stop the trade it persuaded many local people, who considered the Aga Khan to be a "living god", to end their own involvement in it.

The main route now switched to the far south of Tajikistan, the roads leading up from the rugged border regions around Pyandj and Moskovskii, the outer reaches of Russia's lost empire. Russian troops still guarded this border until 2005, but most of their troops were conscripts hired locally, who earned less than $50 per month. Rumours suggested that Russian forces were also involved in trafficking, although officers claimed that the situation had improved by 2001-2.[3] Russian troops withdrew from the border in 2005, and were replaced by Tajik security forces. Whoever was formally in charge, it was relatively easy for traffickers either to avoid border guards in this kind of terrain or to pay soldiers to look the other way.

Once on Tajik territory, the big traffickers were less concerned about police intervention. The authorities seized hundreds of kilo-

---

3 Personal communication, Russian border guards, Dushanbe, May 2002.

grams of drugs every year, but this was mostly from smaller gangs. The major players had high-level political contacts that enabled them to operate with considerable freedom. As a result the drug trafficking had a direct impact on governance: the traffickers required state institutions to remain weak and vulnerable to capture by criminal groups. The trade was immensely profitable, and its constant flow of funds enabled it to ensure the continued connivance of state officials, and to make measures to suppress it too expensive and dangerous to contemplate seriously.

In the main producing area the price paid to farmers fluctuates, depending on demand and supply. Demand in Western Europe remains relatively stable, but supply can change significantly from year to year depending on weather conditions, political interference, and the success of interdiction efforts along the route. At the farmgate, as economists say, in Afghanistan, opium cost about $125 per kilo in December 2006. Once it has undergone the laboratory process to turn it into heroin (about 10 kilos make 1 kilo of heroin), the price rises sharply, and continues rising with every border crossed; the difficulty of the border crossing is reflected in the price paid on the other side of the frontier. The biggest jump, not surprisingly, comes when the drugs cross from non-EU to EU countries; here the security is more effective, corruption is less pervasive (or at least more expensive), and the political will to tackle trafficking much greater. By the time Afghan heroin is peddled around the streets of Glasgow, it costs about $150 a gram. So from Afghanistan to the UK, the price jumps from around $1,000 per kilo to something like $150,000 per kilo. Not surprising that successive "wars on drugs" have been such an abject failure.

Although the most lucrative stages of the transit are geographically at the other end of the road from Tajikistan, enough remains in the hands of Tajik gangs to make their involvement more than worth the small risk. In 2001 the price of a kilo of heroin was reported to rise from $2,000 on the Tajik-Afghan border to $15,000 in Dushanbe.[4] With estimates of drug volumes transiting the country

---

4   US Drug Enforcement Agency (DEA), Afghanistan Country Brief, Drug

ranging from 80 to120 tons,[5] it was clear that the potential profits were huge. The money goes mainly to the top players, and they invest it, more often than not, outside the country, primarily in Russia and in the United Arab Emirates. But a good deal does remain inside the country: many of the gaudy palaces that sprouted in the centre of Dushanbe were clearly financed by money from the drugs trade. By 2004 real estate prices in central Dushanbe were challenging boom town Almaty, as successful businesspeople tried to launder their excess cash. Salaries for drivers and guards, and the broad spectrum of bribery that the trade requires, also left small but important incomes in the country.

If the drugs merely passed through the country, leaving some transit fees with local businesspeople, it might be argued that Tajikistan hardly benefits from any attempt to clamp down on the trade. In reality, of course, the drugs do not merely leave small profits along the way, but wreak their own misery among populations along trafficking routes. Since drug transit began in mass form in the 1990s, the level of drug addiction in Central Asia, and indeed in Russia, has multiplied. Smoking opiates was a traditional and relatively harmless pastime in countries such as Turkmenistan, but the ready supply of heroin has seen a massive rise in intravenous injection of the drug, which gives a much bigger "high" for much less money. Alongside intravenous drug injection has come its malignant twin—HIV/AIDS. A map of the drug routes through Central Asia is almost identical to maps that show increases in HIV/AIDS infection: needle-sharing is quite normal, and the level of knowledge about the dangers of infection is minimal.

The international response to drugs in Central Asia has been to concentrate almost exclusively on interdiction. Initially, this mainly involved providing equipment and training to interior ministry forces or border forces, which were formally mandated to deal with the

---

Situation Report, September 2001, accessed at http://www.shaps.hawaii. edu/drugs/dea0901/dea0901.html.

5 Bureau of International Narcotics and Law Enforcement Affairs, "International Narcotics Control Strategy Report , 2007, March 2007, accessed at www.state.gov/p/inl/rls/nrcrpt/2007/vol1/html/80860.htm

problem. More often than not, these were the very groups involved in the trafficking in the first place, and the international community's well-meaning attempts to bolster their capabilities did little or nothing to improve the situation. The second phase of assistance involved creating independent structures, funded by the international community but formally part of local government, which would be free of corruption and have sufficient capability to tackle trafficking.

One such project was the UN-funded Drug Control Agency (DCA) in Tajikistan, whose staff were appointed by the UN and had their salaries paid by international donors. While other security forces were lucky to get $30 per month, staff at the drug agency were receiving $100 and up, with the senior personnel getting around $600 per month. This was nothing compared with the profits of drug traffickers, of course, but a high salary in Tajik terms. The head of the drug agency, Rustam Nazarov, was widely viewed as an honest officer, but he operated in a political environment in which some people were simply too powerful to be touched. As a result, the DCA tended to go after smaller groups and individuals; in many ways, this merely consolidated the hold of really powerful individuals on the trade, monopolising it in the hands of senior officials. Partly as a result of the establishment of the DCA, Tajikistan recorded the highest seizures of drugs of any country in Central Asia, but even DCA officials admitted that they were probably getting their hands on less than 10 per cent of the total goods in transit.

The never-ending war on drugs seemed destined to fail in Tajikistan, just as it had done everywhere else. Production in Afghanistan continued to soar, despite international initiatives to try and cut cultivation. This failed for simple economic reasons: it was just not profitable for farmers to grow anything else, and in any case the central government was much more concerned with maintaining political stability than it was with tackling the drugs trade. Tajik officials and others often commented on the fact that it was Western demand for the product that was the real problem, which should be tackled as much as the supply side.

The whole international interaction in the drug interdiction game increasingly took on a mechanistic character. Nobody was ready to commit the kind of funds necessary to make mass interdiction a real possibility in Central Asia; and few people were able to take a holistic approach to the problem that would take into account the key role drugs played in the local economy. Above all, no Western countries were prepared to address the key issue of legalisation. While heroin remained an illegal substance, the trade was inevitably dominated by criminal groups, which undermined states across the region.

In some cases, Western intervention just made things worse. Increased assistance and technology given to border guards tended to be used to make border crossings difficult to pass for ordinary travellers rather than for drug traffickers. And noone in the international community could quite bring themselves to admit that their projects in support of counter-narcotics forces were often supporting the very people they were trying to stop.

The corrupting influence of the drug trade was fundamental to the problems faced by Tajikistan in building a viable state. But there were few economic alternatives. The economy remained overly dependent on one single aluminium factory, whose long-term commercial viability was unclear. And while many young men managed to find work in Russia, a large part of the female population was left eking out a living in a rural nightmare of cotton, poverty and disease.

The international attention Rahmonov had gained after 9/11 contributed to his increasing control over the labyrinth of power, and enabled him to move against the political opposition. The neo-feudal structures of power produced a kind of stable paralysis, in which it was difficult to unseat the incumbent president, for fear that the whole structure would collapse. And the fear of a return to war had a kind of numbing effect on the population, dampening demands for political and social change. But the Rahmonov system of power was not tackling the serious social and economic problems the country faced. And that was the problem faced by all the Central Asian countries: strong presidents suddenly appeared weak when faced with serious opposition, because the façade of statehood that they had developed quickly crumbled when faced with a real challenge.

6

THE ISLAMIST CHALLENGE

*"Such people must be shot in the forehead! If necessary, I'll shoot
them myself...!"*
President Karimov on Islamic extremists, 1 May 1998.

It is the summer of 2002, and the height of the Aksy protests in
Kyrgyzstan. Bolot Januzakov, head of the presidential administration, is explaining to me why the Kyrgyz government needed to
clamp down on the peaceful demonstrators. "We have evidence they
might get weapons. And if they get weapons, then it is terrorism," he
explained, waving his arms as if to prove the equation. The logic was
inescapable: as soon as the terrorist label could be applied, new rules
applied. International norms could be ignored, the police were given
carte blanche. All that was needed was to apply the label.

In truth the only weapons involved in the Aksy dispute belonged
to the police, who had shot five demonstrators dead. But it was no-
ticeable that in Central Asia there was a constant attempt to label
oppositionists as terrorists. You could see it in the names of the police departments concerned with internal repression. When the journalist Ruslam Sharipov was arrested in 2003 in Tashkent on politically-motivated charges, it was the counter-terrorist department that
handled his case. In Turkmenistan political dissidents had to deal
with the Department of Terrorism and Outlaws. In Tajikistan the
Democratic Party leader, Mahmadruzi Iskandarov, was sentenced to
23 years in prison after being found guilty of "terrorism".

In no other area was there more myth-making than about terrorism in Central Asia. Under the rubric of the "war on terror", governments used the supposed threats from Islamic radicalism as perfect excuses for increased repression against political opponents. Western military assistance in counter-terrorism training usually ended up with security forces using their new skills against innocent protestors. The skills gained in tackling terrorism—whether it involved monitoring emails, surveillance of mosques, or new police techniques—were all completely transferable to the problem of dealing with peaceful opponents of the government.

In the case of almost every violent act by purported militants in modern Central Asia there has been insufficient evidence to come to a definitive conclusion about what actually happened. In each case, different governments have put up a smokescreen of half-truths and double bluffs that made it possible for different observers to come to completely different conclusions about the reality of radical Islam in Central Asia. In each case, there were at least many unanswered questions, and often some compelling evidence that the "Islamic threat" was being used mainly to justify internal repression or as part of intra-elite struggles for power.

However, the misuses of counter-terrorism and the constant exaggerations by governments of the "Islamic threat" did not mean there was no security or political challenge from Islamist groups. On the contrary, Islamist armed groups were active in the region, while radical but ostensibly non-violent organisations like Hizb ut-Tahrir grew rapidly in membership. However, because the governments in the region so frequently misused the terrorist label, it was easy for many people to believe they were exaggerating the threat.

Under Soviet rule, Islam throughout Central Asia had been driven underground, but even Soviet totalitarianism could not suppress it entirely. Thousands of mosques were closed; many were destroyed; others were turned into museums or warehouses. The main visitors to the few remaining mosques tended to be elderly men. Instead of going to the mosque, young people joined the Soviet youth organisations, the Pioneers or the Komsomol. Nevertheless, in most communities, the older generation passed on the knowledge of Islam to their children.

For 70 years of Soviet rule Central Asia was on the very edge of the Islamic world, with no contact with the major centres of Islamic civilisation. The great 20th century disputes around the role of Islam in politics, the Islamic revolution in Iran, the Palestinian issue and much more had largely passed them by. Their religion was quietist, following the generally apolitical Hanafi school and incorporating many rituals that purist Muslims found anathema: pilgrimages to the graves of local saints were one popular local tradition. This Sufi tradition remained strong in Central Asia, and it was very resistant to political radicalisation.

Under Soviet rule, religious observance continued underground among Uzbeks in the Fergana valley and some other rural areas of Uzbekistan, and in many parts of Tajikistan. The Kyrgyz, Kazakhs and Turkmens, however, had been late converts to Islam, and had taken a fairly lackadaisical approach to its strict observance. Among the Kyrgyz and Kazakhs there was a good deal of traditional shamanic ritual thrown into the mixture. And without settled communities, they had few permanent mosques, and had always had somewhat more enlightened views on the role of women and other social freedoms than their more conservative settled neighbours.

In 1991, as borders reopened, the Central Asian states were suddenly thrust back into the main current of a turbulent global religion. The region's leaders were often poorly informed about Islam: most had read more of Lenin than of Mohammad, and their secularism was hardly dented by the vestiges of cultural practice that recalled the great Islamic traditions of the past. However, many ordinary people began seeking religious answers in the ideological vacuum that followed the collapse of Communism. Missionaries from the Middle East were only too happy to provide simple answers to the complex questions of identity and purpose that accompanied the political turmoil of independence.

Some Uzbeks, mainly from the Fergana valley, had fled to Saudi Arabia after the 1917 revolution, and their descendants were at the forefront of a drive to build new mosques and spread the word in

185

Central Asia. In some cases, they were engaged in real charity work, but more often than not their role was to criticise the traditional form of Islam that predominated in Central Asia, and spread the more purist school of Islam often termed Wahhabism, the predominant form of Islam in Saudi Arabia. In most cases, this did not signify support for political violence or terrorism; many adherents found these Salafi doctrines attractive because they considered local Islam to be irredeemably corrupted. For many, particularly for the young, Salafi Islam had the same attraction as evangelical Christianity did to members of the Orthodox church. It was a rebellion against the old men who dominated local mosques, but knew little about the detailed doctrine of their religion. It outlawed activities such as lavish weddings or drinking alcohol, which had become prevalent among local Muslims, and it strictly condemned (rhetorically at least) cheating at the bazaar or corruption by officials.

Saudi-inspired Wahhabism served as the first stepping-stone for some Central Asians on the road toward the politicisation of Islam and subsequently more militant activities. But Wahhabism in its pure Saudi-imported form did not receive widespread acceptance among Central Asians, and was still considered very much a fringe activity, even without the repressive attitude of most states towards any sign of Wahhabi tendencies. However, if Wahhabism did not provide all the answers for most people, it nevertheless demonstrated clearly that there was an important question being asked. Islam in Central Asia was dominated by a stagnating clergy, who were largely apolitical or pro-government. For younger men, undergoing social and economic upheaval and seeking answers to philosophical questions, these supine and ill-educated imams favoured by governments had few answers. It was more radical imams, and later underground radical groups, who often found ready listeners among young men, disenchanted with the existing social and political order.

The first sign of a resurgent Islam came in 1992, in the Fergana town of Namangan. This unprepossessing town, with its crumbling jumble of Soviet concrete apartment buildings looming over the occasional tea-house, challenged the government in a way that

186

was to shape Uzbek politics for years to come. Central power had almost collapsed in Uzbekistan in the early 1990s: in Fergana the most powerful force was a local mafia group, with a strong Islamic identity, which took over control of the streets and the bazaar, enforcing elements of Sharia law with a good deal of brutality. Really, they were just petty criminals. Their leader, Juma Namangani, was a train robber. None of them had much in the way of a religious background, but they combined Uzbek Islamic conservativism with a mafia-style control of the local bazaar economy.

Karimov personally went to talk to these new local leaders, but in a fateful meeting in Namangan in 1992, was heckled by a crowd of Namangani supporters, and forced to flee the town. He never forgot. In reality, the Namangani group had little popular support: they were easily forced out of positions of power, and most of their motley band fled to Tajikistan, where they fought on the side of the opposition for several years until the peace accord was signed there in 1997. Meanwhile, in Uzbekistan, the government began a crackdown on non-mainstream Islam, arresting many clergy who were accused of being Wahhabis, and closing some of the thousands of mosques that had sprouted after the collapse of the USSR.

By the mid-1990s Saudi missionary activity was banned in Uzbekistan, and was more closely monitored in Kyrgyzstan and Kazakhstan. Students going to study abroad were also under closer surveillance, although from Bishkek and Almaty there was no real way of checking up on young men travelling to the Middle East or Pakistan, and many did end up studying in *madrasas* linked to radical Islamist groups in Pakistan and elsewhere. Meanwhile, in Afghanistan radical Islamists in the Taliban movement were moving inexorably northwards towards the southern borders of the Central Asian states. In the chaos of post-independence Central Asia, Islamist militants began to coalesce into discrete groups, some with foreign connections, others very much home-grown. But for the militantly secular governments in the region, they were all enemies, dangerous adversaries in a very local "war on terror".

Islamic groupings

Government propaganda tended to lump all pious believers into a broad melting pot of Islamic radicalism, but different groups had very different ideologies and tactics. Some were committed to violence, such as the Islamic Movement of Uzbekistan (IMU), a group that eventually became closely linked first to the Taliban and then al-Qaeda. Others, like Hizb ut-Tahrir, sought radical change but proclaimed their commitment to peaceful means; still others sought to operate within the existing legal environment and sought merely a constitutional place for political Islam within the political system. Often the different groups were divided by ideology and personality; at other times they saw common cause, in their opposition to the Uzbek regime for example. But they seldom cooperated openly, and most suffered from the tendency of all radical movements to endlessly fracture and split into myriad groups over strategy, personality and money. Most of them had no publicly known ideologues; they wrote little and spoke less. Their activities were sporadic and poorly planned, and often seemed to provide no evidence of a great overarching plan. All these facets of their activity made them difficult to research, but some general groupings were clear.

The Islamic Movement of Uzbekistan

In 1999 Juma Namangani, the train robber from Namangan, suddenly reemerged on the scene in spectacular fashion. In February 1999 a series of car bombs exploded in Tashkent, including one at the entrance to a government building on the vast Independence Square, where Karimov was due to hold a cabinet meeting. Nearly 20 people were killed, but Karimov escaped unhurt. The government announced that the bombings had been the work of Islamic extremists from Namangani's group, with support from the secular opposition leader-in-exile Mohammad Solih. A massive crackdown followed, in which young men were simply rounded up from mosques and from local communities. At its height the repression affected anyone who looked at all suspicious, who was seen reading a Koran, wore a beard, or had a known history of mosque attendance. In 1999-2000 up to 5,000 people may have been arrested.[1]

The reality of the February attack—as with many subsequent incidents—was endlessly disputed.[2] Some oppositionists claimed Karimov organised it himself to justify a subsequent crackdown; others claimed that the Uzbek National Security Service (NSS) had knowledge of the plot, but either failed to stop it or deliberately allowed it to go ahead. Alternative versions suggested it was the result of internal rivalry within the government. The idea that Solih and the secular opposition had been involved was dismissed by independent observers. However, real evidence that the Islamic Movement of Uzbekistan, as Namangani's group began to call itself, was resurfacing as a potent force emerged in June 1999, when IMU fighters crossed the border from Tajikistan into Kyrgyzstan, and kidnapped four Japanese geologists who were working in the mountains and some Kyrgyz government officials, and held out against a weak and disorganised Kyrgyz army for several months. Only when winter closed the mountain passes did the IMU retreat; the hostages were released a few weeks later after the Japanese government paid a multi-million dollar ransom. The IMU staged other smaller incursions in 2000 and 2001, but finally the Tajik government persuaded it to move away to Afghanistan, where the IMU became an increasingly close ally of the Taliban, eventually merging with other foreign fighters into the 055 International Brigade.

The successes enjoyed by the Taliban in 1999-2000 extended their control over much of the northern territories bordering Central Asian states. Only in the remote Badakhshan region did the anti-Taliban Northern Alliance hang on. Turkmenistan was the first Central Asian state to recognise the Taliban, and in mid-2001 Uzbekistan, despite its previous rejection of any negotiations with Islamist radical groups, also began negotiating with them about possible recognition.

---

1 There are no accurate figures. Tolib Yakubov, a human rights activist in Uzbekistan, has suggested that as many as 10,000 were arrested.

2 For an overview of the different theories, see Abdumannob Polat and Nickolai Butkevich. " Unraveling the Mystery of the Tashkent Bombings: Theories and Implications", accessed at http://www.iicas.org/english/Krsten_4_12_00.htm.

With the IMU based in Kunduz, and the Taliban effectively on Uzbekistan's frontier, the regime in Tashkent was growing increasingly nervous.

IMU camps near Kunduz were among the first targets of the American bombing campaign in October 2001. In one attack, Juma Namangani was reported killed, along with many of his supporters. When US troops overran his base, a huge array of documents, videos and training manuals were left behind. The IMU had become a significant ally not only of the Taliban, but also of al-Qaeda, although its literature still reflected a focus on its Central Asian political goals.[3] However, as in other essentially local conflicts—such as Chechnya—Islamist groups placed domestic grievances in a global context of attacks on Islam, giving local concerns an important global context that not only provided more meaning for local activists, but also encouraged funding from radical supporters in the Middle East.

Despite the many deaths in Kunduz of IMU supporters, a large number fled ahead of advancing Northern Alliance and coalition troops. Some melted back into the countryside in remote Badakhshan, where they were later reported to be involved in cross-border drug smuggling and other low-level crime.[4] Another faction travelled south with al-Qaeda and Taliban leaders, first to the Afghan-Pakistan border areas, and then across the border into Waziristan. Here they settled, largely immune from Pakistani attempts to uproot them. From 2004 onwards there was increasing pressure on President Musharraf of Pakistan to deal with the al-Qaeda and IMU camps, and there were several attacks by the Pakistani military on Uzbek encampments. These continued until 2007, although the reality of the IMU presence on the ground in these areas was difficult to discern.[5]

The IMU was now led by Tohir Yuldash, a former deputy to Namangani, although he was reported to have been injured in one Pa-

3   Marcus Bensman, "IMU in Retreat", Reporting Central Asia, IWPR, 19 July 2002, at http://iwpr.net/?p=rca&s=f&o=175706&apc_state=henirca2002.

4   Personal communications, diplomats, Dushanbe, December 2003.

5   For a sceptical view, see David Hoffman, "The IMU in Pakistan: A Phoenix Reborn, or a Tired Scarecrow?", The Roberts Report (http://roberts-report. blogspot.com), 7 April 2007.

kistani attack in March 2004. He reemerged in public in September of that year, denying that he had been wounded, and vowing that the IMU was still a fighting force. But the movement itself seemed to splinter, with some militants keen to get back to their initial goal, of ousting Karimov and installing an Islamist government in the Fergana valley, while others were more and more integrated into al-Qaeda and Taliban groups, with their emphasis on fighting in Afghanistan and planning for terrorist activities on a global scale.

In Central Asia the impact of the US-led intervention in 2001 was immediately felt. The threat from the IMU, if not completely removed, was sharply reduced, and most of the states in the region felt considerably more secure against further intervention by insurgents. Some claimed that the movement had renamed itself the Islamic Movement of Turkistan, reflecting its recruitment of other Central Asians, including Tajiks and Kyrgyz. But in reality the IMU seemed to be a spent force by 2004, and governments were concentrating on new groups and organisations that seemed to be emerging in its wake.

Its abilities in any case had always been exaggerated by the Uzbek government: it had little popular support, and its actions—even if all the Uzbek government versions were accepted—were all characterised by remarkable incompetence and strategic failure. It seemed likely that it had long ago been penetrated by Uzbek government agents, and its real security threat to Uzbekistan was minimal after 2000. But its continued existence was extremely useful to the Uzbek government for internal repression, and for US support in the "war on terror". If the IMU had never existed, the Uzbek government would have had to invent it.

The 1999 bombings in Tashkent had led to thousands of arrests in Uzbekistan of suspected "Wahhabis", or followers of related Salafi movements. Many of those arrested had nothing to do with the IMU or any kind of radical Islam, but were arrested for being "too pious" or too political. The Uzbek government was never able to distinguish between Salafi movements which concentrated on religious teaching and public morality, and were largely opposed to the overthrow of governments in Muslim countries, and "jihadi" Salafis, which were engaged in armed struggle against the West in particular.

191

Despite the mass arrests, some people who adhered to the Wahhabi school of religious thought remained at large in Uzbekistan. One such family was still living in a suburb of Tashkent in 2003. The male members of the family all wore traditional Arab robes, the elderly ones were all bearded; it was clear they were very zealous in their observance of religious rituals. They were scathing about traditional Muslims in Uzbekistan, whom they viewed as dangerously syncretic in their practices. They were critical of traditional Uzbek rituals, such as the Uzbek wedding, with its huge expenditure and frequently large doses of vodka. "Islamic" weddings were becoming more popular, with little of the pomp and circumstance that most Uzbeks enjoyed on these occasions. Most of their concerns were associated with similar religious ritual and social norms, rather than political systems. They claimed to be opposed to al-Qaeda and its violent methods. The other major target for their criticism was the Hizb ut-Tahrir group, which they claimed was not really Muslim at all and was far too lax and modern in its attitudes.

These isolated Wahhabi families posed little real threat to the authorities. But they were under constant surveillance from the security forces. Hundreds of similar groups had suffered arrest and imprisonment on terrorism charges. In the mid-1990s they had begun to develop a certain following in several towns in Fergana, but their purist and rather ascetic views found fairly limited support. For younger people, who had grown up in the Soviet system, its conservative notions on everyday behaviour fitted poorly with the reality of most people's lives. Both Wahhabis and traditional clergy found it difficult to communicate effectively with younger people, who had more exposure to secular forms of communication, including the internet, and were unlikely to know Arabic or to have any deep grounding in Islam. Instead, many turned to a new group, the Hizb ut-Tahrir al Islami or Party of Islamic Liberation.

Hizb ut-Tahrir

Aziz looks uncomfortable in the dirty surroundings of a ramshackle house on the edge of a small village in the Uzbek Fergana valley.

He is wearing a smart suit, and has a new sedan car parked outside on the dirt-track road. He settles himself down and opens a pack of Marlboro cigarettes. He wants to talk politics. He reminds me of the students I've met at Tashkent universities—curious, but slightly narrow-minded; like them he has been the target of ideologically-charged education. He wasn't brought up to be religious. His grandparents were religious, but his parents were in the Communist Party, and did not visit the mosque. Aziz was confused about religion, he explains, until he met some members of Hizb ut-Tahrir. "They're the only ones who talk about politics the way it really is", he smiles slightly, in between puffs of smoke. [6]

Intense young men like Aziz are the backbone of Uzbekistan's biggest opposition movement. Highly illegal, it operates in networks of sympathisers throughout the Fergana valley. At least 5,000 alleged members of the group are in prison, serving sentences of anything up to 20 years, often simply for possessing a leaflet published by the group. The group has never been proven to engage in terrorist activities, and it rejects terrorism as a political tactic. But it wants to see the revival of a utopian Islamic caliphate, beginning with an overthrow of Karimov, whom they always call "The Jew-Karimov".

The IMU had never been able to recruit significant numbers of followers within Central Asia: there simply was not the appetite for their form of violence among most of the population, who remained largely sceptical of Islamist promises of utopia through terror. Hizb ut-Tahrir offered a similar future utopia, but also eschewed violence as a political tactic. It was particularly attractive to men with some aspirations in life, who found their choices blocked at every turn. These were the lost lower-middle classes, who had prospered so much in the Soviet Union and now were either condemned to a life of selling Chinese nick-nacks at the bazaar or gradually falling in with a criminal group. Instead, HT offered an alternative community, and some sense of mutual support. It gave a purpose in life, and explained life's questions in language these semi-educated secular young people could understand. They were astonishingly successful

---

6   Personal interview, June 2003.

in winning recruits, mainly among ethnic Uzbeks, both within and outside Uzbekistan's borders, but also among some Kazakhs, Kyrgyz and Tajiks.

Hizb ut-Tahrir was a marginal group in most Muslim countries. Set up by a Palestinian Islamic scholar and political activist, Taqiuddin an-Nabhani, in 1952, it combined many aspects of socialist party organisation with a commitment to the creation of an Islamic state, the restoration of the original Islamic caliphate.[7] Hizb ut-Tahrir sought the overthrow of all Muslim regimes, since they had failed to implement Islamic norms, and the unification of all Islamic countries in a recreation of the Caliphate, which had been abolished in 1924. In reality, the Caliphate had never played the role that Hizb ut-Tahrir saw for it, and their historiography was at times profoundly mythical. Tactically, HT saw itself as a movement apart; it did not join coalitions with other groups, and it refused in most cases to work within legal constraints or constitutional systems. In the Arab Middle East it was outflanked on the one hand by movements that joined the constitutional process, and on the other by much more radical groups, such as the PLO, which began to use terrorism as a powerful tactic in their war with Israel.

HT instead proposed a very different strategy, and made its political tactics an absolute part of its ideology. It divided political struggle into three stages. The first stage involves propaganda and recruitment, and what HT literature calls a "stage of culturing", building up a membership base which is entirely loyal to the party's principles. The second stage involves propaganda within the wider Muslim community, seeking to persuade them of the rightness of their ideas, without necessarily persuading them to become members. In this sense, HT is much more like the ideal of a Leninist-Bolshevik party, seeking to be the "vanguard" of the working class, rather than a mass membership organisation. The third stage is the most vital: with an active and consolidated membership, and wide support in the wider Muslim community, HT seeks to overthrow governments and im-

---

7   Suah Taji-Farouki, *Hizb al-Tahrir and the Search for an Islamic Caliphate* (London, 1996).

plement its version of an Islamic political order immediately. There is no gradualism, no compromise in these plans, but there is also very little clarity about how to jump from stage two to stage three.

HT rejected terrorist activity as a political tactic, but it is far from pacifist. In a stifling, empty breakfast room in a grimy hotel off the Gloucester Road in London two senior HT members tell me how the Islamic caliphate would seek to develop nuclear weapons. These are not crazed marginals, or poverty-stricken unemployed drop-outs, but well-educated professionals, born and bred in the United Kingdom. Their arguments about global politics are convincing and well laid out. They would fit neatly with many leftist critics of US foreign policy worldwide. As with Aziz in far-away Fergana, there is not much about religion. All the talk is of Iraq, Palestine, Uzbekistan, Kashmir, the litany of perceived injury to Muslims worldwide.

Given the failure of HT to develop a significant following in the West Bank, or in Pakistan, it may seem surprising that its main strongholds have become Western Europe and Central Asia. In fact, the two share some obvious similarities. In both places young Muslims have been brought up in secular environments, despite the conservative religiosity of their parents or grandparents. Both find it difficult to relate to conservative religious leaders, who are out of touch with contemporary realities and are seen as acquiescent in the face of anti-Islamic governments. In both places, young people feel frustrated by their inability to integrate fully in society, and seek alternative outlets that would give them a new identity and a new purpose in life.

In Central Asia the group began in the mid-1990s, apparently started up by a visiting missionary. It grew quickly despite the government's attempts to repress it. After the Tashkent bombings of 1999, many of its members were arrested and sentenced to long terms of imprisonment. But HT's impressive organisational skills used the prison network to their advantage, in some cases recruiting ordinary criminals to their cause. Some were hardened by their experienced in prison, and went home more radicalised than when they entered. Others were broken by the experience, turning to drink or drugs to try and forget.

The government's repression has also forced HT to operate even deeper underground than before. It has always been organised along semi-conspiratorial lines, although in Western countries it has recently become much more open, with spokesmen appearing on media and on their websites. In Central Asia, however, they have continued to organise in small five-member cells, apparently to avoid any one member knowing too many other members in case of arrest. In reality, this strict structure does not appear to be so closely followed in everyday life, and many HT members know perfectly well who is also involved in the group.

Its membership was at first confined to ethnic Uzbeks, based in eastern Fergana and in southern Kyrgyzstan. It grew quickly among ethnic Uzbeks in the Kyrgyz cities of Osh and Kara-suu, although latterly it seems to have captured some support in the north of the country also. In Uzbekistan, it has continued to grow, and some government sources claimed it had more than 10,000 members. Since 2001 its recruitment has been boosted by international events, notably the war in Iraq, and also by apparent US support for Karimov, which feeds into their simplistic view of the world, in which the US and Israel are leading an anti-Islamic crusade with the assistance of existing Muslim regimes around the world.

Despite Uzbek government claims to the contrary, there was never any evidence that HT was involved directly in any violence in Central Asia. The group's ideology precluded terrorism as a tactic, although it was often slow to condemn terrorist acts against Western targets. The Uzbek government claimed that it was closely linked to the IMU, but contacts seem to have been intermittent at best.

In reality, HT did not do very much. Its most frequent activity was the distribution of one-page leaflets. Initially, it distributed them publicly, at bazaars or on buses, but this led to significant levels of arrests, and in later years it mostly delivered leaflets to houses at night or left them behind in bus-stops or other locations. The leaflets were often well-written analyses of political problems that struck a chord with readers, whose only other source of news was state television. HT wrote mostly about Uzbekistan, about the closure of bazaars, about repression of its members, and also about the US military presence in the country. Interspersed with these issues of local concern were pamphlets dealing with international politics.

The main concern with HT was that it would eventually tire of its opposition to violence and reinterpret its ideology to permit some kind of armed resistance to the government, or else that it would experience a split, with some followers moving into a more active, and violent, phase of their political struggle. There were frequently rumours of such splits, and occasionally new groups sprouted briefly. However, considering the way most movements and groups in Central Asia inevitably splintered into competing, personality-centred factions, HT was surprisingly successful at maintaining at least a semblance of unity, perhaps a result of its strong emphasis on ideological indoctrination, although by 2005 there was increasing evidence that this ideological unity might be breaking down.

There were certainly differences of opinion among many members, however. Some supported suicide terrorism in Palestine, for example, while others were opposed to all violence. There was no evidence of HT being involved in suicide attacks, although there was a strong streak of martyrdom among many members. Some almost courted arrest by giving out leaflets openly at bazaars, but it appears that this tactic was later discouraged by the leadership because it was decimating the ranks of young recruits. Members also had different opinions towards the IMU and other armed groups: some saw them as mistaken in their tactics, but most viewed them as ideological brothers, despite the differences in their theological and political outlooks.[8]

More formal splinter groups emerged in the 1990s: one group, Hizb an-Nusra, emerged from the Tashkent group of HT, apparently dissatisfied with HT tactics, but it quickly faded from view. Another group was established by Akram Yuldashev, who retreated from HT's emphasis on global revolution to address much more local affairs through social activism and the development of Islamic-focused self-help groups in business and everyday life. The extent to which this group, known as Akromiya, really established itself

---

8 Based on interviews with HT members in Uzbekistan, Kyrgyzstan, 2003-04.

formally is hard to ascertain, but it was accused of organising the Andijan events in May 2005.

Some analysts of HT have used the easy label "conveyor-belt of terrorists" to discredit the group. This is rather a glib characterisation of a more complex reality; there is some danger that its ideological indoctrination does start the recruit off on a path towards violent radicalism, but there is only evidence for this in a small number of cases, which might of course have occurred without HT's involvement. The problem is that viewing HT simply as a kind of proto-terror group inevitably invites repressive measures against the group, which tend either to reinforce its influence because its members are imbued with the mystique of martyrdom, or to encourage members to split with the movement and move towards violent resistance.

Nuances of this kind were not lost on some more enlightened officials in Uzbekistan, but for the most part public policy towards Hizb ut-Tahrir was primitive in the extreme. Labelled as terrorists, some were condemned to long periods in prison for possessing leaf-lets, reading Hizb ut-Tahrir literature or simply attending one of their political circles out of curiosity. Repression increasingly forced them underground, and their activities were severely curtailed. By 2004 there were fewer and fewer leaflets being printed and distrib-uted, and the ground was left open for a new wave of activists, and a renewal of the violence of the late 1990s.

Tashkent bombings: 2004

Tashkent is largely a modern, Soviet city, with wide boulevards and nondescript architecture. There is little to delay tourists on their way to the more historic cities of Bukhara and Samarkand, but most like to spend a couple of hours at Chorsu bazaar, where some of the traditional atmosphere of an Eastern market can still be felt. Behind the bazaar are the remains of Tashkent's old city, with its winding alleyways and dusty courtyards. It is a particularly poor part of town, and attracts many of the incomers to the city from the more con-servative countryside. Chorsu itself is always teeming with traders and shoppers. If anybody wanted to cause mass civilian casualties with a bomb, this would be the place to do it.

At 8.20 am on 29 March 2004 a woman walked up to a police post at the market and blew herself up, killing two policemen in the explosion. Fifty minutes later, after the market had been partly cleared by arriving police, a second woman walked into a crowd of policemen and detonated a bomb she was carrying. On the previous evening, it began to emerge, a home-made bomb had apparently exploded in a house in Buhara, killing several would-be terrorists. Further incidents followed over the next three days, including a shoot-out with a group of militants in a Tashkent suburb that left 20 armed men dead. In total, over 40 people were reported to have died in the incidents.[9]

This was the official version, and the Uzbek government immediately blamed international terrorists for the incidents, comparing them overtly with the bombings of public transport by an Al-Qaeda group in Madrid a few weeks earlier. But the differences were more obvious than the similarities. In the first place, the whole chain of events was confused and contradictory. The authorities provided no evidence to back up their claims of multiple terrorist-related incidents. Secondly, the militants had apparently not attempted to target civilians but had attacked almost exclusively the police. One woman in the block of flats in which some militants were eventually killed told reporters that one of the armed men had escorted her indoors with her child to safety, claiming she would be in danger from the police if she stayed outside.[10]

Finally, and perhaps more telling, there was the public response. In Spain hundreds of thousands had marched through Madrid to denounce the terrorists. In Tashkent nobody marched. On hearing that police had been killed, many people who worked at Chorsu bazaar seemed to think they deserved it. Traders told reporters that only the day before the bombings, police had beaten an old man to death

---

9   See Alisher Ilkhamov, "Mystery Surrounds Tashkent Explosions", *Middle East Review*, at www.merip.org/mero/mero041504.html

10   Personal communication, 2004.

in public because he had argued with a policeman. The police had spent the past several months extorting money from traders under the pretext of new government regulations. Nobody seemed to have much sympathy for their demise.

The government immediately saw the hand of Hizb ut-Tahrir in the attacks, although there was no evidence for HT involvement, beyond a few leaflets found at one of the houses in Bukhara where explosives had been found. Planting HT leaflets was a familiar police tactic, however, and it was impossible to know any more about the connections. Slightly more convincing were claims that the bombings had been planned at least partially among Uzbeks in Kazakhstan. In the south of Kazakhstan there were many religious Uzbeks who had fled the country to avoid repression, and there was a growth of both neo-Wahhabi groups and also HT cells in areas around Shymkent. Rather than there being a plot by HT or the IMU, it seemed more likely that a new group was emerging, although given the incompetence with which the attacks were carried out, it seemed unlikely that many had undergone much serious training in Afghanistan or elsewhere.

There were further bomb attacks in Tashkent July 2004. Three suicide bombings were reported, targeting the US embassy, the Israeli embassy and the Prosecutor General's office.

Inevitably the 2004 bombings soon became a matter of dispute between the government and independent observers. The former British Ambassador Craig Murray claimed that the suicide bombings were not all they seemed, after he visited the sites of the alleged bombings. He concluded that "…these events were a combination of a series of extra-judicial killings covered by a highly controlled and limited agent provocateur operation."[11]

A group calling itself the Islamic Jihad Union claimed responsibility for the bombings, and Western governments duly listed the group as a proscribed international terrorist group. The reality was impossible to determine, given the secretive nature of the Uzbek state, but it seemed likely that there was some kind of real group of militants

---

11 Craig Murray, comments on his weblog. http://www.craigmurray.co.uk/archives/2005/10/hazel_blears_li.html

involved; however, there may also have been a linkage to internal disputes within the Uzbek state. The latter theory was given some basis by the story of the mother of one of the suicide bombers. She contacted the NSS to say her daughter had disappeared, and had even set up a meeting with the man who had apparently taken her away. But the NSS refused to intervene, claiming that they had the situation fully under control, fuelling more rumours that they were somehow involved in the incidents.

The bombings were notable for the apparent use of suicide bombing, the first time this had occurred in Central Asia. The women involved in the suicide bombings were apparently from fairly middle-class Tashkent families and not from impoverished rural areas. This sociological snippet also reflected similar trends in Palestine and elsewhere. In reality urban lower-middle class families were just as impoverished as some of their rural counterparts, and their children far more vulnerable in some cases to ideological temptation, given their relative education followed by frustrated ambitions.

The 2004 bombings, whether involving *agents provocateurs* or not, suggested that the traditional analysis of Central Asian militants—the pro-violence IMU, and the radical propagandist approach of HT—was inadequate. The IMU was no longer—if it ever had been—a monolithic force, and lots of splinter groups were emerging. By 2005 the HT also seemed less unified than it had been, and a more amorphous network of Islamist groups seemed to be emerging in Central Asia, some moving towards more community-based activism, while a small minority supported more violent approaches to the Uzbek state. Increasing pressure on HT had probably led to more limited communication with their leaders abroad, and greater local autonomy in their reaction to events. This did not necessarily mean they were becoming more radical. In parts of Kyrgyzstan, HT began getting involved in some charitable work, which was explicitly outlawed by their literature as being a distraction from their main aim of political struggle.

There was also growing evidence of the links between criminal groups and Islamic activism. The southern Kyrgyz crime leader Bayaman Erkinbaev for a while had a shop called "Bin Laden". He later said it was just a joke, and thought up a new name, but he also had a small army of young men who were trained in martial arts, who were at least outwardly very pious. A group discovered in northern Tajikistan, called Bayat, was also primarily a criminal group, but with religious overtones. Members were allegedly involved in the murder of a Christian pastor. And in northern Kyrgyzstan Muslim sects, particularly the Tablighi Jamaat, a Pakistan-based group, were recruiting heavily among former criminals.[12] Most used their new-found religious fervour as a way of getting over their criminal past, but there was a fear that these groups might also become involved in criminal or nationalist activity. And although Tabligh liked to describe itself as apolitical, some of these young men held strong political opinions. These groups were in their infancy, but they were thriving in the atmosphere of an inactive and uncaring state, and found remarkable resonance among young, often criminalised men, who found society changing in ways that they could hardly comprehend, let along come to terms with. The challenge of Islamism seemed set only to grow in Central Asia, but the response of governments in the region to this emerging threat often seemed likely to only make things worse.

Counter-terrorism

If a definitive account of the "war on terror" is ever written, a whole chapter could easily be devoted to the failures of counter-terrorism policy in Central Asia. Uzbekistan, which faced the most serious threat of Islamist militancy, was also the most ineffective at dealing with it. Central Asian leaders came ill-equipped to deal with this new threat—they had never faced the problem of mass revolt or terrorist activity in the Soviet period, and their militantly secular background gave them little insight into the minds of these new revolutionaries.

Nowhere in the Islamic world did religion play such a minimal role in public life as in Central Asia. Even in Turkey, where secularism was constitutionally guaranteed and backed up by a dominant military, Islam always hovered around the edge of the public sphere, and from time to time parties with an Islamist tinge took power,

---

12 Personal communicatons, police officers, Issyk-Kul region, March 2005.

culminating in Tayyip Erdogan's government in 2003.[13] In Central Asia all the states banned political parties with any religious element, except in Tajikistan where the Islamic Rennaissance Party of Tajikistan (IRPT) was legalised as part of the peace settlement.

The IRPT was an anomaly, but it demonstrated that there was a constituency in Tajikistan willing to vote for an Islamic party, however emasculated and however restricted by the authorities. In other areas, the Tajik government was extremely cautious about any rise in Islamist influence. Through a hand-picked Council of Elders it controlled the *imams*, rooting out any who seemed likely to take an independent line. The government also tried to register all mosques, although it was not always successful, and attempted to clamp down on the growth in *madrasa* education. Most children went to secular state schools, if they went to school at all. Attempts by mosques to get involved in social or humanitarian work were quickly suppressed by the authorities. They had learned much from the experience of Algeria, Lebanon and Palestine, where the work of Islamists in tackling social and health problems had resulted in broader popular support.

The Tajiks achieved much of this control without using overt repression, largely because the civil war had inoculated much of the population against Islamism: rightly or wrongly many blamed the Islamists for the violence of the 1990s, and popular support for Islamist movements was limited.

In Uzbekistan, for at least a part of the population, anything seemed better than the continuation of the Karimov regime. Its repression of Islamic groups in the 1990s was popular with some secular Uzbeks, but such repression merely engendered further underground militancy and the continuing existence of the IMU outside the country. Uzbekistan, having failed to adequately contain the problem itself, simply exported its radicals, first to Tajikistan, then to Afghanistan, and finally to Pakistan.

---

13 Analysts who advocate Turkey as a role model for Central Asia underestimate the concern with which Uzbek officials, in particular, viewed developments in Turkey, especially after 2003.

The Uzbeks imposed serious restrictions on all religious activity, closing many of the mosques that had been set up in the 1990s, although there were still far more operating than during the Soviet period. Any organised religious instruction of children was illegal. Any discussion of religious or political issues in the mosque was also effectively outlawed, and the themes for mosque sermons were issued by the central muftiate in Tashkent, an institution that had little respect among believers. This central control of imams ensured a fairly compliant group of clergy, but the downside was the loss of respect for them among the broader population. Many were accused of corruption, which made them even more dependent on the authorities, and few were able to counter the attraction of more radical movements through theological argument. As a result, alternative religious authority figures emerged, many not part of the official structures. The former Mufti Muhamad Sadyk Muhamad Yusuf received a constant stream of visitors at his house on the outskirts of Tashkent. He was an internationally recognised orthodox theologian, and his opposition to groups such as Hizb ut-Tahrir was well known. But he had been exiled by the government in the 1990s, apparently because his authority was beginning to challenge his political masters. He was eventually allowed to return, but was given no official position and kept at a distance from religious life.

The government faced a paradox: it needed strong religious leaders to counteract the threat of Wahhabism and groups such as Hizb ut-Tahrir, but any strong Islamic leader seemed to pose a potential political threat to the authorities. A moral leader could hardly fail to speak out against political repression and government corruption, and this kind of Islamic opposition was much more dangerous to the regime than the emergence of something like the IMU. As a result, the muftiate was packed with government lackeys and NSS officers, and was deeply mistrusted by many Muslims. This uninspiring religious hierarchy and the accompanying repression of independent Muslim activity ensured that much religious activity moved underground. Small groups of men would meet to discuss issues of Islam: most of these were fairly innocent, but a few strayed into political issues or provided space for more radical leaders to gain a hearing.

In Kyrgyzstan and Kazakhstan the context was more liberal, although in both countries the authorities intervened in the case of overt Islamist activity. However, in all countries the same problem presented itself. Religious leaders had little authority among disaffected youth, and were viewed as too close to the political authorities and too mired in corruption to be effective. With the religious establishment unable to undermine support for more radical views, the task of combating religious extremism fell solely to the security forces, who inevitably focused largely on repressive measures to tackle groups such as Hizb ut-Tahrir.

In some cases this repression undoubtedly worked. Some potential recruits were dissuaded from joining radical groups for fear of the consequences. Some who were imprisoned because of their involvement in Islamist groups left prison determined to have nothing to do with them in the future. But in many cases, the opposite happened. Imprisonment embittered many activists; those who had been hardly active members or were simply relatives or friends of activists became more solidly integrated into Islamist networks. Prison acted as a useful propagator of Islamist ideas, and had the added advantage of introducing Islamists to hardened criminals, thus providing potentially violent recruits to the cause. The Uzbekistan muftiate issued a *fatwa* calling on local neighbourhoods to ostracise those arrested for Islamist activity and their families; as a result, they formed their own networks of mutual support. After 2001, women—mostly the mothers and wives of those arrested—started to play an important role, maintaining support networks for HT members inside prison, and staging occasional anti-government protests.

A key tenet of successful counter-terrorist operations has always been to isolate the hard core of activists who will not respond to any concessions, while winning over the broader population with political concessions and economic or social assistance. Uzbekistan's approach was the opposite: arresting thousands of young men, many of whom had little or no connection to real Islamist groups, produced an embittered group of friends, relatives and neighbours, all of whom were less likely to cooperate with the government, and more likely to drift into opposition to the regime. Policies designed to limit terrorist activity—

mining of borders, strict frontier controls, internal roadblocks and the ubiquity of security forces—all fed into increasing dissatisfaction with the government and destroyed many people's livelihoods.

Since the police were given a free rein in dealing with Islamist militants, there was also no way to limit their corrupt activities, which further alienated the population and also ensured that the police had a vested interest in a continuation of the "security threat". The police turned arrests of Hizb ut-Tahrir activists into a thriving business, with those arrested often released after payment of thousands of dollars in extortion money. The government had created an interlocking series of vicious circles, and established a policy which failed completely. The only surprise in Uzbekistan was not the emergence of Islamic radicalism, but that it was so unsuccessful.

In theory, Western powers understood the ultimate futility of the Uzbek approach. President Bush telephoned Karimov after the 2004 bombings to warn against an over-repressive response. US diplomats praised the subsequent "restrained" response to the bombings, despite the hundreds of arrests reported by human rights groups. However, this intellectual understanding of the problems caused by Uzbek repression was entirely undermined by a subtext of sympathy for Uzbek policy. Much was made of the "security threat" faced by the government, and of its "key role in the war on terror". Everyday interaction among security professionals from both sides tended to stress the security approach to Islamist militancy: few were qualified to advise on the political, social or economic aspects of a holistic counter-terrorist policy.

Indeed, few Western officials were qualified to provide any intelligence at all on these groups, since they seemed to rely almost exclusively on Uzbek intelligence, which was working to its own agenda, and could hardly be regarded as a reliable source. On the Islamic Jihad Group, the State Department claimed that "Those arrested in connection with the attacks in Bukharo have testified to the close ties between the IJG leaders and Usama bin Laden and Mullah Omar."[14]

---

14 "US Department of State Designates the Islamic Jihad Group Under Executive Order 13224", 25 May 2005, acessed at http://www.state.gov/r/

But all trial testimony of this sort is staged, and produced under duress by the intelligence services, and is therefore entirely inadequate for real intelligence assessments. Indeed, there was never even any real evidence that the Islamic Jihad Group, the Islamic Jihad Union, the Islamic Movement of Turkestan, the Islamic Movement of Central Asia, or any other of the myriad alleged terrorist groups allegedly involved in these plots actually existed. In October 2006 Makhmasaid Jurakulov, the head of the Department to Combat Organised Crime in Tajikistan's Ministry of Internal Affairs, claimed that the Islamic Movement of Turkestan had been invented by the Uzbeks, in an attempt to characterise it as a threat to the whole of Central Asia, although it seemed to remain focused only on Uzbekistan.[15] Uzbek intelligence reports seem to have been swallowed blindly by some analysts, without any corroboration, the result being some very warped views of the real threat in the region.[16]

The failure to develop good independent intelligence on Central Asian Islamic radicalism contributed to the failure of Western governments to challenge Uzbek counter-terrorism policy. It left Western intelligence agencies dependent on the dubious investigative skills of Central Asian intelligence services, which were following their own political agendas. And the use of torture to extract information not only led to misleading intelligence and analysis, it also spurred a moral debate about whether Western intelligence agencies should be using material that had been obtained in this manner.[17] It was just another step away from the kind of moral values that the international community repeatedly claimed to uphold.

---

pa/prs/ps/2005/46838.htm.

15 For discussion of this, see "Is the Islamic Movement of Turkestan and invention of the Uzbek SNB?", 17 October, 2006, at www.roberts-report. com.

16 A good example is Frederick Starr, Svante E. Cornell, Zeyno Baran, "Islamic Radicalism in Central Asia and the Caucasus: Implications for the EU", Silk Road Paper, July 2006, at http://www.silkroadstudies.org/new/docs/Silkroadpapers/0607Islam.pdf

17 The former British Ambassador in Tashkent, Craig Murray, has written widely on this issue.

7

GAMES PEOPLE PLAY:
CHINA, RUSSIA, AND THE EDGES
OF AMERICAN EMPIRE

When everyone is dead, the Great Game is finished. Not before.

Rudyard Kipling, *Kim*.

Journalists visiting Central Asia for the first time seldom managed to write an article without invoking the 19th-century "Great Game" of espionage and geopolitical intrigue, when British spies would thread their way through the mountains and try and blend in with the population in the bazaars of Central Asia, or bring lavish presents to the emirs of Bukhara. Then, of course, it was the expanding Russian empire and the remote reaches of British India which had collided in northern Afghanistan and Central Asia. Now it was the clash between a post-colonial Russia, in reluctant retreat from its former colonies, and the advancing financiers and military advisers of the Western powers. An expanding Chinese economy, in constant search for energy resources, was also quickly increasing its influence in the region, and formed the final angle of a complex diplomatic triangle.

Russia sought to re-establish its former zone of influence in the region, promoting its own economic imperatives, particularly in the energy sector, and focusing on symbolic security and political ties. China sought to stop any cross-border influences on its own restive Muslim minorities, particularly the Uighurs, and also sought to gain access to the region's major raw materials and energy commodities. The US, meanwhile, also saw Central Asia as an alternative energy supplier, but after 2001 US policy was increasingly focused on security ties, seeking strategic partners for its military actions in Afghanistan, and potentially in the future with Iran. From time to time, masked by a host of inconsistencies, the US also sought more open and democratic societies in Central Asia.

These interests all contradicted each other. Russia and China were united in their opposition to a US presence in the region, but their alliance in Central Asia papered over a number of important differences. The US's unilateral approach did little to improve its standing in the region. Governments became adept at playing one power off against another, seeing a way to escape necessary reforms by playing the game of geopolitics. Even where there was some symbolic unity among the powers—in the war on terror for example—different interpretations of the same security threats divided rather than united these countries.

Beyond the big three, there were other countries with interests in the region. In the 1990s there was competition between Turkey and Iran for influence, but interest on the part of both countries has faded in recent years. Turkey's brief flirtation with a wider Turkic world largely ended in mutual disappointment in the early 21st century: Central Asians did not enjoy swapping one "big brother" for another so quickly. The Turks realised that Central Asia needed vastly greater resources than they could provide, and that business opportunities were not as great as they had expected. Moreover, the primary focus of Turkey remained on Europe and the EU, and only nationalist dreamers viewed Central Asia as a top priority for foreign policy. Iran's early efforts to expand influence also came to nothing. It had little to offer these secular governments, and was more concerned about stability than the export of revolution. Only in Tajikistan, where it had considerable cultural relations, did it retain a more significant position, although its cultural links did not really extend to political influence.

Russia: retreat and revanche

For any Russian diplomat flying home to Moscow for the New Year celebrations in 2001, the wait in the departure lounge of Bishkek's Manas airport must have been a painful experience. Easily visible through the glass window, lined up like grey, bloated slugs along the tarmac, were lines of C-130 Hercules cargo planes. On their sides were the words "US Air Force". Bored US soldiers hung around the airport shops, and flirted with waitresses in the cafes. As the plane took off, through the window you could catch a glimpse of the first temporary tents of US Air Force base Ganci.

For many Russian officials the US military presence in Central Asia was the most visible evidence of the humiliation of Russia in the post-Soviet period. Since 1991 Russia had been in retreat from Central Asia, concentrating instead on retaining the rebellious southern fringes of its own federation in the Caucasus. True, it had kept troops on the ground in Tajikistan, but in the rest of the region its security ties were diminishing. The Central Asian states joined NATO's Partnership-for-Peace programme in the mid-1990s, and there were increasing ties between their militaries and those of Europe and North America. Kazakh and British forces held joint exercises, and many officers went to Europe and the US for training.

During the 1990s Central Asia also tried to diversify its economic ties, bringing in Western investors to develop the oil resources of the Caspian basin, and seeking financial support from Western-dominated international financial institutions, such as the World Bank and the EBRD. Russian economic influence dwindled as Soviet-era heavy industries collapsed, and with them the ties that bound these republics so closely together. Trade with Russia dropped sharply as Central Asians sourced imports from Turkey and Dubai, or from China and other Asian partners.

Culturally and socially too, Russia seemed to be in retreat. Russian was once the second language for almost all Central Asians, and for many urban elites it was their preferred tongue. With the onset of independence, indigenous languages came to the fore, especially in Uzbekistan, Tajikistan and Turkmenistan. Use of Russian dwindled

211

in rural areas, and fewer young people received Russian-language education in schools. Partly this was for political reasons—in Turkmenistan and Uzbekistan there were conscious efforts to diminish the role of Russian, both through closing of many Russian schools and through the Latinisation of the Uzbek and Turkmen alphabets.

These developments were compounded by mass out-migration. Central Asia experienced massive social change in the 1990s: millions of Russian-speakers—ethnic Russians, Ukrainians, Tatars, Germans, and others who had Russian as their native tongue—had left the Central Asian republics, fundamentally changing the ethnic balance of the populations they left behind. There were still sizeable minorities remaining, particularly in Kyrgyzstan and Kazakhstan, but in most cases the best educated had left, depriving the region of teachers, technical staff, engineers and other key workers.

The discontent among Russians with their new status in the independent republics seldom translated into political activity. They were very different from the remnants of other empires, the so-called *pieds-noirs* (European settlers) in Algeria for example. Russians had no real sense of collective identity in these new states. Many had been born and raised in Central Asia. For many Russia was almost a foreign country, rather than a homeland to return to. And many were too busy trying to survive in the new economic conditions to try and slow the inexorable end of empire through political activity. In any case, the Soviet empire differed from its British and French counterparts in important respects: there had never been a significant anti-colonial movement, either among Russians in the metropolis or among non-Russians in Central Asia. There was not even a widespread acceptance of the terms "empire" and "colonialism". The Soviet Union was an empire which did not accept the label, and even promoted anti-imperialism as one of its most important slogans. Speaking to Russians in Central Asia at the beginning of the 21st century was a little like discussing British India with an elderly generation in the UK. There was much talk of ungratefulness on the part of the locals, and frequent comments that all the infrastructure in the region had been built by Russians, and that local people had no real understanding of how to maintain it. Attitudes ranged from the overtly racist to the patronising, but there was no acceptance of any kind of guilt for the colonial past.

In response, attitudes towards Russians were also ambivalent. There had been no fight for freedom from the Russians, at least not since occasional uprisings in the 19th and the early 20th century. There was little of the overt hatred of Russians that you found in the Baltic states, although there was occasional low-level antipathy that sometimes broke out into incautious sloganeering. But more common was a kind of grudging respect, a sense that Russians had contributed to Central Asia's development and still represented a culture and state to which many Central Asians still aspired. But there was also very little understanding of the historical relationship between Russia and the Central Asian states: Soviet teaching had emphasised exclusively positive benefits from this relationship, and any reaction against that view after independence had been so heavily politicised that it was difficult for many people to have a clear view of this relationship in the past. Both Uzbekistan and Turkmenistan had introduced new historical ideologies, blaming Russia for past and present failures. But the everyday problems that independence brought undermined these new nationalist historiographies.

This relatively positive attitude towards Russia was fuelled by an almost universal nostalgia for the old days of the Soviet Union, a period looked back on as a kind of golden age by many Central Asians. Partly this was a false memory—few people recalled the petty tyranny, the fear, the shortages—but Brezhnevite socialism had indeed been relatively comfortable for many non-Russians on the periphery of empire. Everybody received a salary of sorts, there was widespread access to education, there was little crime, and there was above all a universal belief that tomorrow would be very much like today. With independence, that belief in a stable future disappeared, but many still saw Russia as a guarantor of some kind of stability and a natural partner, even as new governments opened up links with all manner of other foreign states.

Russia did not use its natural cultural and historical ties in the region well. In many cases it tended towards a patronising arrogance that went down badly with locals, and it seldom had much insight

213

into the internal dynamics of the region. Although Russian officials tended to believe that they were uniquely equipped to understand the social and political dynamics in the region, as opposed to naive Westerners for example, in reality they often misjudged the situation. Part of the problem was that the Russian Ministry of Foreign Affairs had little in-house expertise on Central Asia—the region had not of course been considered part of its remit in the Soviet period. And it was hardly the destination for its top diplomats, although the level of representation began to improve after 2001.

Russia began to take Central Asia more seriously after 2001, expanding its diplomatic and intelligence presence in the region, seeking more economic influence, through both investment and control over labour migration, and where possible by expanding military influence. Initially, Russia seemed to face serious obstacles in retaining its influence in the face of an expansionist Western presence: superficially, it seemed to have little of the political or economic attraction of a relationship with the US, and business investment from Russia always came with a multitude of financial and political strings that made it often unattractive. Nonetheless, Russia had a number of advantages—geography and familiarity above all, but also a rebounding economy—that it began to use to restore its influence in the region.

The Russian military had been fundamentally opposed to the establishment of US bases in Central Asia, and were critical of Putin's apparent agreement to the US initiative. In reality, the Americans never really consulted the Russians about the basing, and Putin had little choice but to agree to a *fait accompli*. But the military fought hard to reassert their influence in the region. They managed to retain a military presence in Tajikistan, and in 2002 Moscow announced an agreement to open a base in Kyrgyzstan, at Kant, some 60 km from the American base at Manas. Many saw this as a reassertion of Russian military might in the region. The quiet reality, however, was the shocking comparison between the two militaries, with the coalition base far superior in funding and equipment to the Russian presence, which consisted initially of a couple of rusting aircraft and a small symbolic squadron of underemployed soldiers. A local newspaper demonstrated how low things had shrunk for the Russian military when it launched a charity drive to collect second-hand newspapers and books for the apparently undersupplied Russians. Nor did the base have any discernible purpose, except to demonstrate that Russia still had the ability to project power into its former colonies.

The real breakthrough for Russia in Central Asia came after the revolts in Georgia and Ukraine in 2003/4. Suddenly, beleaguered regimes in Central Asia started viewing America as an unreliable ally, and began turning back to Russia for political support. However, Russia was badly damaged by its intervention in Ukrainian politics, backing the losing candidate and being accused of involvement in an assassination plot against the eventual winners Viktor Yushchenko. As elections approached in Kyrgyzstan in 2005, Russian support for President Akaev was much more muted. In any case, Akaev was mistrusted by many in Moscow, primarily because he was seen as pro-Western and because of his willingness to host the US base at Manas airport. Russian officials started talking to potential opposition leaders, including Kurmanbek Bakiev, who they thought might turn out to be more pro-Russian.

These "pro-Russian" and "pro-Western" labels were widely used by Russian diplomats but were largely meaningless in everyday life in Central Asia. There was little ideological commitment to any foreign policy orientation among most Central Asian political figures; they enjoyed playing off different powers against each other to produce the most advantageous political and economic benefits. Bakiev was thought to be pro-Russian, simply because he had a Russian wife. Some saw Feliks Kulov, on the other hand, as pro-Western, because his wife and daughter were living in the US. Both these views turned out to be largely meaningless when the two men came to power: Bakiev agreed to retain the US base in Kyrgyzstan, despite heavy pressure from Russia; Kulov was less amenable to Western pressure on governance and other issues than some had envisaged. Nevertheless, the Russians' more cautious approach ensured that they did not end up supporting Akaev to his inevitable end, although they did offer him and his family refuge when they fled the country.

However, the big prize for Russia was still seen as Uzbekistan. It had been working slowly to reassert political and economic influence since 2003, chiefly through Gulnora Karimova, who had moved to Moscow, and begun working with Russian business to invest in gas, telecoms and other Uzbek ventures. Russia tried to build on Uzbek concerns over the relationship with the US, particularly the criticism by the US over human rights and the lack of agreement on payment for the US base. But until May 2005 there was no real sign that cooling relations with the US would necessarily turn Tashkent towards Moscow.

However, after the Andijan massacre, Russian support was crucial for Karimov. By July it was clear that the whole US-Uzbekistan relationship was in doubt. The Uzbeks announced the closure of the US base at Karshi, a major coup for the Russians, although they did not go as far as offering the base to the Russian military, and remained wary of reentering Russian security structures. There were also more opportunities for Russian business in Uzbekistan, although few were attracted to any investments outside the energy sector.

Russia's growing role as a world energy superpower was also reflected in its dealings with Central Asia. Apart from its long-term relationship with Turkmenistan, it also began investing in Uzbek gas production, and increased its purchases of Uzbek gas, mainly for further export to Ukraine. In the less glamorous field of electricity generation the Russian giant RAO-UES, under the leadership of Anatoly Chubais, was extremely successful in reintegrating many Central Asian generation and distribution networks into the former Soviet grid. Indeed, the RAO-UES grid was planning to be even more integrated than under the Soviet Union, slowly reuniting Kazakhstan, Kyrgyzstan and Tajikistan in one generation and distribution grid. True, Kazakhstan retained control over transit across its territory, but nevertheless this was a lucrative and politically powerful source of Russian influence. It was also potentially good for Central Asia, because potential exporters of electricity, notably Tajikistan and Kyrgyzstan, finally had a chance to reach potential markets. Russia offered investment in long-standing projects, such as the Rogun hydroelectric station in Tajikistan and an equally ambitious dam and power station in Kyrgyzstan.

Although Russian leaders publicly offered support to any beleaguered dictators in Central Asia, in reality Russian support was just as unreliable as American backing. In private the Russians were frequently discussing alternative leaders for the future. In Turkmenistan they had been seeking an alternative future leader for some time among the diaspora, with little success. In Uzbekistan too they had been following the power struggle at the top of the political pyramid with interest for years. More recently Moscow had been talking to Russian Uzbeks, such as Alisher Usmanov, a major business magnate in the steel industry, to try and ensure the succession of a future pro-Russian leader.

Despite a widespread Russian attachment to the rhetoric of confrontational geopolitics, and an almost Cold-War mentality sometimes among diplomats, in reality many officials in Moscow understood that Russia was no longer able or willing to take on responsibility for Central Asia alone. A serious Western disengagement from the region would leave Russia almost alone to cope with a rising tide of migration, the increasing threat of Islamist violence, and a massive drugs trade. Russia was neither able nor willing to confront all these challenges alone, and some officials in Moscow understood this. However, the rising tide in Moscow of anti-Western paranoia, which accompanied the rise of former KGB officials in Russian politics, ensured that too much of its foreign policy was viewed in simplistic cold war, geopolitical terms. And it was all too easy to provoke the emotions of post-colonialism: those massive US planes sitting on the runway in Bishkek were the kind of visual irritant that no amount of sober geopolitical thinking could soothe.

The unknown neighbour: China

The idea that Central Asia will inexorably come into a greater Chinese economic or political zone is widespread in Central Asia, and there is considerable fear of what a Chinese-dominated future might entail. Admittedly, since the early 1990s when discussions with Kyrgyz or Kazakh officials about the Chinese were like entering a comic book discussion of the "Yellow Peril", attitudes have become more realistic and less fanciful. There is more appreciation of the economic benefits of neighbouring China, but still the fear of Chinese expansion lurks not far below the surface.[1]

Central Asians had little knowledge of China when the borders first opened in the early 1990s. What they did know tended to come from Soviet-era propaganda, where the Chinese were portrayed as a mortal threat to the Soviet Union. After the 1960 Sino-Soviet split, the Chinese were viewed as the main enemies in the Cold War in Soviet Asia, and no political lesson in school was complete without a caricatured portrayal of Mao Zedong's China. With the break-up of the USSR, the Chinese were seen as threatening neighbours, who would take advantage of their smaller neighbours, given the slightest opportunity.

In reality, the Chinese had very limited ambitions in Central Asia in the 1990s. Their main concern was to settle border disputes, on their own terms, and prevent any influx of instability across the border that could unsettle their own Muslim minority, the Uighurs, some of whom had been involved in a militant campaign for independence. During the 1990s there were frequent bombings and shootings in Urumchi and elsewhere in the Xinjiang Autonomous Region, and the Chinese clamped down hard on any sign of political restlessness. While the Soviet Union was in place there was no safe haven for these separatists, but with the creation of Muslim states on the other side of the border, China was extremely concerned that they might provide passive or even active support for Muslim peoples within China itself.

There was some sentimental support for the Uighur cause in both Kazakhstan and Kyrgyzstan in the 1990s, but this seems to have faded

---

1 Popular fear of China's billion-strong population is expressed in a rather bitter joke about a Chinese-dominated future. The Kyrgyz Defence minister is having an argument with his Chinese counterpart. "We will fight you know," says the Kyrgyz general, "if you try and seize our land". "Ah, but we are not going to fight you," smiles the Chinese official. "We will just cross the border with our army and surrender."

slightly by the early 21ˢᵗ century, perhaps because of broader antipathy to anything that was reminiscent of militant Islam in general, and also because of a somewhat more favourable view of the Chinese among the general population as interaction and trade increased. Certainly governments were largely supportive of Chinese demands to suppress signs of Uighur political activity, and often deported Uighurs suspected by the Chinese of carrying out "separatist" activity. The discovery of several Uighurs linked to al-Qaeda in Afghanistan and their transfer to Guantanamo Bay by the US merely heightened government suspicions of the Uighur cause. Nevertheless, in January 2002, the Kazakh media were vocal in their criticisms of Beijing's particularly harsh stance towards Uighurs in the wake of September 11ᵗʰ.[2] In reality, most Uighurs had nothing to do with terrorism, but they were frequent targets of the security services in Central Asia, partly because they were usually businesspeople, and therefore were tempting objects for extortion.

The first phase of Chinese interaction with Central Asia focused primarily on border disputes which had remained unresolved in the Soviet period. Frontiers had been closed to both Chinese and Soviet citizens, and borders were heavily defended on both sides. Gradually the Chinese opened up border crossings that had been closed for decades, but frontiers remained heavily guarded and travel across the border was tightly controlled.

Driving from Kyrgyzstan over the Torurgat crossing remained an exercise in patience even in 2004. From the nearest town of Naryn it was a four-hour drive up to the first Kyrgyz border check-point, where young conscripts insisted on all manner of written permissions to enable a car to continue. A further hour's drive crossed a kind of no-man's land—Kyrgyz territory in which nobody was permitted to live. Finally, cars arrived at a customs check-point, where Kyrgyz customs officials hung around a bare room, waiting for the day's shipments of scrap metal to come past. This was Kyrgyzstan's sole

---

2　Mark Berniker, "China's Uighur Policy Draws Critics in Kazakhstan", *EurasiaNet*, 29 January 2002, accessed at www.eurasianet.org/departments/ rights/articles/eav012902.shtml.

export to China, and was an extremely lucrative business. The remains of thousands of Soviet factories, vehicles and machinery were sold as scrap, loaded onto old Kamaz trucks and shipped across to Kashgar, where they could be sold at relatively high prices to Chinese merchants. One driver claimed that a lorry-load of scrap had to pay $500 in bribes to pass the Kyrgyz border, but even with such high costs it was still an easy way to make money.

From the customs post, there is another drive along a narrow road, past more trucks laden with scrap, until, fluttering in the breeze, a Chinese flag indicates the border post. From the top of the pass, a green valley stretches out into the mist, the beginning of an almost incomprehensible expanse of Chinese territory. The Chinese also have a "forbidden zone" on their side of the frontier, and it is another long drive before arrival at Chinese customs and immigration posts. After the ramshackle nature of the Kyrgyz authorities, suddenly the Chinese officials seem efficient and smart. This is clearly the border of a major power.

The contrast between Kyrgyzstan and China as states could not be greater. When the two sides discussed border disputes in the 1990s, the Kyrgyz were almost hopelessly outclassed in negotiations, with few qualified cartographers, international lawyers, or other technical specialists on border issues. The Chinese were in no mood to make concessions and they came away from the talks with a favourable deal, in two agreements signed in 1996 and 1999, which transferred some 125,000 hectares of Kyrgyz land to Chinese sovereignty. Realistically, it is hard to see what else the Kyrgyz government could have done, and some officials claimed that the outcome could have been even worse. In any case, most of the land was in mountainous regions where there were no residents and little or no economic activity.

Nevertheless, the hard Chinese stance confirmed the fears of some Kyrgyz, and it proved a highly contentious issue in domestic politics, where opposition politicians seized on the issue in their ongoing battle with President Akaev. When the agreements came up for ratification in 2002 they sparked sharp opposition and anti-government demonstrations. Similar concessions by the Kazakh government in the mid-1990s were seen as so contentious they were kept secret until 1999, for fear of a political revolt over the issue. China's aggressive stance over border negotiations merely confirmed historical fears over Chinese expansionism. In reality, China had no interest in territorial expansion, but was concerned primarily with stability on its western frontier, and secondly with improving economic ties across the borders. But its hardline stance in frontier negotiations won it few friends in the Central Asian states.

Paper Tiger? The Shanghai Cooperation Organisation

Much of China's negotiations with the new Central Asian states took place on a bilateral basis, but by the mid-1990s Beijing was searching for a multilateral organisation to help channel its political goals in the region. In April 1996 Russia, China, Kyrgyzstan, Kazakhstan and Tajikistan held a summit in Shanghai and formed a loose grouping, called the Shanghai Five. At first, the grouping was concerned almost solely with borders, visas, and military confidence-building measures along the frontier.

In time it evolved into something more ambitious, first embracing trade issues and then, at a summit in Bishkek in 1999, internal and transnational security issues, particularly those China termed the "three evils": terrorism, separatism and extremism. In July 2001 the grouping evolved into a permanent organisation, the Shanghai Cooperation Organisation (SCO), and Uzbekistan was persuaded to join, partly because of the organisation's new mandate in counter-terrorism, which focused on the local security concerns of member-states rather than global threats. According to China's foreign minister, Tang Jiaxuan, "all [SCO] members are supportive of China's position concerning East Turkestan terrorists, and of Russia's stance on Chechen terrorists, and regard these efforts, as part and parcel of the international fight against terrorism."[3]

The sudden appearance of US forces in the region, and Uzbekistan's new pro-Western stance, seemed to have dealt a blow to the SCO's ambitions in the region. A planned summit for June 2002 was postponed, and the Chinese leadership seemed unable to coordinate a

---

3   Ibid.

united front in the new geopolitical constellation. Uzbekistan, in particular, showed no enthusiasm for its new membership of the organisation. Western diplomats in Tashkent quipped that Uzbekistan tended to undermine almost any organisation it joined, and the SCO would be no exception. They spoke too soon, however; gradually the SCO reasserted its role in the region.

Perhaps even more than Russia, China was deeply concerned by the presence of US troops in the region, particularly those close to its border at Manas in Kyrgyzstan. When rumours were reported that the US might also consider a base in Kazakhstan, the Chinese foreign ministry protested strongly to the Kazakhs. For the Chinese, the Central Asian bases looked like part of a long-term effort at encirclement of China, despite US protestations that the bases were only to be used to support US forces in Afghanistan. This paranoia was fuelled by statements before 9/11 that pointed to China as the key potential adversary of the US in the 21st century, and the ongoing pro-Taiwan and anti-China position of some individuals close to the Bush administration. Few observers believed that either Manas or Karshi would be short-term bases, and rightly or wrongly many analysts pointed to their proximity to China as reasons for their long-term utility for the US.

Despite their public unity, there were fundamental contradictions among members of the SCO. The Central Asian states were suspicious of Chinese ambitions in the region, and although Kyrgyzstan and Kazakhstan were happy to cooperate on economic affairs, Uzbekistan had effectively declared a blockade of Chinese consumer goods entering the country through Kyrgyzstan. On security concerns too, the Central Asian states had rather different priorities from those of the Chinese, and tended to see the Uighurs as far less of a threat than did their counterparts in Beijing. And although Russian and China were happy to cooperate, particularly in opposition to the US, the two major regional powers also had contradictory policies at times, particularly in economic competition between the two states over Central Asia's energy resources. Lastly, attempting to counter Chinese influence was Japan, which was one of the most lavish donors to Central Asia, and the object of much admiration among Central Asian leaders for its modern polity and economy. Nevertheless, as the US presence in the region became more troubling for Central Asian leaders, the SCO began to make a comeback. In June 2004 its members met in Tashkent, a key piece of symbolism, demonstrating that Uzbekistan was increasingly keen to balance its pro-US stance. The group agreed to set up an anti-terrorist centre in Tashkent, although its remit remained very unclear. The group also began to expand, with Mongolia added as an observer, and talks opened with Afghanistan. In 2005 the SCO also agreed to Iran, Pakistan and India joining the organisation as observers. Informal approaches by the US to gain such status were firmly rebuffed.[4]

Throughout the 1990s China had stayed away from any obvious interference in domestic politics in Central Asia. But after 2001 it began to take more interest, troubled by any sign of potential instability, and ready to back the region's leaders as much as possible. However, its understanding of the political dynamics on the ground was often limited, and led to poor decisions.

In March 2005 Chinese diplomats in Bishkek, who had apparently reported that Akaev was in trouble, seem to have been subsequently ignored by Beijing, which continued to support Akaev until the end. China was deeply unsettled by his ousting, and particularly by the unrest it generated; some of the looting seems to have targeted Chinese and Uighur traders in particular. There was little public response from Beijing, but it was concerned by the potential for the new regime to be more democratic than its predecessor—and hence less willing to cooperate with the Chinese on suppression of Uighur political activity—and also concerned that the new regime would be even closer to the US, and possibly willing to countenance a permanent future for the US military base.

Neither of these fears were realised, although the threat of instability remained real. But the new Kyrgyz leadership insisted that there would be no change in Sino-Kyrgyz relations, something confirmed

---

4   Personal communication, US State Department officials, Washington D.C., December 2004.

by prime minister Feliks Kulov during the SCO summit in Moscow in October 2005. However, Kyrgyzstan agreed to permit the US to retain its base, largely because of the financial benefits the host country gained as a result and its political use as a bargaining chip in relations with China and Russia. This decision effectively undermined a joint statement by the SCO in July 2005 that requested a timetable for the withdrawal of US military forces from the region.

However, it was in Uzbekistan that Beijing made its most overt statement of support for one of the region's ill-fated leaders. Just one week after the suppression of the uprising in Andijan, President Karimov visited Beijing and was given full support by the Chinese leadership for his actions. The foreign ministry said it supported Uzbekistan's measures to crack down on "the three evils" (extremism, separatism and terrorism) and to maintain domestic and regional stability. As in Kyrgyzstan, China had little insight into the nuances of domestic politics, but it was easy to persuade Beijing that the forces in Andijan were just the kind of oppositionists who might be sympathetic towards Uighur aspirations too.

Talk of fighting the "three evils" hid a much deeper Chinese fear, that the inspiration of popular revolutions in Ukraine, Georgia and Kyrgyzstan might spread further east. The protests in Ukraine were horribly reminiscent of the thousands who had protested in Tiananmen square in 1989, and Uzbekistan's brutality was all too familiar to the Chinese, who had also crushed the Tiananmen protestors with military force. The Chinese joined the Russians in warning against the "import" of US values of democracy to Central Asia; China's *People's Daily* accused the US of shaking the "ideological mindsets and cultural foundations" of other countries by exporting US-style values of "freedom and democracy".[5]

For most Central Asians, these grand political themes were less important than the Chinese impact on the economy. Most people's experience of China came from the bazaar, where cheap Chinese

---

5   Mure Dickie, Richard McGregor, "Fear of a 'colour revolution' behind China's new clampdown on free media", *Financial Times*, 18 November 2005, at www.ft.com/cms/s/8013c7da-57d7-11da-8866-00000e25118c.html.

consumer goods came to dominate the stalls by the late 1990s, undercutting more expensive goods from Turkey and Iran, not to mention local products. Most of these goods were brought across from Urumchi by so-called "shuttle traders", both Uighurs and Han Chinese from China, but also Kyrgyz and Kazakhs, who travelled by train, bus and plane across the border, and came back laden with bags full of every conceivable consumer item. This travel also played a part in changing Central Asian perceptions of China: Urumchi was a thriving economic metropolis by comparison with Central Asia's cities; the Chinese economic miracle, even in the far west of the country, could not fail to challenge historical stereotypes.

Gradually this trade became more regulated, and larger businesses, and powerful political figures, took over much of it. Most of the goods ended up in markets in Almaty, Bishkek, and Osh. From there the trade went back to individuals, who were forced to smuggle most goods across the border into Uzbekistan, because of the government blockade on imports. Police along the road from Fergana to Tashkent frequently confiscated Chinese goods from the groups of women who dominated the trade; more frequently they were paid a bribe and the traders went on their way.

More serious Chinese investment was limited in the 1990s, but developed much more quickly in the 21st century. In Kazakhstan the level of investment was particularly high, with a $9bn deal to build a pipeline from western Kazakhstan's oilfields across the entire country to the Chinese border, and a $4 billion investment in PetroKazakhstan in August 2005, a deal that caused some concern among Kazakh businesspeople, worried about potential Chinese domination of the economy.

Elsewhere in the region, investment was more sporadic. Chinese companies were searching for oil and building roads in southern Kyrgyzstan, but there were few resources to exploit in that state. In Uzbekistan there were promises of investment, and some soft loans, largely to demonstrate political support, but only limited commercial investment. In most cases, it was Russian companies that seized on Uzbekistan's estrangement from the West, winning contracts in the oil and gas sector and in mobile telecommunications, probably the

225

only really profitable sectors for any outside investor. Except for the Kazakh deals, China had little chance in the short term of breaking Moscow's domination of gas and other energy exports from Central Asia. It was in this sphere that future competition between the two powers seemed likely to surface, with discussions continuing on a gas pipeline from Turkmenistan that would directly challenge Russian control of that state's energy exports.

Overall, Chinese penetration of Central Asia was a strange mixture of success and failure. Overreaching diplomacy, particularly over borders, ensured that Kazakhs and Kyrgyz remained highly suspicious of Chinese intentions. Repression of Uighur political activism had a broader impact on foreign policy, which ensured that China was always on the side of governmental repression; its fear of any democratic tendencies among its own people merely intensified this attitude. And it was always concerned about stability and prevention of conflict. But China's approach was one that tended to lead it to overestimate Central Asian governments' legitimacy. Having misjudged the longevity of Akaev, the Chinese gave their total support to Karimov. But whatever the lack of nuance in the Chinese political approach to Central Asia, there was a creeping inevitability about Chinese economic penetration of the region. It seemed that neither the West nor Russia might ultimately be able to compete with the competition from the East.

The West in Central Asia

It was tempting to characterise international relations in Central Asia as a kind of new Cold War, with the West battling for influence against a resurgent Russia and the new China. On the ground the reality was slightly different. These often formalistic regional groupings and shifts in foreign policy did not have much impact on most people's lives. If it was a game, it was a virtual one, with most of the moves played out away from view, and with little effect on everyday life. But some foreign policy shifts had more impact than others.

From a practical point of view, relations with Russia were of most importance for ordinary people. Russia was the key trading partner and the source of millions of dollars' worth of remittance income from Central Asian workers living there. Relations with China evoked strong emotions in the popular consciousness, but China was also a key trading partner for Central Asia's bazaars. With the US, things were different. There was virtually no significant trade, and little investment, and only small elites were interested in the political significance of a strong relationship with the US. True, the US provided aid, but much of it was invisible to most people, or was directed primarily to small political elites—either in the government, or in civil society and democracy-promotion programmes.

It was sometimes hard not to feel sorry for the architects of US foreign policy. Take Kyrgyzstan. From 1991 to 2005 American taxpayers contributed more than $300m in bilateral aid, not to mention US funds channelled through the World Bank, the UN and other multilateral institutions. American charities were also generous. US diplomats repeatedly intervened on behalf of human rights activists, journalists and other civil society representatives. They pushed for free elections, and supported the new government after the March 2005 upheaval. But opinion polls and anecdotal evidence suggested that the US was still broadly mistrusted by many Kyrgyz, who still viewed Russia as their closest ally.

In large part, these attitudes could be traced to a lingering Soviet-era distrust of the US, or to the consistently biased Russian news reports that most Kyrgyz watched. Similar Russian-inspired views of the US were present throughout the region, with Russian news the most important source for many people, only partly countered by the more objective approach of Radio Free Europe and similar outfits. However, it was not merely the filtering of news that informed views of the US. They evolved in response to world events, with at least part of the antipathy towards the US (which was not accompanied by antipathy to Americans as such) certainly informed by the US interventions in Afghanistan and Iraq, and by well-publicised abuses in Abu Ghraib and Guantanamo Bay.

The war in Afghanistan was supported by many Central Asians, who had little sympathy for the Taliban; Uzbeks and Tajiks had a positive attitude towards their compatriots in the north of Af-

227

ghanistan, who were allied for the most part with US forces. The war in Iraq was a different matter: opposition was not vocal but was widespread, although both Uzbekistan and Kazakhstan publicly supported the Americans, and the other Central Asian states took an equivocal stance. There were occasional exceptions: opposition figures in Tashkent took some heart from the overthrow of Saddam Hussein, and wondered why the US was not equally firm with their own dictator.

However, the excesses of American foreign policy seriously undermined the US's ability to promote the very values they claimed to be fighting for. As news of abuses emerged in Abu Ghraib prison by US military personnel, it became much more difficult to criticise the Uzbek government over its much more extensive and brutal torture regime. For years Western governments had tried to convince the Uzbek government to adopt the legal principle behind *habeas corpus*; while detainees were kept in Guantanamo Bay or at Bagram air base for years without charge, accusations aimed at these governments about detaining opponents without charge sounded hollow.

The condition of prisoners in Guantanamo was better than in, say, the Jaslyk prison camp in Uzbekistan. But the perception of US wrongdoing gave huge scope to those government officials and their propagandists who tried to draw up a spurious balance sheet of moral equivalence. The situation was made worse by the increasing perception of US double standards. It was never clear to Uzbek democrats why the US government was so supportive of their oppressors when it was so critical towards governments in, say, Belarus and Ukraine.

The US was not alone in this. European governments were often even less responsive to concerns about human rights. The key European partner for Central Asian states, Germany, followed the US lead in trading pressure on human rights and political change for the right to maintain a military base at Termez. Germany pushed repeatedly in 2006-7 for EU sanctions on Uzbekistan to be relaxed, despite the government's failure to make any progress on an investigation into the Andijan massacre, or on broader human rights issues. Meanwhile, in Turkmenistan, Daimler-Chrysler translated Niyazov's disastrous *Ruhnama* to ensure that he continued to buy their luxury cars. And western banks were more than happy to provide a safe home for the billions of dollars embezzled by Niyazov from the Turkmen state. Meanwhile, back in Tashkent, Bremen cotton buyers happily traded in Uzbek cotton, picked by hand by child labour.

Multilateral institutions, including the UN, were also for the most part unable or unwilling to address uncomfortable issues for their host governments. The EBRD and the Asian Development Bank both lent hundreds of millions of dollars to Turkmenistan and Uzbekistan, without achieving any level of economic reform. In all, Western policy towards Central Asia's two most desperate regimes was a litany of compromise and inconsistency that was hardly justified by legitimate security concerns, and in both cases allowed their leaders to continue along a path towards long-term instability.

Negative views of the US in Central Asia were reinforced by a constant stream of Russian propaganda, which tended to portray the Americans in the worst possible light. There was no adequate response from the US; American diplomats tended to be seen as somewhat aloof, and had problems connecting with local people in a meaningful dialogue. Concerned by security issues, US embassies gradually moved out of city centre buildings to new high-security compounds on the edges of cities. These concrete boxes, surrounded by high security and topped by the paraphernalia of electronic technology, embodied a political discourse of mutual distrust.

The US could never really compete with Russia in economic terms. Economic survival was the fundamental issue for millions of families, and foreign policy links that tended to support their quest for economic prosperity were bound to gain more support. In almost every case, this meant closer ties with Russia. Russia meant jobs and more prospects of significant investment. Closer security ties between Uzbekistan and the US brought no significant commercial investment from US companies; a shift back to the Russian sphere of influence was expected to produce Russian investment and, more important, greater opportunities for work in Russia for Uzbek citizens.

There was little the US could do about its lack of investment in the region. These economies were simply not attractive for Western companies, outside the extractive industries sector. In truth they were not very attractive for Russian companies either, but geography made investment slightly less risky for them than for US companies. In any case, US legislation that outlawed corruption, and US corporate governance, made it even more difficult for US companies to compete against Russian and Chinese rivals, who had few qualms about playing according to local rules.

There was seldom an appreciation of the importance of Russia and China for Central Asian economies among Western diplomats. International aid projects tended to favour infrastructure and policies that excluded rather than included Russia. The EU's TRACECA project sought to recreate an East-West Silk Road, which would provide an alternative to the north-south routes that had grown up to serve Russian markets. US trade projects tried to bring the five Central Asian states into agreements that had nothing to do with their predominant trading partners to the east and the north, and offered complex infrastructure projects that tried to link Central Asia to Afghanistan and Pakistan, but seemed to deny the commercial advantages to Central Asians of their economic ties to the north.

Geopolitically, also, the US tended to develop approaches that excluded regional powers. The US-led GUUAM organisation brought together the former Soviet states of Georgia, Uzbekistan, Ukraine, Azerbaijan and Moldova. These states had very little in common apart from a generally pro-US foreign policy. Indeed, the organisation seemed to have no purpose in life except to needlessly irritate Russia. One day in 2003, Uzbekistan announced that it would withdraw from GUUAM, implying that it was little more than an expensive talking-shop. Two days later, it rescinded its decision, after considerable US pressure. Too often the US wasted political capital on issues like this, which could have been better spent on pushing for domestic reform, rather than geopolitical advantage. Similarly, gaining support for the war in Iraq, achieving immunity for US troops from the International Criminal Court, and a myriad other US global concerns all took time out of a focus on the region's more immediate problems.

Adventures in Central Asia tended to underscore the limits of American empire rather than its global reach. Geography was against the US playing a more significant role than either China or Russia. The region was not attractive for US investors, it had little exposure in domestic media, and had no vocal diaspora to push for more aid or support. Once attention shifted from Afghanistan to Iraq there was even less geostrategic interest in a region which posed significant problems for political or economic engagement.

However, it was not simply a matter of geography or short atten-tion-spans. The US was committed to "transformational diplomacy" on a global scale, not only in selected areas of the world. The US sought changes in behaviour by Central Asian regimes, but did not have the power to force or persuade them to take those steps. Its military (hard) power was not applicable, and its ability to project "soft power" was fatally undermined by its declining reputation both within Central Asia and elsewhere in the world. Low levels of for-eign aid and a huge shift in resources from Central Asia (including Afghanistan) to the Middle East left it unable to use economic power as a lever for change.

In the end, it seemed unlikely that geopolitical dynamics alone would determine the internal development of these states. Both Rus-sia and China were wedded to existing dictatorial leaders, while a significant minority of the population in each state was keen to see a change of regime. This left both states in something of a problematic posture. Supporting only the status quo, they had little to offer in the case of significant political change. In the long term, the popular desire for more responsible government and economic change could cause serious problems for both Russia and China. As Russia be-came more authoritarian, it offered less of a role model for moderate political figures in Central Asia. And while the Chinese model of economic development was attractive, its political repression under-mined its attractiveness for some political elites. For Central Asia to achieve its full potential, it needed to harness the economic growth of its two major neighbours, while remaining open to broader en-gagement with Europe and the US. However, the disappointments of the dalliance with the West after 2001 made a new relationship with the world outside Central Asia far more difficult than it might otherwise have been.

Conclusion

In the centuries of history of Central Asia, these few years at the beginning of the 21ˢᵗ century may one day be seen as merely a small blip of international interest. Yet they represent more than just an unsuccessful flirtation between the West and Central Asia: they represent a much wider range of themes in contemporary international relations and in US foreign policy, in particular, that will continue to shape the world throughout the 21ˢᵗ century.

By 2007 the West was in retreat in Central Asia. It had failed to make any impression in Turkmenistan, where a new leader seemed set to continue the repressive state his predecessor had constructed. In Uzbekistan, too, the West was squeezed out, replaced by Russia and China in both political and economic ties. Tajikistan was still talking, but the increasing inequalities of that country, its role in the drugs trade, and the authoritarianism of the government were taking their toll on the relationship with both the US and Europe. Russia remained its key security partner. In Kyrgyzstan the new government was significantly less friendly towards Western partners, and the new elite had little apparent interest in or knowledge of the wider world.

Russia was enjoying some of this Western retreat, but it could hardly afford to be complacent over events in the region. All the states examined in this book faced huge obstacles to their stability over the next decade, and as Russia became more influential in the region, at least some Russian officials were concerned that they would be drawn into future political instability, and possibly outbreaks of conflict.

Failure to develop viable and effective states with popular legitimacy ensured that the possibility of state failure was almost always in the air. This was particularly linked to the inevitable problems of succession that faced all the region's leaders. The overthrow of President Akaev in Kyrgyzstan demonstrated the weakness of that state's institutions, once the personality of the leader was removed from the political equation. In Turkmenistan and Uzbekistan, the long-term prospects were poor, unless effective state structures that could manage internal and external shocks were developed. Kazakhstan demonstrated an alternative model of relatively liberal economic advancement, combined with a sometimes ruthless political monopoly of power. But the inefficiencies of its political system were camouflaged by its revenue stream from energy resources. And in any case, as was pointed out in the introduction, its history places it in a different tradition from that of the other Central Asian states.

Part of the West's retreat was ensured by objective factors, such as geography and the natural rebound of Russia from its temporary weakness in the 1990s. But there are also good reasons inherent in US policy in particular that damaged the credibility of the West, and of ideas of democracy and open economies, in the region. Part of the problem was the geopoliticisation of values, with democracy becoming a foreign policy tool for the US rather than a common good of value regardless of geopolitical tendencies. The nationalist discourse of US foreign policy, explored so well in Anatol Lieven's *America, Right or Wrong*,[6] has undermined the universal values it seeks to promote. This geopoliticising of democratic values and human rights permitted anti-Americanism to translate into opposition to all forms of political change.

The close relationship with the Karimov government served a similar purpose, particularly with those already suspicious of American intentions. US basing in Central Asia did nothing to bring democracy or smarter economics in its wake. In reality, it simply intensified Russian and Chinese concerns that the "temporary bases" would gradually turn into permanent military presences, and so caused the two regional powers to intensify efforts to turn local governments against Western influence in general.

In retrospect, the failure to understand the post-colonial reality of Central Asia, and above all the importance of its continuing relationship with Russia, was one of the most profound mistakes of Western policy in the region. The Cold War hangover that affected so much of American foreign policy, even after Communism had collapsed, led to a damaging overemphasis on separation from the former imperial power as a precondition for a strong relationship with the US. These

---

6   Anatol Lieven, *America, Right or Wrong: The Anatomy of American Nationalism* (2005).

attitudes were evident in the repeated references to supporting the "independence of Central Asian states", diplomatic code for shifting out of the Russian sphere of influence, the overt support for Turkmenistan's "neutrality", and the little lamented GUUAM organisation.

This in turn led to a failure to consult over US bases in Central Asia, and a myriad of smaller policy moments that made it extremely difficult to develop any cooperative approach with Russia in the region. However, good relations with Russia were vital for Central Asian states, for trade, for transport, for cultural development and for security. And paradoxically, the more countries tried to limit Russian influence, the worse their internal situation became, in both economic and political terms. There were some other reasons for this, of course: the pro-US period in Uzbek foreign policy also coincided with a period of extremely poor economic decision-making. However, a close relationship with the US provided Uzbekistan with an excuse to retreat along the path of autarky, something that was much more difficult for states such as Kazakhstan and Kyrgyzstan, which were linked with Russia by a number of trade and security agreements.

Russia had retreated from its empire in Asia with a speed unmatched by any other European empire. It had also been an entirely peaceful retreat. But the speed of withdrawal was a major problem for Central Asia's weaker states, who overnight were forced to confront major problems of modernisation on their own. Attempts to replace Russian cultural hegemony with Western influence were largely a failure, with only small elites responding to the allure of American-dominated global culture. However, a reassertion of Russian culture also met resistance, while the failure of local cultures for the most part to respond adequately to the challenges of modernisation gave room for those seeking cultural fulfilment in the global call of both radical and mainstream Islam.

These cultural processes went largely unnoticed by the international community, which tended to deal mainly with small English-speaking elites and so gained a false sense of the potential for reform and progress. The real decision-makers were seldom part of their dialogue; they did not speak English, their views were a long way away from the acceptable noises made at round-tables and seminars, and they were often closely linked to semi-criminal activities. This failure to identify key players and underlying social and historical factors led to a critical failure of intelligence, particularly with regard to the authoritarian states of Turkmenistan and Uzbekistan. It was easy to believe that these were authoritarian but modernising states, if you limited interaction to a few mildly progressive officials in the ministries of foreign affairs. Anybody who dug a little deeper could immediately see the fairly nasty reality underneath this façade.

This kind of approach was also endemic in the activity of donor organisations. Loans and grants were provided to government partners, but donors wanted control over where the funds were going, and developed an artificial bureaucracy within ministries. Thus in many cases, the international community was dealing with a virtual state, centred around "Project Implementation Units" within the government, more enlightened officials from the ministry of foreign affairs, and a small but sometimes vocal NGO community. When much of this façade was stripped away during the Kyrgyz revolution, diplomats found themselves face to face with a more ugly reality, in which narcotraffickers and racketeers vied for parliamentary seats, and bureaucrats known mainly for their corrupt past dominated the new government.

This engagement with the virtual state contributed to the mistakes of US policy in Uzbekistan, where a kind of group-think set in: the desire of the US to see signs of reform made it easy for Uzbek diplomats to offer small evidence of change without actually changing the system at all. The desire for change led to a widespread belief among US officials that change was actually occurring, and that a long-term partnership with the government was feasible. In reality, this kind of engagement merely delayed the inevitable, and provided a comfort zone for governments who had no real desire to embark on difficult and complex reforms.

In 2001 many Central Asians saw a new era of partnership with the West as a possible breakthrough in their desire to build new lives and emerge from the collapse into penury and brutality that had marked the 1990s. Five years later most of those dreams were in shatters, left on the bloody streets of Andijan, or buried by the bureaucratic and criminal takeover of the Kyrgyz revolution. Many erstwhile democrats simply upped and left, retiring to fight another day. Others battled on, but with little optimism that there would be any change in the near future. Their place as intellectual leaders was increasingly taken by nationalists and Islamists, who found plenty of fertile ground among the impoverished youth of Central Asia. The new generation, which was supposed to have left behind the mind-set of the Soviet past, was embarking on the future with ideas even more alien to the West than those of their parents' generation.

Fifteen years after independence the future looked gloomy for Central Asia. Kazakhstan was the only exception in an otherwise failing regional economy. Kyrgyzstan was the only partial exception to a series of repressive autocracies, and all the states were run by neo-feudal presidents, who combined autocratic political powers with significant control by their families over major parts of the economy. It seemed unlikely that many of these regimes would last another fifteen years. But when they do disintegrate, the consequences may be far worse than anything we have seen so far.

Many of the problems faced by Central Asia in the 21st century are rightly laid at the gates of the lavish presidential palaces of the region's leaders, but the West also must take some of the responsibility for the way events unfolded. Sidetracked by the temptations of tyranny, and its alluring but false promises of security and modernisation; blinkered by the prism of the "war on terror", and an ill-informed obsession with radical Islam; or distracted by the allure of democracy on the cheap and the idea of revolution; at every turn the West failed to answer the real needs of ordinary Central Asians, and instead capitulated to the narrow visions of their self-appointed leaders.

INDEX